Critical Studies in Native History
(continues Manitoba Studies in Native History)

Jarvis Brownlie, Series Editor

Life Stages and Native Women

Memory, Teachings, and Story Medicine

Kim Anderson

Foreword by Maria Campbell

University of Manitoba Press

Life Stages and Native Women : Memory, Teachings, and Story Medicine
© Kim Anderson 2011
Foreword © Maria Campbell 2011

25 24 23 22 21   8 9 10 11 12

University of Manitoba Press
Winnipeg, Manitoba, Canada
Treaty 1 Territory
uofmpress.ca

Cataloguing data available from Library and Archives Canada
Critical studies in Native history ; ISSN 1925-5888 ; 15
ISBN 978-0-88755-726-2 (PAPER)
ISBN 978-0-88755-405-6 (PDF)
ISBN 978-0-88755-416-2 (EPUB)
ISBN 978-0-88755-248-9 (BOUND)

Cover design by Mike Carroll
Cover image by Leah Dorion, "Midwife"
Interior design by Karen Armstrong Graphic Design

Printed in Canada

A portion of royalties from this book will be donated to the Gabriel Dumont Institute and to the Ontario Federation of Indian Friendship Centres Strong Women Scholarship with the National Aboriginal Achievement Foundation.

The University of Manitoba Press acknowledges the financial support for its publication program provided by the Government of Canada through the Canada Book Fund, the Canada Council for the Arts, the Manitoba Department of Sport, Culture, and Heritage, the Manitoba Arts Council, and the Manitoba Book Publishing Tax Credit.

Funded by the Government of Canada | Canadä

Contents

To Maria Campbell,
for her dedication to storytellers, young and old

Acknowledgements

Most acknowledgements leave the thanking of families to the last, but there is no question here that my immediate family deserves an upfront acknowledgment, as they have sacrificed the most so that I could take on a book project.

First, there is David, who makes everything possible. In addition to being a single parent during my absences, taking on the added domestic work that fell to him, spending his vacation time following me around on the research trail, booking flights, managing computer issues, and generally acting as the executive assistant I really need, Dave offered many valuable insights into my intellectual work, as he so often does. After all the above-mentioned tasks, he still managed to listen to me and respond with remarkable acuity as I rattled on during one of the late nights or early mornings when we found some time to talk. My first debt of gratitude always goes to Dave.

Sixteen years ago, Dave and I began a family, and it is this monumental undertaking that guides my work. The birth of our first child, Rajan, launched a desire in me to learn about how I could raise a healthy community member and a curiosity about how Indigenous societies might have done this in the past. I felt a duty to see this child through a series of life passages; to celebrate him and honour him at each stage of his life; to find a way to build community for him and to instil responsibility. The birth of our girl child, Denia, inspired a need for more knowledge about the lives of girls and women in the past, and her unrelenting feminine spirit has given me joy by witnessing the power of the feminine every day. Denia has also taught me how this book project has represented a certain amount of "fasting" on the part of the family. To Dave, Rajan, and Denia: I love you. Thank you for being so patient.

My extended family also stands behind this work. My dad passed away the spring before I started the PhD that led to this book, but he always encouraged education and would have been so proud. My mom, who always worked while raising children and who changed career a number of times, continues to inspire me with her spirit of engagement and perseverance. Thanks to David's parents, Barb and Dwaine Dornan, for their support, and for providing a much needed vehicle for the field work in Saskatchewan. And of course, there are Doug, Jennifer, and Nigel, our "baby bear" who has recently come into the family and reminds us of the beauty and joy that new life provides.

In the Indigenous community we often talk about "families of the heart." Through the course of the ten years since I first approached Maria Campbell about collaborating with me on a life stages book project, Maria has become an older sister, auntie, teacher, friend, and grandmother to me and my family. Our work is ongoing and is grounded in the love and kinship that have grown out of what we have done together. Maria, I am so grateful.

I have gained other relatives in the course of this project, and would like to acknowledge the generosity of each of the participant historians:

To Mosôm Danny: I feel blessed that you gave me so much time and were always open to do "one more interview" each time I called. I am rich from our time together in that space of knowledge and story. You are magnificent.

Elsie, I could talk to you forever, you are so insightful. I admire you for being such a supportive auntie and grannie to young (or younger!) women, including me.

Gertie, I keep coming back to you because your stories, experiences, and insights set off countless "aha" moments in me. Thank you again, my long-time friend.

Hilary, I so appreciate your e-mail messages of encouragement about my work overall. I loved your little girl stories and value the time we have spent together. There's more shopping and visiting to be done yet!

June, thank you for trusting me and letting me share your experiences. They will go a long way towards helping our people.

Madeleine, my friend, mentor, and co-woman warrior in the health and wellness sector, thank you for working with me again. I keep your words of encouragement pinned to my bulletin board.

Marie, although you are no longer with us, your stories are alive and will contribute to change many generations into the future. Thank you for being such a warm and engaging teacher.

Olive, I hold onto the blessing you gave me one sunny day as I left your apartment in Saskatoon. You told me in a loving way that I was doing good work, and as fragile as I was feeling, I knew, then, that it was all going to be okay.

Rebecca, I always feel like a special niece in your presence. Thanks for adorning me with beautiful things, for treating me to sumptuous meals, and for being such a steadfast supporter of my work over the years. I greatly appreciate all that you do, as the knowledge you share of women's ways carries infinite possibilities.

To Rene, our "akiwenzie" and uncle in Guelph, thanks for teaching Anishinaabemowin through story. We are blessed to have you in our community. And thanks to Joan for helping!

Grandma Rose, you have taught me many things about the generosity and love of a grandmother. Your energy and drive are astonishing; you show us granddaughters across the country how, truly, a woman's work is never done.

Rosella, I greatly appreciate your open nature, and your beautiful artwork that you gifted to me. I can't believe all that you accomplish as a teacher, leader, and great-grandmother. I will see you on the land!

Sylvia, you were a great "mom" to me; feeding me, making a cozy room so I could rest when I really needed it, showing me jigging, and teaching me to bead. I'm so glad I've had time to be a small part of your wonderful family. I'll be back!

While not a participant historian, Jane Middelton-Moz deserves a hearty thanks for providing me with an interview so I could put all of this history into the context of contemporary healing. Thanks, Jane, for welcoming me into your home, feeding me lunch, and giving me all the time we needed to start off the dialogue on how to apply this work around "the old ways." Your work is a great gift of hope and inspiration.

In addition to these new relatives, I have one more "other mother" to thank for this project. It was my friend Linda Crawford Teasdale who first conceived of the idea of doing some kind of book on life stages of women according to Anishinaabek teachings. Linda passed away in 2000, but she never abandoned me or the project. Wherever you are, Linda, here's my final tobacco for this one. Thanks and Chi Meegwetch. (I DID IT!!)

Of course, this kind of work would never get done if it were not for financial support. My first thought in terms of this kind of support goes out to Bill and Anne Brock, who generously provided the funding for the

University of Guelph Brock Doctoral Scholarship that saw me through a PhD and the first stages of this book. It was a pleasure getting to know them, for they, too, are storytellers. I was also financially supported by the Social Science and Humanities Research Council, the Indigenous Peoples Health Research Centre out of the University of Saskatchewan, the Indigenous Health Research Development Program at McMaster University/University of Toronto, and the Centre for Research in Inner City Health, St. Michael's Hospital, Toronto. Early funding from the Canadian Research Institute for the Advancement of Women allowed me to start thinking about this topic.

As this book began as a PhD thesis, my supervisor, Terry Crowley, had a great hand in what you will read here. As a senior academic, he was able to both appreciate and encourage some of my (perhaps unorthodox) methods, and to shepherd me through the requirements of doing a PhD in history. I am also thankful to Terry for teaching me how to improve my narrative writing style and how to better integrate voice into the text.

I was grateful to have enlisted the assistance of Winona Wheeler, first as a course instructor and then as a member of my dissertation and defence committees. In addition to being a mentor as an Indigenous scholar, she brought invaluable expertise in oral history and in community-based research with Algonquian peoples.

Wendy Mitchinson, another PhD committee member, brought wisdom, curiosity, and encouragement throughout the course of my degree. Thanks to Jennifer Brown for her careful and insightful work as my external examiner, and to Linda Mahood for being so encouraging as the internal/external examiner at my defence.

The Aboriginal Resource Centre at the University of Guelph is a special place that provided me with an office for five years while I worked on my PhD. The folks at the Centre made it feel like my home away from home. A special thanks to Dr. Jaime Cidrio and Dr. Cara Wehkamp, sisters on the academic journey. I am so proud of you women!

Other friends along the way include Danielle Terbenche, my PhD sister, the Sorsdahl family who often hosted me in Saskatoon, and Liza Brown and Leah Dorion who hosted me and helped me find historian participants in northern Saskatchewan. Lila Tabobondung and Dave Munroe hosted me and helped me find research participants around Wasauksing. Dave Munroe came to Guelph and spent several days painting my office at the Aboriginal Resource Centre just the right shade of yellow to set me off on my PhD. I am very sad that he died suddenly a month before I defended my dissertation.

As the thesis moved into a book, I acquired new friends at the University of Manitoba Press. In particular, I want to acknowledge David Carr for his support and friendship over the years. Thanks, too, to the academic peer reviewers for the feedback—I hope I have done it justice! I am also grateful to have community-based peer reviewers and supporters, including Sylvia Maracle and Carlie Chase, who reviewed the book draft.

Finally, the book would not be what it is without the skilful work of Beth McAuley, my editor and friend. Thanks, Beth, for sitting with me by the water, and for listening once again.

Foreword

by Maria Campbell

Like many women of my generation, I grew up with stories; lots of them, and all kinds. Some were nonsensical, others were riddles. There were *ahtyo-kaywina*, the sacred stories, and others that were *tahp acimowina*, the family histories. But it was the stories about the women that I loved best, stories about strong, courageous women and about weak, foolish ones, stories of births and deaths and women's cycles; of bad love affairs, brutal husbands, and yes, strong and gentle men. Some of the stories were told while we worked, cutting up meat and packing jars for canning or while smoking and drying fish. Some were told on the way to the berry patch.

"Look, that's the place where your cousin Jenny was born," the story went. "Your auntie was craving Saskatoon berries, but she was told by her mother and the old midwives not to go berry picking because she was almost ready to deliver her first baby. Of course she didn't listen, the *mut sti quon* that she was, she snuck away. Well wouldn't you know it, another *mut sti quon*, a young black bear, had slipped away from her mother and, like your auntie Betsy, was gobbling berries as fast as she could. When your auntie Betsy came around the bush she bumped right into her. They both screamed and ran. I don't know what happened to the young black bear, but your auntie Betsy tripped and fell and, not long after, Jenny arrived. Good thing Betsy had a good set of lungs. Her mother said she was screaming so loud her voice echoed all over the valley. It was hard to know if one woman was having a baby or ten. Yes, this is Jenny's berry patch."

Our nohkoms would laugh whenever they stopped at the place where they found Betsy. To this very day, that particular place on the side of the hill is still called "Jenny's berry patch." It is one of the family and landscape stories of our area.

I loved all these stories, and whenever I saw two women together—old or young—I was there like a shot, pushing my hair behind my ear and listening as hard as I could so I wouldn't miss anything. The place to hear the best stories was with my Cheechum and nohkoms and their old lady friends and relatives. I danced with excitement when these friends and relatives began arriving to spend a week or two or three with us, as they did every summer. While Dad was putting up the big tent for them, I helped my nohkoms carry bedding inside for they always moved into the tent with the visitors and I as their helper moved with them. As we spread the floor covering and blankets down, my Cheechum always made my bed beside her. I would be happy knowing that the nohkoms wouldn't try to chase me away if I was by her side and the discussion was getting too risqué.

Some of the old ladies were midwives and medicine women, meaning they knew and doctored with plants. One of them was also a ceremonialist. They were, with the exception of my Cheechum, all practising Catholics and Anglicans, which was not uncommon in those days. They were all deeply spiritual rather than religious, but at the same time they were completely sacrilegious. They ate, gambled, and sewed while they visited and told one story after another. Some so scary they would make your hair stand on end, others so sad you wanted to cry. Some were so outrageous you laughed till you were sick, as I often do today when I get together with my cousin Hilary and we retell these stories while we sew and bead. Even the funny ones, when the two of us discuss them, contemplate them, or have ceremony with them, will open doors to knowledge we thought was lost to us. When this happens, it's like a miracle and we are in awe.

It was with these old ladies and with our moms and aunties that the young girls in our family learned about "woman's stuff." No one ever explained about menstrual cycles, menopause, or being an old woman—or for that matter about how babies came to be. They just told stories about events and experiences. The rest we figured out on our own. Sometimes the figuring out on our own was an experience in itself and made for another funny story.

Like Mary Beth, one of my friends, who told me when we were comparing stories about birthing that her mom had told her that angels put babies inside of mothers, and her being a good Catholic she assumed that meant babies came in the same way that the baby Jesus came to the Virgin. She was twenty-two when she married and found intercourse a fun pastime, but she believed an angel was responsible for her pregnancy. She also believed babies came out of the navel. Well, surprise, surprise.

I knew where babies came from, as my nohkoms were midwives, but I believed you got them from kissing boys. You can guess my anxiety after my first kiss. I jumped off the barn and galloped my horse recklessly around the countryside because I'd heard one of the old ladies say a woman miscarried because she rode horseback. It has always been amazing to me how, as a little girl and young woman, I was taught so much about birthing, life, and death but nothing about the actual act of sexual intercourse and its role in giving life. Perhaps it was because the old way of being put out on the land for your first moon cycle was no longer practised when I was young, at least not in my community. And perhaps because the old women whose job it was to put us out were no longer able to do that, and so our "period" was dealt with by our Catholic mothers who shamefully whispered the barest of information and the whole thing was kept a secret where once it would have been a time of rejoicing and celebration. The fear of the church was deeply ingrained and, for many families, it was best to leave those old ways alone because they didn't want their children to suffer the consequences. It is hard to understand this unless one knows the history of the churches and their absolute power in the lives of our peoples.

So for my nohkoms, perhaps the power that was left for them was the stories they knew and the storytelling they did. In addition to the *acimowina*, like the one about Auntie Betsy, my Cheechum also told the *ahtyokaywina*, which were told only in the winter beginning with the first snowfall and ending in the spring when the frogs started to sing. *Ahtyokaywina* told how we came to be here as well as taught us the taboos and laws of our people. Some of these stories were *Wesakachak* stories of foolish and heroic deeds that taught the young how to live "a good life" and reminded the old to stay on that path. The stories were multilayered with knowledge and teachings interwoven into each of them. The keeper of these stories was Notokwe Ahtyokan, the old woman spirit who was the first grandmother, and as the keeper of the *ahtyokaywina*, she was also the keeper of family and community law.

Everyone knew some of these stories, but my understanding is not all people could tell them in their entirety, as that was a learned thing. One had to be gifted to do this, just like a person was gifted to heal with plants or ceremony. In a family there was one person, usually the old grandmother, who was this keeper and teller, and that was also true of the larger extended family/community as well. She was loved and respected by the people, and the stories gave her authority. Her loyalty was to the children and she was responsible for passing on to them this knowledge so they could have a good life and, if they were ever lost, the lessons in the stories would guide them home. As a child I understood this old grandmother spirit who looked after us and I knew about the responsibility of this "keeping role." My Cheechum was a good role model, but I never saw myself as an old woman. Who does when they are a child?

For a time I left those ways behind, believing they could never be a part of this new life. I got into trouble in the city and for a while I was lost, but times were changing in the 1960s, especially in Indian country. The old people had become "radicals," or so they were called by some officials. They travelled the country holding cultural and spiritual teaching sessions wherever they could find a space, and young people came from everywhere, hungry for their knowledge. It was their stories that brought us back and launched what we now know as the Aboriginal healing movement. Their stories taught us to decolonize ourselves and reclaim our communities. Through them we were then able to engage in our own radical activity, because the old people and their stories brought us a sense of safety and gave us courage. I felt this when, lost and sick, I came home and attended my first sweat lodge. It was conducted by an old lady and, when she sang the opening song, I knew I was home and I was going to be okay.

I felt this, too, when I met up with my first old man teacher, Peter O'Chiese. It was Peter who told me, "Speak, speak up! You have to get rid of that white man's notion that Indians don't talk, don't ask questions and don't do any critical thinking. It was not easy to live in the old days. If you were to survive you had to rely on *ki mamtonaychikunn, kaytay acimowina akwa* [and he would chuckle here] *mistahi mamaskatch*: A good mind, old people's stories, and a good dose of wonder and curiosity."

The storytellers of today are no different from Peter or those old people of the sixties or the old women of my childhood. The elders that share stories in this book continue to give us a sense of place, a sense of safety, courage, and vision. Their stories make us laugh and teach us to be better people, families, and communities. And, as this book demonstrates, we can also call on the stories we find elsewhere. I learned from old Peter how important it is to think, to ask questions, and to discuss with others. He never put down Western ways of knowing, he just warned me to always remember it was not "our" way of knowing. But he encouraged me to read everything, especially the writings of anthropologists and ethnographers.

One day, to illustrate why it was important to do this, he picked up a jigsaw puzzle my children and I had just completed. He lifted it high and dropped it. Pieces flew all over the room. "That's what happened to *wahkotowin* and to our stuff," he said. "Our kinships, our lives, and our teachings are all over the place. Those anthropologists and people who came to our elders to get stories and knowledge recorded everything and took it away. Our old people talked to them because they knew it was the only way they could save it. Maybe it is not complete, maybe pieces are missing, but if you know the language and some of the stories, then you have a big piece. And if you work with others who have pieces and you read the writings and listen to the tapes those people collected, then you will put our life back together, and when another generation of young people come along and ask questions, you will all be able to share your stories with them and our people will live. That is old man's dream."

This book has been constructed from multiple layers of stories in that spirit of rebuilding, and I am proud to be a part of it. I am grateful to have grown up with knowledgeable elders and to have met other elders/teachers who had the courage and commitment to teach me and others to be a part of the rebuilding. In my older years I have also been fortunate to work with a new generation of storytellers/scholars, like Kim Anderson, who has carefully pieced together all the different kinds of story medicines to write this book. I am sure our first grandmother Notokwe Ahtyokan is walking with us on this journey as we do the work of communicating our family histories and community laws in new ways.

I thank my Creator, my Cheechum, and my nohkoms. I thank Peter, my uncle Smith, and Rose Auger. They have all gone home now but their spirits, memory, and stories will always be here to guide us. I thank Kim Anderson and the other scholars who are a part of my life and who teach me so much.

Respectfully,
Maria Campbell
Gabriel's Crossing
April 3, 2011

Life Stages and Native Women

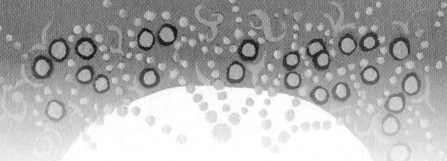

Introduction

Digging Up the Medicines

We never had any doubt that women were the centre and core of our community and our nation. No nation ever existed without the fortitude of our grandmothers, and all of those teachings have to be somehow recovered. And it will be up to these young people—well, like yourself—young women that are just digging up and going around—they've got to *dig up the medicines*, to heal the people. And the medicines, in this case, are the teachings. They've got to dig them up! You've got to find them.

—Mosôm Danny Musqua

*W*riting a book is an arduous process that can take one on an emotional roller coaster, and during the five years that I worked on this book there were many times when I felt lost and discouraged. I begin with this quote from Saulteaux Elder[1] Danny Musqua because this is what he said to me during the summer of 2007 at one of those times. Mosôm[2] (Grandfather) Danny didn't know about my anxieties; these words came up in the middle of an interview we were doing for another piece of work.[3] But what he said could not have been more fitting as a reminder of why I had decided to write a book on life stages and Native[4] women. I therefore offer Mosôm Danny's words as a point of entry, for this book is based on medicines that I have dug up through listening to the oral histories of Michif (Métis), Nēhiyawak (Cree), and Anishinaabek (Ojibway and Saulteaux)[5] elders. My intent is to offer these medicines as a contribution to the healing process we call decolonization and, in particular, to encourage dialogue about the role that gender can play in that process. The book is based on northern Algonquian stories—as these are the people I come from—but I believe the teachings and stories will be both familiar and applicable to Indigenous peoples across Turtle Island (North America). I hope that other peoples in North America and beyond will also take inspiration from the beautiful teachings represented in these story medicines.

Like Mosôm Danny, I believe that the recovery of our peoples is linked to "digging up the medicines" of our past. Knowing our history is an integral part of recovery for us as Indigenous peoples and for our communities in general, and it is in keeping with the adage that one often hears in "Indian country": "You have to know where you are coming from to know where you are going." We know that the more we understand about Indigenous experiences in the past, the better we will be able to shape our future; the more we understand about colonization, the better we will be at decolonizing ourselves and our communities.[6] It also means learning about the brilliance of our traditional cultures; the systems that can inspire us today as we reconstruct. When it comes to addressing issues related to Native women, this process involves understanding how gendered and intergenerational relations worked in the societies of our ancestors; about how our foremothers and grandmothers defined and then lived their identities, roles, and authorities,[7] and about how much of this was lost.

As with others doing healing work in Native communities, I too have drawn on Anishinaabe life cycle "teachings"[8] for grounding and inspiration. In my interpretation, Anishinaabe life cycle teachings stress (among other things) that the health and well-being of the individual is dependent on how well she or he fulfills his or her life stage roles and responsibilities. Whereas these teachings can be applied to anyone, I have used them here to explore how the roles, responsibilities, and practices related to various life stages contributed to the health of Native women and girls in "traditional" (i.e., land-based) communities.[9]

My interest in Indigenous women's history in particular has been driven over the years by a curiosity about the non-patriarchal and non-hierarchical social structures of many land-based Indigenous societies. We live in a world where it is hard to imagine a society without patriarchy, but the study of Indigenous cultures in the past can offer glimpses of this kind of world. This is the world that Mosôm Danny speaks of when he encourages us to dig up medicines about "the fortitude of our grandmothers." On numerous occasions he has expressed concern to me about the subjugation of Aboriginal women, noting that it is the direct result of colonization. He has also talked about how this subjugation stands behind much of the social disorder and ill health we see in our communities today. Cherokee scholar Andrea Smith has written extensively on this subject, asserting that the introduction of patriarchy, gendered violence, and social hierarchy were colonial responses to the "threat to counter imperial order" that Indigenous women represented, coming from the societies that we did.[10] I have often wondered about the kind of fortitude our ancestor-grandmothers had, and about the counter-imperial positions and egalitarian roles they held; this book provides some material to satisfy that curiosity. Although the twentieth-century period that I write about certainly manifested many of the social ills that Mosôm Danny and Andrea Smith refer to, vestiges of the traditional power of women were still operational. I write more about the complexities of this world when I introduce the oral history-tellers in Chapter 2.

I first started thinking about the significance of the life cycle and Indigenous women while writing the book *A Recognition of Being: Reconstructing Native Womanhood* (2000).[11] In that work I explored Native female identity based on the life histories I had recorded of forty women from across Canada. Because of my long-standing interest in gender equity, the first section of *A Recognition of Being* included an exploration of how functioning systems of gender roles, responsibilities, and relations were dismantled through colonization. In *A Recognition of Being*, I mapped the movement from gender equity, to the subjugation of Aboriginal women, to resistance and recovery. In addition, I discussed how the recovery of gender equity is essential to the recovery of Indigenous societies overall. The book was about decolonization through "reconstructing Native womanhood," a process which involves identity formation at the individual level as well as collective thinking about restructuring social relations in our contemporary societies.

As I was finishing *A Recognition of Being*, I began to think about how Indigenous identities are defined by life stages as well as gender. Although this could be said of any society, I was curious about the distinct way in which the responsibilities of different life stages played into the organization of Indigenous societies. If roles and responsibilities, privileges and authorities were determined according to gender as well as age, the way in which these elements worked together factored into a person's purpose as well as his or her position in society. I was intrigued by how the well-being of a community was apparently linked to interdependency and how well people worked and interacted across the life stage continuum. This book thus explores how changing roles and responsibilities throughout the life cycle of girls and women shape their identities and their place in Indigenous society. I see this exploration as part of my ongoing inquiry into "reconstructing Native womanhood" and, by association, reconstructing families and communities.

Finally, I was moved to do this research because of my role as a parent. As a new mother in the mid-1990s, I was overcome with a desire to learn about Indigenous customs related to pregnancy, childbirth, infant care, and ceremonies that honour children's life passages. Now, as a mother of teenagers, it has been helpful to explore teachings and stories about adolescence from an Indigenous perspective as I continue to work at knowing and honouring my children. As a middle-aged woman, life cycle teachings offer me reminders on how to respect and care for myself in the work that I do. And as I grow into an old lady, I will take inspiration from the stories about the power of age! Some Indigenous people have more immediate access to this knowledge through teachers or lived experience, but this was not my experience as a young woman. So I took Mosôm Danny's advice and kept digging, and I'm very glad to share what I have found.

"How It Was": Looking for Native Women's History

My inquiry into the life stages of northern Algonquian women began with some basic questions about "how it was"[12] during the childhood years of our current generation of elders. Other historians have used the life cycle approach to examine the different ways that people understood life stages in the past, and they have examined changing experiences of these stages as well as the rituals and ceremonies associated with them.[13] I knew that this type of exploration fit well with the oral history research I wanted to do, especially considering that there is very little historical literature, or any other type of literature, on life stages and Indigenous women. I had long been interested in the ceremonies, practices, and protocols that accompany transitions between life stages and I wanted to learn more about them, so I could incorporate them into my own family life.

These objectives gave me a general direction for inquiry, and they set the basic framework for understanding the life stages of the women I interviewed. But as I have mentioned, I was intrigued by deeper questions; questions about how life stage roles and responsibilities were a part of defining identity and citizenship, that is, "the status of being a citizen," of having "membership in a community," and "the quality of an individual's response to membership in a community." [14] I wondered how this fostered the creation of *mino-pimatisi-win*—a term used to describe holistic health and wellness, including physical, emotional, mental, and spiritual states of being. [15] These questions took root over the many years of my listening to the teachings of Anishinaabe and Haudenosaunee Elders on the life cycle continuum. I was fascinated by the way these teachers spoke to the value accorded to each life stage, and by their descriptions of how different generations worked interdependently to uphold the spiritual, social, economic, and political order of Aboriginal societies. In particular, I was struck by their respect for elders and children; the honouring of their contributions, as opposed to seeing them as a responsibility or, at worst, a burden. Framed in this way, life stage identities and practices defined each individual's purpose as well as his or her community responsibility throughout the life cycle, and these responsibilities were critical to the health and well-being of both the individual and society. These teachings gave me a strong foundation from which to begin, and for this reason I would like to offer a brief review of their importance and meaning.

Life Cycle Teachings of the Anishinaabek

As the knowledge keepers of our societies, Elders will point out that Indigenous teachings related to the life cycle are complex and can take many years to master. In order to learn and especially to become a teacher of this knowledge, one must engage in multiple practices of Indigenous knowledge transfer. This can involve a combination of doing "sweats" (sweat lodge ceremonies), fasting, being adopted into families that carry the knowledge, and learning the protocols around sharing the knowledge. I have not lived long enough nor have I done all of the work that is necessary to carry this knowledge. I can, however, impart what I understand of the teachings as I have learned them through hearing them told in community settings and through reading about them in the literature I will reference in this chapter. Most of what I will share comes from the Anishinaabek.

Among the Anishinaabek, life stages are typically described as having either four or seven levels. In *Ojibway Heritage*, Anishinaabe author and ethnologist Basil Johnston describes the stages as "the four hills of life," which progress from infancy, to youth, to adulthood, to old age. [16] These physical life stages have corresponding moral stages of development, which are preparation, quest, vision, and fulfillment of vision. [17] Johnston's teachings emphasize the difficulties involved in physical survival and highlight the challenges presented by undertaking a moral journey through life. Youth are required to acquire skills such as hunting and fishing, sewing, and cooking.[18] Adults are responsible for ensuring survival through caregiving and providing,[19] while also carrying a moral responsibility for living out the vision that was given to them in their youth.[20] Whereas the physical challenges might be formidable, Johnston points out that it is the moral journey that gives meaning to human life. Moral development through fulfilling one's personal vision marks the difference between merely existing and fully living.

In this teaching, infants and children are portrayed as "frail and help-less," but their traditional role has been to bring "happiness and hope to all," because they represent potential and the future.[21] Infancy and childhood is a time of preparation for the vision quest, which takes place in youth. Youth is defined by the quest; it could begin early (among those "hardly out of in-fancy")[22] and end late, taking as long as necessary. Johnston points out that a person cannot proceed to the adult stage until he or she has received a vision particular to his or her life's purpose.[23] Visions are achieved through fasting and isolation, where the individual has the opportunity to seek communion with his or her inner self.[24]

Johnston describes how the principle of non-interference is key to fulfill-ing a vision: individuals are to live out their vision according to "the laws of the world and the customs of the community,"[25] but at the same time, no one is entitled to interfere with the vision of another. In old age, individuals are to take on a teaching role, because "by living through all the stages and living out the visions, men and women know something of human nature and liv-ing and life."[26] Their wisdom will be respected and adhered to, providing they have lived out their vision.

In *The Seven Fires: Teachings of the Bear Clan as Told by Dr. Danny Musqua*, Mosôm Danny discusses human development according to Saulteaux oral tradition. He describes it as the progression through seven fires: conception and life in the womb; birth to walking; walking to seven years of age; little men and little women; young adults; adult development; and old age and death.[27] This model includes three types of elders: "community elders, cer-emonial elders and earth elders," categories which are "based on the specific areas of knowledge that have been attained."[28]

Mosôm Danny teaches about life as a learning journey in which one's spirit strives to learn about the physical state of existence in this world. He describes how the spirit is more conscious in the earliest stages of life, particularly when in utero and to some extent during infancy. Because of the shock of arrival in the physical world, the spirit enters a subconscious state early in its lifetime, and from there it progresses through the remaining life stages in pursuit of awakening the spirit.[29] Danny notes that ceremonies are an important part of this learning journey, as they acknowledge the spirit and mark important milestones in the life of an individual.[30]

As with Johnston's teaching, Mosôm Danny's teachings tell us that life is a journey through various stages of consciousness; stages which are both facilitated and celebrated through ceremony. Danny's teachings define certain roles and responsibilities for these different stages. Infancy and early childhood involve being nurtured, being dependent on others, and developing trust.[31] As children grow older, they learn about discipline and taking up responsibilities. Youth is a time when individuals begin to assume adult responsibilities and are charged with caregiving duties for the young and old in the community. As Danny puts it, this is a time when there is plenty of "volunteer work."[32] Adults carry responsibilities of providing for family, and elders are the teachers and keepers of knowledge, law, and ceremony.[33]

The Midewiwin, a spiritual society of the Anishinaabek, also define the roles and responsibilities of the life cycle as having seven stages. These stages include infancy and childhood ("the good life" or "spirit life"); youth ("the fast life"); young adulthood ("wondering/wandering life"); middle adulthood ("planning/planting life"); mature adulthood ("doing life"); and elder years ("elder life").[34] As with the other teachings, in this model the individual progresses from being the recipient of care and teaching, to seeking and fulfilling one's purpose, to becoming the teacher. Odawa Elder Liza Mosher describes how one can get stuck at any stage if one doesn't go through the appropriate experiences and lessons that need to be learned. She gives the example that if someone has been overly disciplined as a child or youth, they might end up "running around" or engaging in immature behaviour in adulthood.[35] Each stage must be completed in order to successfully achieve the next, and there are many who reach their senior years without achieving elderhood because they have not done the necessary work of growing and becoming responsible.[36]

The Midewiwin framework also defines the privileges and responsibilities for each life stage. I am most familiar with the way these stages have been adapted and how they are currently being applied in the health and healing work I do with Native peoples in Ontario. As a community-based educator, I have facilitated workshops using a model based on the Midewiwin framework and developed by the Ontario Federation of Indian Friendship Centres.[37] In this model there are not seven, but eight stages of life: infants, toddlers, children, youth, young adults, parents, grandparents, and elders. The added stage of young adulthood is useful in terms of the work that we do to validate the complexities of moving through these youthful years in modern society. In general, I have seen how this model lends itself to healing because it reintroduces concepts of individual purpose and community cohesion. The intent of these workshops is to help us mitigate the violence, social dysfunction, and trauma that are the legacy of colonial interference. Life cycle teachings help us to do this.

Through applying the teachings as they are used in community-based workshops, I have learned that there are responsibilities for each group. Infants are responsible for bringing joy to the family; this is their job. Because of their proclivity to curiosity and the need to explore, toddlers remind us of the importance of maintaining a safe environment. Children bring truth because their honesty demands it, and youth offer challenges to the precepts of the community. Young adults are responsible for doing the "work of the people"; they can be called upon to do whatever labour is necessary to ensure community survival. Parents are providers, and grandparents are life teachers. Elders are highly regarded, because they are the "spirit teachers."

These teachings speak to life stage roles and responsibilities, ceremonies, and interdependency that are so crucial to the health of our communities. They demonstrate how teachings can change over time as circumstances and audiences change; they change in response to the needs of the people and the times they serve. Johnston's emphasis on the frailty of young children, for example, likely comes from his teachers who had lived in the early 1900s when families were suffering from high rates of infant mortality as a result of widespread tuberculosis. The life stage teacher in Johnston's narrative speaks of "the coughing sickness," stating that "few, in relation to the number born, live on."[38] As noted above, teachings that are provided in workshops today are placing more of an emphasis on young adulthood/adolescence. One reason for doing so is because this stage of life has become more pronounced over the past fifty years or so. In the period covered in this book, the 1930s to the 1950s, youth did not go through extended periods of adolescence like young people today: as soon as an individual passed through puberty, she or he was expected to meet the responsibilities of adulthood. Young people today go through a longer period of transition from childhood to adulthood, and in our communities they are facing many challenges. Contemporary teachers work in communities that may, for example, be coping with epidemic rates of adolescent suicide,[39] so teachings about purpose, life stages, and belonging could never be more critical. It is important to note, however, that although certain aspects of a teaching can change depending on the context, the teaching's core substance and values do not change.

I have been in workshops where we use life cycle wheels and models to reflect on our past and to think through what we need to do in terms of moving forward in our development. My experience of using these teachings in modern settings fostered my curiosity to see how they were manifested in the lives of Aboriginal peoples in the past. I knew that that our current generation of elders could speak to a time when communities were still largely living off the land, where kinship systems were more intact, and when communities had to work together to ensure survival. I explore the meaning of these teachings in more depth in the following chapters.

Overview of the Book

I have divided the life stage findings into four chapters (Chapters 3 to 6) roughly based on Anishinaabe life cycle teachings, although this division was greatly influenced by the amount of material I collected about each life stage. For example, I found a lot of material about women in their early years and elderly women but less about women in their young adult years and middle-aged women. Therefore, all of the material on "adult" women from the time of puberty to menopause is included in a single chapter. Although these chapters rely primarily on information provided in the oral histories, they also draw on literature that contains information about the life stages of northern Algonquian women.

Oral history work is as much about process as it is about product, so Chapter 1 is devoted to an examination of what oral history involves in an Indigenous context. I thought it was important to provide the reader with a behind-the-scenes look at both the theory of Algonquian oral history and how it worked out in my experience of writing this book.

Chapter 2 provides a look at who the oral historian participants were and where they came from. I also provide some historical context to give the reader an idea of the bigger picture surrounding the lives of the historian participants.

Chapter 3 is about pregnancy, infancy, and the toddler years. It begins with a look at family planning, which was typically handled by the "old ladies." I then provide information on some of the protocols related to the care of pregnant women. Birth and newborn care is then described. This care included the practices pertaining to the umbilical cord and placenta; customs which were widespread and long-standing in northern Algonquian communities. I write about names and naming ceremonies for babies, and finish with what is known about "walking out" ceremonies for toddlers.

Chapter 4 is about childhood and youth, and shows a consistency in parenting styles from the earliest European observations into the twentieth century. I discuss how non-coercive and indirect techniques were the hallmark of Indigenous childrearing. Children were taught to be self-reliant while learning a sense of responsibility to the community, and co-existing principles of independence and interdependence were the foundation for raising Indigenous children. Chapter 4 also includes an extensive discussion about practices around puberty. This life passage brought about rapid change in the status of the individual, who was now expected to fully contribute to the adult work of the community. I write about puberty fasts and seclusions, drawing on information I found in the literature and then share stories about the experiences of the historian participants.

I begin Chapter 5 with what struck me the most regarding young and middle-aged women: how hard they had to work to ensure the survival of their families and communities. This was part of living a land-based lifestyle, but women's work was undoubtedly also compounded and complicated by poverty and discrimination. This meant that women had to be extra resourceful in managing the material necessities of their communities, such as food and clothing. The value placed on their home-centred work meant that women had their own circles or "jurisdictions" from which they were in charge of not only the material resources but also the social relations of the community. I discuss how they were also the "keepers of relationships," forming strong bonds among themselves and taking responsibility for teaching family law to youngsters.

Chapter 6 is about elderly women. The story medicines in this chapter inspired me because they showed that "old ladies" had power and authority that were at odds with western patriarchal family structures up into the 1960s (the end of my period of analysis). It was the old ladies who held responsibilities for leadership and governance, teaching, and managing the health of their communities. There were a number of stories about elderly women who were leaders in their extended families; the *gii maa kwe* (head woman) was the final decision maker in many cases. Old ladies were valued for how they looked after the communities through their attention to kinship, through how they managed the health, well-being, and spirit connections of community members. As with the younger women, elderly women worked hard to ensure the survival of the community, contributing to the very end of their lives.

I conclude the book with a summary of what I have learned and with some reflections from a conversation I had with Jane Middelton-Moz, psychologist, author, and educator. To me, Jane is like an eagle, flying over Indian country, watching and addressing trends in social well-being through her work as a trainer in intergenerational trauma and community intervention. As I have stated, the intent of this book is to assist with decolonization. I knew that Jane, with her extensive experience travelling to Indigenous communities across the continent, would be able to speak to how the story medicines in this book might be applied to Indigenous lives today. I am grateful to Jane for helping me end the book, and to Maria Campbell who starts it off. Their pieces are the bookends to the participants' stories and my analysis. Maria's foreword offers us a place of beginning with Notokwew Atayokan, the old lady who is the keeper of the laws and who will always be with us to sustain our peoples through teaching the power of our traditional ways. Jane's conclusion offers us a perspective of Indian country today, allowing us to see the possibilities of how learning about and applying "the old ways" can help us move into the future.

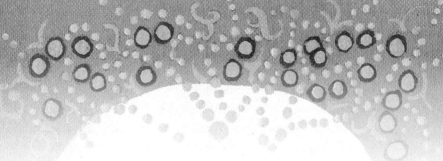

Chapter 1

Weaving the Stories

*T*his book represents a weaving together of stories from multiple sources, both written and oral. Whereas the foundation of the book is the oral history that I gathered from the historian participants, I have also used materials that I've read in books and articles to add depth and context. My aim was to put all of these sources together to build a rich and multilayered story.

Perhaps the most important thing I learned from working on this book is that the *process* of doing oral history work is as important as what is *produced* at the end. Whereas the gathering of written sources was a process of collecting information that would develop and support a historical profile of Algonquian women, the process of collecting oral history was much more of an exercise in learning about how story medicines can work, and gradually finding my place within that work. Because this element is so important, I have devoted this chapter and the next to describing the sources I drew from, the process it involved, and how I wove it all together. I begin with a quick glance at the written sources before getting into considerations about Indigenous oral history.

Written Sources

Although there is very little in terms of focused literature on life stages of Native women, it was possible to glean some information by combing through many different sources, disciplines, and literary genres.

I began with the history books, but soon found that in spite of the increasing production of women's history since the 1970s, the lives of Indigenous women are still largely invisible in that genre of literature. There are some exemplary historians who have written about Algonquian women's lives in the fur trade era and up into the nineteenth century,[1] but histories about the distinct experiences of northern Algonquian women in the twentieth century are generally lacking. When I read twentieth-century history about mainstream North American women and girls, I often think about how different the lives portrayed in the literature seem from what I know of Native women's lives during the same time periods, and I think about what we are missing in our North American history texts as a result. Where are the stories of kokum (granny) teaching the four-year-old how to hunt; the depictions of infants in moss bags watching siblings and female relatives pick berries or Seneca root; the puberty fasts; the fiddle dances and the Sun Dances; the women's councils; the old woman doctoring with plant medicine? Many of these things were going on in Native girls and women's lives, even up to the time when mainstream teens of the 1940s danced the jitterbug and 1950s housewives grappled with "the feminine mystique."[2]

If you are looking for information about these distinct Indigenous worlds, it would be better for you to go to the ethnographic and autobiographical literature. Although the earliest autobiographical works that cover the pre-reserve and early settlement period are written by men, one can mine them for information about women's lives.[3] Later autobiographical works written in the 1970s provide information about mid-century Cree and Métis communities through the eyes of Aboriginal girls.[4] Northern Algonquian voices also come through in edited collections of oral history. Freda Ahenakew, for example, has been prolific in recording and publishing stories of Cree elders. Ahenakew's material offers rich information about women's lives in the first half of the twentieth century, and there are other collections of northern Algonquian oral history that are informative in this way.[5]

Ethnographies offer the most explicit sources of information about the life cycle of Algonquian women, especially those that were researched and written during the early twentieth century.[6] While these ethnographies were typically written by outsiders and must be reviewed as such, they are nonetheless built out of interviews with "informants," many of whom were the oral historians of their early-twentieth-century Indigenous communities.[7] Because of the urgency to document the cultures they believed to be dying out, these ethnographers often interviewed elders, asking them to speak about "traditional" societies. One must take male bias into consideration, given that many of the anthropologists during this period were males who spoke exclusively to male informants. There are works by a number of female ethnographers, however, and several ethnographies contain information from female informants.[8] Many of these stories can be historically situated within the late pre-reserve and early reserve era.

I was able to find a fair amount of information in the ethnographic material related to the work that women did in land-based societies, and these depictions of "women's work" provided a backdrop for writing about middle-aged women. There was also a fair amount of information in the ethnographic literature related to marriage, family structure, and kinship obligations, and there was some information about the roles of older women. These roles included working as herbalists and midwives, looking after children and being teachers of the younger generations. Information about children often focused on their contributions to community in terms of work and child-rearing practices and styles. I was surprised to find that there was also plenty of information in the ethnographic material about ceremonies for infants and girls, particularly naming ceremonies and puberty rites. After years of yearning for more information about these ceremonies, I realized that there are descriptions in the ethnographic literature! Of course, there are people who carry this knowledge and continue to do the ceremonies, but documentary information can be helpful and perhaps more accessible to those who don't have teachers in their own circles.

My review of all this material reinforced what Maria Campbell has encouraged me to do in terms of working with literature. As Maria describes in her preface to this book, the late Anishinaabe Elder Peter O'Chiese always stressed to her how important it is for Indigenous people to sift though ethnographic literature because it can be helpful to us as we put the pieces of our cultures back together. The message is to read as much as you can, while being aware of the limitations. I always bear in mind the lesson from my friend the Sto:lo Elder and healer Dorris Peters, who remembers her uncles telling the craziest stories that they made up on the spot to have fun with the anthropologists who came around in the 1930s! For this reason, it is important that we work with our elders and oral historians at the same time as we read the literature. As I demonstrate in the next section, this work with oral history involves much more than collating information and checking for "facts." It is about working with story medicines.

Purpose: Listening for Stories that "Work like Arrows"

> Clearly, Indigenous oral histories do not abide by conventional disciplinary boundaries. They are about relationships and generational continuity, and the package is holistic—they include religious teachings, metaphysical links, cultural insights, history, linguistic structures, literary and aesthetic form, and Indigenous "truths."
>
> —Winona Wheeler,
> "Decolonizing Tribal Histories"[9]

As Winona Wheeler indicates, Indigenous oral history contains many elements that take it beyond the goal of showing "how it was." There is often an overt sense of purpose to oral history work, and this book is definitely built on that element. I share my sense of purpose with a number of other Indigenous scholars who have framed the writing of Indigenous history as a project in decolonization.[10] With reference to how Cree oral history works, for example, Neal McLeod writes, "Cree narrative memory is an ongoing attempt to find solutions to the problems we face today, such as breakdown of families, loss of language and general loss of respect for ourselves and others."[11] According to this approach, oral history serves our communities by providing insight and vision and inspiring change for the better.

In addition to providing insight and vision, one of the primary characteristics of Indigenous oral history is to delineate the world view of the people it serves.[12] Rather than offering a chronicle of events, Indigenous oral history typically works to confirm identity and remind the listeners of the social and moral code of their society. "History," writes ethnohistorian Raymond Fogelson, "is not something that happens to Indians; it might better be conceived as a potent force that they actively utilize to refashion, and manipulate as a survival mechanism."[13] This point is demonstrated by Dakota historian Waziyatawin Angela Wilson, who gives the example of how this played out in the work she did with Dakota historian/Elder Eli Taylor. Although she originally set out to record a "Dakota historical perspective on specific events," it soon became apparent that the material was more significant for the information it provided "about the meaning of being Dakota."[14] The truths we seek in this work are thus more about the truths of who we are and want to be as a people, rather than the "truths" about "what happened."

Whereas academic historians may be reluctant to engage in this kind of history-telling, anthropologists have been recognized and rewarded for their Indigenous oral history work. Anthropologist Julie Cruikshank is often cited for the work that she has done with Elders Angela Sidney, Kitty Smith, and Annie Ned in the Yukon. Cruikshank has written about how she originally went looking for narratives about events (in particular, how the Klondike gold rush affected women's lives) and was confounded when Elders provided traditional stories instead. She later realized that the Elders' allegorical stories underpinned the narratives and events of their own lives. Their traditional stories provided a code by which one could live a good life, a "life lived like a story."[15] According to Cruikshank, the Elders might say that stories "are not even really about facts or events." Rather, "they are about coming to grips with the personal meanings of broadly shared knowledge and converting those meanings to social ends."[16]

In the field of linguistic and cultural anthropology, Keith Basso has been recognized for his award-winning books that explore this function of story among the Apache. Basso has documented how Apache stories often "work like arrows," acting as piercing missives, sent out to "make you live right."[17] He demonstrates how many traditional Apache stories are connected to particular places, allowing the land to continuously remind people of social and moral code even when storytellers are absent or deceased.[18] Basso also explores the notion that "what matters most to Apaches is where events occurred, not when."[19]

I offer these considerations because, as a historian working with Indigenous oral history on this project, my aim has been to foster healing and decolonization by delineating a world view and creating a sense of identity and belonging. Judging from the standards of conventional history, some might find both the individuals' stories and my overarching narrative too idyllic. But one must bear in mind that my intent was to create a story that "works like an arrow,"[20] or, in Neal McLeod's words, allows us to "conceive of a different way that people might live together."[21] What I have provided for the reader are glimpses and threads of a world in which identity and belonging were fostered and nurtured in childhood; where women had authorities that were rooted in cultures that valued and respected equity; and in which "old ladies" ruled. The reader will not find stories of violence and abuse here, although these things were also happening in northern Algonquian communities from the 1930s to the 1960s. There are other works that tell stories of domestic violence, fallout from residential schools, and communities in crisis. Although such works are important to consider for the truths they tell, this is not the focus of the stories in this book.

Building on Relationships

Another important lesson I learned in this oral history work was about the significance of relationships.[22] I had been doing qualitative research with Native peoples for about fifteen years as a community-based consultant, scholar, and researcher prior to beginning this project, and was therefore quite familiar with conducting interviews on a variety of subjects. Based on this experience, I figured I would need to interview about forty people to do the book I had in mind. When I made this suggestion to Cree scholar and historian Winona Wheeler she responded, "Forty is way too many! Try six." Winona then made the distinction between doing grounded theory (within social science) as opposed to oral history. Whereas the latter can be built out of one-time meetings and interviews, it can take much longer to build the types of relationships that Indigenous oral history requires. Winona did not say much more at the time, leaving room for me to discover this distinction for myself. Yet her words corresponded to what Maria Campbell had also been teaching me over the years; that the quality of oral history is based on the quality of the relationship between the teller and the student. Maria had also advised me that it was better to work with fewer people, but to do more interviews.

Of course, I didn't listen to my teachers at first, and set off in search of an indefinite but plentiful number of oral historians. I was driven by curiosity and a concern for seeking out the "truth." I wanted to find out, for example, how widespread some of the lifecycle ceremonies had been at mid-century. Because of this I felt compelled to interview a larger number of people—certainly more than six. But as Trickster would have it, I was limited in the number of historian participants because I had a hard time finding individuals who were keen to be interviewed. This led to other considerations about doing Indigenous oral history. When I shared my woes with Mosôm Danny, he suggested that elders might feel intimidated when asked to play the role of oral historian. Perhaps humility and shyness play a part. But Danny made the additional point that "sometimes elders run away from telling their history, more out of fear that people are going to say, *Oh, you are just making things up.*" Danny spoke about his own experiences in developing the confidence to engage in oral history work:

> I know what that feels like [to be fearful of speaking]. I was there until I was forty-five years old and I decided to fast. That's when I

found the fire and the desire to do this. Finally I was brave enough. Now I don't give a darn what anybody says…. I was born to hear these stories and to remind people that they need to be revisited in order to understand the full impact of the loss of our people's way of life. I'm just telling what I heard and that's it. Let them find the rest—because the time is here to put all this information together. With one parcel of information here, and another parcel over here, we will put it all back together. Eventually the teachings will be there.

I appreciated this encouragement because I had made contact with a number of elders who agreed to be interviewed but then cancelled when the time came to do the work (a situation I had run into with my own father over the years in my attempts to do oral history with him about his upbringing in Manitoba). Danny's comments and my experiences made me reflect on how elderly Indigenous people can suffer from the traumas and ambiguities of their particular histories. For people who have been colonized and oppressed, "history" is not always a pleasant place to go. Whereas establishing trust is a necessary part of any interview process, it is perhaps even more significant (and difficult) when there are traumas, pressures, and expectations from the community around what is shared.

The relationship between the storyteller and the story listener is thus paramount, and so it was a blessing that I ended up working with only fourteen participants—far fewer than originally planned! According to Winona Wheeler, "The social relations between a teacher and student, more specifically the degree of commitment on the part of the student determines, to a very large degree, the quality and depth of knowledge the student receives."[23] One only has so much time to build relationships, which includes plenty of informal time outside of the interview process. Even working with fourteen was a lot. As I describe later, I was able to get into depth with some participants more than others because of limitations on time.[24]

Writing about his work with Cree Elders, educator Walter C. Lightening demonstrates another point in terms of the significance of relationships. He describes how "thinking mutually" works between the storyteller and the listener.[25] The position of both the listener and the teller will thus have an impact on what is told, and both parties carry responsibilities for the knowledge. Because the telling will depend on what the student is ready to hear, each telling will be different, or, as Walter Lightening points out, "Elders' teachings are individualized."[26] Lightening further notes that often stories can be coded and structured with multiple layers of metaphor, which unfold over time as the listener becomes ready to receive the knowledge.[27]

In their work with Cree Elders, Walter Hildebrandt, Sarah Carter, and Dorothy First Rider have also remarked on this characteristic of Indigenous oral history, writing that "some stories ... need to be absorbed over many tellings before the significance of the message as it relates to the social context provided by the teller and the occasion can be understood: such stories cannot be superficially analysed for meaning."[28] They point out that "oral testimony cannot be sifted for 'facts' alone. The importance of the speaker and the forum must be appreciated as well."[29]

Although some stories maintain consistency over time,[30] some stories change with time. These stories vary according to the life stage of the participants telling them or according to what is important to them at the time of telling.[31] Because the subjectivity of the storyteller is understood, it is without question that stories of the past will reflect the needs of the present. One must therefore pay attention to why a storyteller chooses to tell a particular story to a particular audience at a particular time. As noted above, there is a purpose in every telling, which is not seen as detracting from the "truth."

My subjectivity in writing this book is thus evident if one considers that I was a listener/student of the individual storytellers as well as the person engaged in telling/writing the larger story represented by the book. On the most obvious level, the individual stories reflected my interests because they were told to me in response to my questions. But as I have learned over the years, people don't always answer the questions you ask—they choose which stories to tell and how to tell them. I also chose which stories to tell when it came to writing the book. My purpose in doing so involves wanting to make a contribution to family and community healing.

More analysis would be necessary to uncover how the storytellers spoke to me specifically as a listener, gauging what I was ready to hear and so on. I also feel that I only got part way into the storytelling process with a number of the participants, because I had to stop doing interviews in order to get the writing done! Then there is the added complexity that I was listening not only for myself but also for a future readership. At this point, it isn't possible to assess how all these elements factored in, nor how lessons or insights from the stories might reveal themselves over time. There were some "mythical" stories, for example, that I did not include because I felt I needed more time with them and a better understanding of how to apply them in this context. These stories and considerations will be part of my story bundle as I work more with the material in the future.

Responsibilities

In working with oral history, one must also be aware of the protocols that centre on knowledge sharing. This is particularly important when it comes to traditional or sacred knowledge, which typically belongs to the collective. As Winona Wheeler has remarked, "In the Cree world all knowledge is not knowable. Some knowledge is kept in family lines, other kinds of knowledge have to be earned."[32] This is true of a number of Indigenous nations, and there are often protocols around the sharing of stories.[33] Oral history work can also involve taking on responsibilities that carry on long after the project is done, for as Wheeler says, "in the Cree world our sources are our teacher and the student-teacher relationship prescribes life-long obligations and responsibilities."[34] I can now see how this applies because of the sense of duty I feel towards the storytellers. I once heard Cree elder Pauline Shirt remark that her grandmother would finish telling a story with "now you owe me."[35] Within this tradition, I am indebted for what has been provided.

I have only recently begun to understand what it means to take responsibility for the knowledge you gain as a storyteller. When I was finishing writing this book, I began to reflect on a conversation that I had had with Maria Campbell when we first spoke about doing this work together. Maria had agreed to do the research and writing about life stages of Indigenous women with me, but only if we focused on Cree and Métis women, the people of our mutual heritage.[36] She wanted to do this because, as she said to me, "that way you will have something you can teach." At the time I took this to mean that it would be fitting for me to have knowledge of my own people that I could bring to the classroom as well as to the community-based types of teaching that I do. Now I realize that there are other applications for this knowledge. For example, there are ceremonial and healing responsibilities that I gained through the process of doing the oral history for this book. Although I do not want to write about these responsibilities here, it is important to note that there is often a parallel track of learning and apprenticeship that goes on for Indigenous academics and community teachers who engage in a quest for traditional knowledge. The learning and the work that come with it continue long after the book is done.

Working with the Historian Participants

In the end, the fourteen historian participants I worked with resulted in fourteen different types of relationships, histories, and experiences. As noted previously, Maria Campbell and Mosôm Danny had distinct roles in terms of the overall framework and direction of the project. I had originally approached Maria in 2000 to see if she wanted to co-write a book on the subject of life stages of women. As time passed, she was unable to take on the work involved in researching the book, but she continued to provide me with guidance and teaching. Maria also became one of the primary oral historians, spending plenty of informal time with me—driving, working, doing theatre productions, having late night teas, or enjoying long winter breakfasts during which times many of the stories came out. Along with this informal teaching and storytelling, we recorded eleven interviews. During the course of the project, Maria also hosted me (and my family) in her home for months at a time while I worked with the oral historian participants in Saskatchewan. The student–teacher relationship we developed along the way falls within traditional models of education and oral history, where the student and teacher become interwoven within each other's lives.

Danny's contribution was twofold: as an oral historian participant and as the Mosôm (Grandfather) who provided a theoretical framework for the book. I have already outlined Anishinaabe life stage teachings, which include those shared by Mosôm, and I begin each chapter with a quotation that offers his teachings. I typically refer to him as "Mosôm," for he is "the old man" of this project. I also refer to him as "Danny" in each of the life stage chapters. As with the other participants (whom I also refer to by first name), Danny provided life history stories that exemplify the teachings.

As this is a work about women, some might question why I chose a man to provide the theoretical framework, or why Danny and Rene Meshake (another male participant, introduced in Chapter 2) were participants. In truth, I had originally wanted a female teacher to speak to the life stage teachings, but was not successful in securing one. In the meantime, I had met Danny while I was doing research in Saskatchewan and was both astonished and enraptured by his storytelling ways. I discovered that he had a wealth of knowledge related to my book project, and that he had published on life stages as well. Danny's teachings are applicable to men and women, and his respect for women's historical authorities fit well with what I was looking for. Ultimately, Mosôm shared what he knew with a magnificent and loving generosity of spirit, telling me "this knowledge belongs to you; it belongs to the nation." I worked with both Danny and Rene because they made themselves available to me as teachers, and because I knew from listening to them previously that they had rich and powerful stories to share about the women in their communities.

In working with the oral historian participants, I tried to follow Maria's advice to do multiple interviews. I made the effort to interview each of them at least twice, and at least half provided four or more interviews. I conducted close to fifty recorded interviews in total, and engaged in plenty of other visiting where discussions were not recorded. In the process I learned that not all of the knowledge one is seeking comes from recorded interviews. For example, I was only able to do two recorded interviews with Sylvia Wuttunee, but I enjoyed a weekend stay with her during which she fed me, looked after me, and gave me my first lesson in beadwork. Together, we beaded the feathers that are part of my "story listening" bundle. I carry these items with me now as I go about listening to stories and sharing them with others. As such, Sylvia contributed enormously to the storytelling process, teaching me a lot about the roles and responsibilities of Cree women. Like Sylvia, each storyteller made a distinct contribution.

When it came time to conducting the interviews, I asked general open-ended questions about the communities the historian participants grew up in. I have found in previous work that those with more experience and training as storytellers require less questioning. As a trained oral historian, for example, Mosôm Danny can talk for hours with very little prodding or interruption. This does not mean, however, that the role of the listener is inactive; as indicated previously, the quality of listening will determine what is told. My experiences working with Danny taught me about the spiritual nature of knowledge transfer, as this kind of sharing involves work that I can only describe as unlocking the space between the teller and listener so the story can enter. The success of our history-telling sessions was related both to how I prepared for the interviews and to Danny's facility as a storyteller to move into that space.

Maria is also an experienced storyteller, although as I suggest above, the process I undertook with her was different in that it was more long term and involved other types of responsibilities on both of our parts. My experience working with Maria over the ten-year period since we first entertained the idea for this project has taught me about the kind of knowledge that can come out of building a "traditional" student–teacher relationship. The time we spent together made it possible to delve into layers of memory and analysis that were not immediately apparent—even to Maria—in the first few interviews. We had to work to get there at times, and there were many lessons that happened when we were doing something else with no voice recorder in sight. In turn, Maria and I grew into other types of responsibilities to one another: family responsibilities, student–teacher responsibilities, and mutual responsibilities to community. I wasn't able to get to this level of work with all of the participants, but I made many new relationships along the way. I spend the next chapter introducing those relatives, new members of my family of the heart.

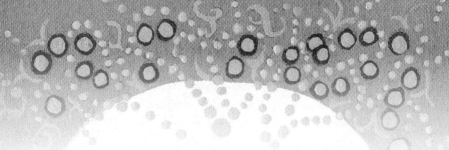

Chapter 2

People and Places

Michif, Nēhiyawak, Anishinaabek: Locating the Oral Historians

The women and men who participated as oral historians in this book were from Michif (Métis), Nēhiyawak (Cree), and Anishinaabek (Ojibway and Saulteaux) communities in the Prairies or in Ontario. I chose to base this life cycle book on Indigenous women in these groups because of my personal ancestry and my community connections. I also wrote about these peoples[1] together because they are part of the same language family and, at mid-twentieth century, they had many similar cultural characteristics in terms of hunting/harvesting life ways, social and political organization, and the ceremonies and teachings that supported these worlds. This is not to discount the diversity between, and indeed within, Nēhiyawak, Michif, and Anishinaabek peoples and communities, then or today. There are certainly marked differences in experiences related to whether the participants grew up on reserve; in Métis settlements or communities; in "the bush" or in small towns; in Christian, "traditional," or mixed spiritual communities; within different economies, and so on. But it is fair to say that all of the historian participants had a connection to the land of their ancestors and the teachings that come from that connection.[2]

Many of the historian participants were from the Treaty 6 area in Saskatchewan. This is because the teachers I had sought out to help me frame the research (Maria Campbell and Mosôm Danny Musqua) live in Saskatoon. I spent three years going back and forth to Saskatchewan, basing myself in Saskatoon and in Batoche, building relationships and interviewing those who came from areas north and west of there. Others were from Ontario, because this is where I live and where I have connections to various Anishinaabe communities. Although I had known some of the participants previously, others were introduced to me by friends and community members. The widespread and seemingly haphazard geographical representation of oral historian participants is thus based on my personal network of relationships, rather than a regional or territorial focus. For example, Rene is the only participant from the Treaty 3 area, but his participation in this book is due to the fact that he works as an Elder in the city where I live and has been a long-time friend and teacher to me. At the same time, I knew that Rene had wonderful stories as a result of being raised by a formidable Anishinaabe grandmother. Like Rene, most of the oral historian participants now live in urban areas, but the stories they told come from their rural or on-reserve childhood communities.

The Times

In the previous chapter I noted that the stories I collected were focused on the positive elements of social organization in northern Algonquian communities at mid-century. While these stories provide a refreshing and uplifting perspective on northern Algonquian life, it is important to provide some basic historical context, as the Michif, Nēhiyawak, and Anishinaabek were under tremendous stress during the mid-twentieth-century timeframe of these stories.

If we begin with the parent and grandparent generation of the historian participants, we see that they had come through times of great repression and change. Those who had lived through the late nineteenth century saw the loss of traditional territories that had sustained their economies and life ways for centuries. Late-nineteenth-century First Nations peoples found themselves parcelled onto reserves and subjected to a "pass system" that gave Indian agents control over where First Nations people could go, when they might leave the reserve, and when they had to return.[3] These "prisons of grass"[4] had marked the beginning of an era of increasing oppression and control of Indigenous peoples on the part of church and state. Historian Olive Dickason has written about the staggering loss of traditional and reserve lands, the intensified federal control over Indigenous lives, and the enforced assimilation attempts that characterized the late nineteenth and early twentieth centuries. While noting that unscrupulous land surrender and expropriation had begun for First Nations in Ontario after the war of 1812, Dickason points out that, between 1896 and 1911, more than one-fifth of reserve lands on the prairies were surrendered. Further lands were then expropriated without surrender by municipalities and companies for their use.[5]

Politically, First Nations peoples were grappling with the enforcement of an Indian Act governance system; a system which, among other things, stripped First Nations women of officially engaging in the governance of their nations. Whereas they had held traditional governing authorities previously through hereditary chieftainships, as clan mothers, through women's councils or other governing structures aimed at maintaining balance, under the Indian Act they could not vote, run for leadership, or even speak at public meetings. In terms of the general political climate, Olive Dickason notes that the power of the Indian Agent grew "steadily more arbitrary," adding that "their duties accrued until they were expected to direct farming operations; administer relief in times of necessity; inspect schools and health conditions on reserves; ensure that department rules and provisions were complied with; and preside over band council meetings, and, in effect, direct the political life of the band."[6] While Métis communities were not subject to this particular authority, they were nonetheless subject to colonial authority through game wardens, local politicians, the RCMP, and other policing mechanisms.

Socially, Indigenous families experienced tremendous stress because of interference with their extended family systems. Although many Indigenous families today still enjoy the benefits of extended families and clans, twentieth-century interference on the part of the church and state is certainly behind much of the crisis and social dysfunction where it exists in contemporary communities. Jessica Ball and I have written about how the dismantling of Indigenous families was a tremendous blow, noting that among First Nations and Métis families prior to the twentieth century, the family "underpinned everything from economics to politics, law, and social order, and so the health of the family and family systems was paramount."[7] In terms of economics, people lived in extended family groups that allowed them to harvest and share resources, and their societies were organized around these extended families and clans. Late nineteenth- and early twentieth-century colonial policies were introduced to encourage removal from the land and the dismantling of land-based societies by introducing individualism, private land ownership, and male-dominant nuclear families.[8] Native women were slandered as lax and slovenly in their mothering, and missionaries and representatives of the American and Canadian governments were then sent out to train them into being docile housewives.[9]

All of these policies were aimed at breaking down the powerful kinship systems that sustained communities economically, politically, socially, and spiritually, and which had made them both resistant and resilient to the colonial processes. Two colonial tools aimed at dismantling traditional kinship systems were particularly devastating: residential schools and the child welfare system. Operating from 1879 to 1996, residential schools ripped the heart out of communities by taking their children to institutions where many were physically, sexually, emotionally, and spiritually abused. Ernie Crey and Suzanne Fournier have written that by 1930, almost 75 percent of First Nations children were in residential schools. Following on this, child welfare authorities began to remove children from Native homes and communities in the 1950s, leading into what has been coined the "'60s scoop" where children were removed in record numbers from Indigenous homes. By the 1980s, Native children made up 50, 60, and 70 percent of the child welfare caseloads in Alberta, Manitoba, and Saskatchewan, respectively, even though they represented less than 4 percent of the overall population.[10]

Spiritually and culturally, residential schools were greatly responsible for shaming and beating Indigenous practices out of the child. The schools followed in the centuries-old footsteps of missionaries who had worked relentlessly at converting First Nations peoples, and they reflected the policies of the Canadian state that had banned cultural and spiritual practices. For example, the 1884 "potlatch ban" that threatened the peoples of the Northwest Coast with imprisonment for engaging in their ceremonial feasting and dancing was the first of many restrictions imposed by the state and reinforced by the church. The Sun Dances of the Prairie peoples went underground in 1895 because of federally imposed restrictions, and in 1914 the federal government banned First Nations peoples from appearing in traditional dress and performing traditional dances at fairs and stampedes. As Olive Dickason has pointed out, these bans were "a direct blow to Amerindian community cohesion."[11] These cultural practices were at the heart of spiritual engagement and social organization.

If we look at this history, we can see that the late nineteenth- and early twentieth-century periods had been brutal for the historian participants' families and communities. By the time the first of the historian participants were born in the 1930s, First Nations peoples had endured half a century or more of oppression on the reserves, where movement was restricted and economic activity in terms of hunting, fishing, and farming was thwarted. Métis people had been run off their traditional lands and found themselves "squatting" in places such as the road allowance where they had to "poach" to survive. Several generations of children had already been removed and sent to residential schools, and the child welfare system was moving in to take more. First Nations soldiers were coming home from World War II to find that they were not being respected or given the same rights as white veterans. Women were overwhelmed with large families and were feeling the weight of patriarchy, alcoholism, and violence that their men, powerless to protect and provide for their families, had begun to adopt.

I have painted a bleak picture here because these were bleak years. But it wasn't all bad! The twentieth century also saw new forms of political organization and resistance, with organizations like the Métis Association of Alberta and the National Indian Brotherhood, which were founded in the 1930s and 1940s. Many families and clans held together and supported each other. Women maintained some of their authorities, as will be seen in the stories presented in this book. Spiritual and cultural practices that had to go underground were preserved, and Indigenous men and women did what they could to maintain their land-based economies.

From their own descriptions of their mid-century communities, I learned that all of the historian participants were raised in communities that sustained themselves through hunting, trapping, fishing, gathering plant foods and medicines, and, in many cases, managing gardens or small farms. As well, their communities engaged in the cash economy through casual and seasonal work, which, depending on their location, included trapping, commercial fishing, logging, working as guides, or working as farm hands. Participation in the cash economy was often thwarted through restrictive policies around trade or policies that made it illegal for Native peoples to hunt in their own traditional territories. Many had to resort to "poaching" even to feed their own families.

In general, the historian participants grew up in log or lumber houses that their families had built. It wasn't until the late 1950s and 1960s that people living on reserve began to see the introduction of "that pre-fabricated cardboard housing" (as described by historian participant Gertie). Water was hauled from nearby sources because running water didn't come to most communities until the 1970s. (It is perhaps notable that by 2001, there were still 5,300 on-reserve homes lacking basic water and sewer services.)[12] Most families were still seasonally mobile to some extent, living in tents for their summer excursions and, in some cases, in tents out on the trapline during the winter.

Christianity was well entrenched in all of the participants' communities by mid-twentieth century, but there were still plenty of "traditional" spiritual practices going on in one form or another. It was hard for the historian participants in this project to assess the level of traditional spiritual practices, because much of this was done in secrecy. Most of the communities had one church, while others had several churches or missions, which in some cases caused fractures in the community because of the conflicting denominations.

Western health care was scarce, and usually involved having to travel to the closest town. Women, and older women in particular, were largely responsible for the day-to-day health care in the communities. Schooling involved a mixture of day schooling and residential schooling for First Nations and Métis alike.

Some of the historian participants came from communities where there was little to no interaction with whites, other than with the governing and policing authorities who were in their communities. In other cases, there was interaction for business purposes only. The language in many of these communities was either exclusively Nehiyawewin (Cree) or Anishinaabemowin (Ojibway or Saulteaux), although some grew up with a mixture of Cree, Ojibway, and Chippewyan, along with French, English, and Michif.

Introducing the Oral Historian Participants

When I first began this project, I had hoped to find elders who were in their late eighties and nineties because I wanted to reach into "history" as far back as the interviews would allow. In the end, most of the historian participants I spoke with were in their sixties and seventies, which allowed for storytelling about the mid-century period from the 1930s to the 1960s. This is a generation of "aunties" and "uncles" to me; they are people who are only one generation older than me and who, according to many of the life cycle protocols outlined later in this book, carry responsibilities for teaching me and helping me learn what I need to know. In a number of cases, these aunties and uncles started out trying to connect me with their own elder relatives and teachers, but due to a number of illnesses, winter weather, general reluctance, and perhaps fear arising from the lateral violence that works to silence our storytellers (as described previously by Mosôm Danny), these interviews did not come to pass. I see these aunties and uncles as an interpreter generation; those who lived land-based "traditional" lives but are able to work easily with young people, contemporary realities, and the English language. For that reason, they were more accessible to me.

My oldest participants included Grandmothers Rose (born 1926) and
Olive (1930), and on the other end of the spectrum I interviewed some wom-
en who were born in the early 1950s (Rebecca, Hilary, and Gertie). Although
I made efforts to corral the stories into a specific time period (i.e., the childhood years of the participants that included the 1930s, 1940s, and 1950s), the
book also includes cultural teachings and materials to which the participants
referred, to capture things that happened "long ago." I include these stories
because they are important in terms of achieving my goal of delineating the
world view of those I interviewed, as discussed in Chapter 1.

Table 2.1 offers a glimpse of where participants are from, along with their
ages. I have inconsistent biographical information that I can offer here, as I
had varying degrees of time and accessibility to gather this information and
each participant decided how much he/she wanted to share. There were two
participants who chose to remain anonymous, and so I do not provide biographical information for them. The intent of the biographical sketches that
follow is simply to give more context to an overall understanding of the day-
to-day life in the communities discussed in the book. I introduce the historian
participants from the youngest to the oldest, starting with Grandma Rose.

Table 2.1: The Oral Historian Participants

Name	Childhood Community/ Region	People	Birth Year
Rose Fleury	Duck Lake, Saskatchewan	Métis	1926
Olive Morrisette	North Central Saskatchewan	Métis	1930
Danny Musqua/Mosôm	Keeseekoose First Nation	Saulteaux	1937
Maria Campbell	North Central Saskatchewan	Cree/Métis	1940
Marie Anderson	Wasauksing First Nation	Ojibway	1940
Elsie Sanderson	Northeastern Saskatchewan	Cree/Métis	1943
Rosella Carney	North Central Saskatchewan	Cree/Métis	1943
June King	Central Ontario	Ojibway	1945
Sylvia Wuttunee	Red Pheasant Cree Nation	Cree	1945
Madeleine Dion Stout	Kehewin Cree Nation	Cree	1946
Rene Meshake	Northwestern Ontario	Ojibway	1948
Rebecca Martell	Northwestern Saskatchewan	Métis	1950
Hilary Harper	North Central Saskatchewan	Cree/Métis	1952
Gertie Beaucage	Nipissing First Nation	Ojibway	1954

"Grandma Rose" or Rose Fleury (Métis, b. 1926) is from the town of Duck Lake, Saskatchewan, where she was still residing when I interviewed her. In the 1930s of Rose's childhood, Duck Lake was a thriving centre, where French, English, Scottish, and Doukhobor immigrants had arrived by train in previous decades. The town also included Métis and First Nations inhabitants, and was situated close to two reserves (Beardy's and Okemasis and One Arrow). It was, therefore, a multilingual and multicultural centre where people came to go to church (Anglican, Catholic, Baptist), to shop, to do banking, and to conduct other business. The town had a mill and a slaughterhouse to serve the area's farms and ranches. Rose described her family as "hunters more than anything else," although they also worked as labourers on farms where, in addition to earning wages, they were "paid" with produce and with permission to hunt on the farmer's land. Most families had a small number of farm animals and grew large gardens. During the school year, Rose boarded at the local convent and was schooled there, as her family lived slightly out of town.

Olive Morrisette (Cree/Métis, b. 1930) is a pseudonym for an elder from a Road Allowance community in northwestern Saskatchewan.

Danny Musqua (Saulteaux, b. 1937) is a member of the Keesekoose First Nation, a reserve formed after the signing of Treaty 4 (1874) and located in southeastern Saskatchewan near the Manitoba border. Danny's family were farmers and hunters, and Danny himself farmed for over thirty years. As he was a sickly child, Danny was raised by his grandparents, who instilled in him a lot of the traditional knowledge that he shares today in post-secondary institutions, as well as Native organizations and communities.

Maria Campbell (Cree/Métis, b. 1940) grew up in a Road Allowance community near Prince Albert National Park. Her community and others in the region consisted of families who had moved there following the 1885 (Riel) resistance. After thwarted efforts to homestead in the area, many of these families ended up living on the "road allowance," which was patches of Crown land on either side of the roads. Maria's people lived in this territory in extended family groups that subsisted on hunting and trapping. She has written about these early years in her acclaimed autobiography *Halfbreed* (1973). As an artist, researcher, and educator, Maria has focused on issues pertaining to Métis history.

Marie Anderson (Ojibway, b. circa 1940) grew up on Wasauksing First Nation, an island in Georgian Bay adjacent to Parry Sound, Ontario. Marie went to school on the reserve and to high school in Parry Sound. She graduated from the University of Western Ontario with a teacher's degree and taught for many years. Marie's leadership perhaps came from being the daughter of the acclaimed World War I hero Francis Pegahmagabow, who was also a community leader and the primary informant for the ethnographer Diamond Jenness. Marie was a fabulous storyteller who sadly passed away in 2010.

Elsie Sanderson (Cree/Métis, b. 1943) is from Cumberland House, a Métis settlement on Pine Island in northeastern Saskatchewan and close to The Pas, Manitoba. Because of its location on the Saskatchewan River Delta, the community has a long history as a stopping point on the fur trade route, and a longer history as a meeting place. In Elsie's childhood, the community still emptied out in the fall time and moved out to traplines where they would remain for the winter. When asked how many families would live on the trapline together, Elsie replied, "It's hard for me to say because to me we were all one family." Families lived and worked together in tents within their traditional extended family territories. Furs were sold collectively to a broker who came to the camps, and members would come in periodically for supplies at the Hudson's Bay Company store. During the summer, community members worked in the local commercial fishing industry. In Elsie's youth, the elders spoke Michif, but this has generally eroded and Cree remains the only Indigenous language spoken in the community.

Rosella Carney (Cree/Métis, b. 1943) is from Molanosa, a small community that gets its name from its proximity to Montreal Lake (First Nation) in northern Saskatchewan. Rosella's family were among others who had left the reserve at Montreal Lake to form the small settlement where they were able to trap, fish, and work in logging. In Rosella's family, it was her grandmother who came to Molanosa after having been "kicked off the reserve" for partnering with an outsider. As the community was small, there was very little in terms of infrastructure. Rosella remembers her grandmother travelling by dog team or canoe to get supplies at Montreal Lake, thirty kilometres away. There were no churches, but there was a Mennonite mission where some children were schooled. Others were taught in a one-room school, housed in a donated building in the community.

June King (Ojibway, b. 1945) is a pseudonym for an elder from an Ojibway community in north-central Ontario.

Sylvia Wuttunee (Cree, b. 1945) is a member of the Red Pheasant Cree Nation in Saskatchewan, a community that was established following the signing of Treaty 6 in 1876. When Sylvia was a child, there were about 500 people living on reserve in small "villages" or family communities. Sylvia's mother is Métis and came to Red Pheasant from the Eagle Hill district in the Battlefords to enter into an arranged marriage with Sylvia's father. Sylvia's mother's parents wanted this marriage so their daughter would have treaty status; they told her, "Your children and grandchildren will always have a land base if you marry a treaty Indian—not like the Métis who have no land to call home and have to live on road allowances." Sylvia's parents raised her as a Christian, and they were both strict and loving to her in her youth. Their family lived off subsistence farming along with the wage labour of her father, who drove a truck for the grocery store.

Madeleine Dion Stout (Cree, b. 1946) is from Kehewin Cree Nation, located 240 kilometres east of Edmonton, Alberta. In Madeleine's childhood, families were self-sufficient and there was very little interaction with neighbouring communities, other than the occasional trip to sell cream or where the need arose for western medical care. The language spoken in the community was exclusively Cree. Men from the community had some interaction with farmers, for whom they worked stoking hay or picking up and moving rocks. Families subsisted otherwise on what they acquired by hunting, fishing, and berry picking. Madeleine's family also had a limited amount of cattle, pigs, and chickens, and they lived off the produce of their large garden. Madeleine attended day school until the age of seven, and was then sent to residential school. Madeleine is the niece of Joseph Dion, who is the author of *My Tribe the Crees*, a book I have used in this project.

Rene Meshake (Ojibway, b. 1948) spent his first ten years in his grandmother's traditional territory of Pagwashing, in northwestern Ontario, about eighty kilometres north of the town of Geraldton. This community was built along the Canadian National railway tracks and was "off reserve," although many members were registered with either Long Lake #58 First Nation or Aroland First Nation. In the 1960s, this community was moved onto the aforementioned reserves, a point of rupture that Rene describes as the beginning of the end of their "traditional" ways. In addition to occupations of hunting and fishing, men in Rene's childhood community worked on the railway, built highways, or worked as forest firefighters. Rene's grandmother engaged in fishing, trapping and hunting, sold blueberries, and traded with people passing through on the train.

Rebecca Martell (Métis, b. 1950) spent her childhood in northern Saskatchewan, where the economy was based on mining, trapping, hunting, and fishing. Rebecca's family lived on their own and "in the bush" in the summer, where they resided in a log house or in tents, depending on the activity. During the winter, Rebecca's family would move into town, where Rebecca attended a day school. The languages spoken in the community of Rebecca's youth were English, Cree, and Dënesųłiné (Chipewyan).

Hilary Harper (Cree/Métis, b. 1952) shared stories that come from the time spent with her "little kokum," Celine Morrisette Wright from Moosomin Reserve just outside of Cochin, Saskatchewan. Hilary was primarily raised in Lloydminster, Saskatchewan, but spent a lot of time at Moosomin where her maternal grandparents and great-grandparents lived. Hilary's family had been displaced from a disbanded reserve just outside of Duck Lake, Saskatchewan.

Gertie Beaucage (Ojibway, b. 1954) is from Nipissing First Nation, located on the north shore of Lake Nipissing between Sturgeon Falls and North Bay, Ontario. This reserve consisted of several small villages and was part of the Robinson-Huron Treaty of 1850. In Gertie's childhood, the men in her community worked as wage labourers in farming or fishing, in lumber camps, or as hunting and fishing guides. Gertie's mother also worked seasonally at the tourist resort located on reserve, and her father was one of the few who still worked a trapline on the reserve. Schooling for children at Nipissing was a mixture of day and residential schooling, and Gertie and her four siblings were bused into North Bay where they attended a Catholic day school. Gertie's family was a mixture of Catholics and "traditional" people who resisted the ways of the church.

These fourteen elders provided a wealth of material for me to work with, which I have woven into their stories about their life stages.

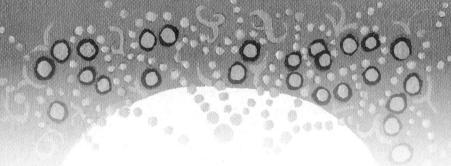

Chapter 3

The Life Cycle Begins:
From Conception to Walking

> A sense of self, a sense of purpose; a sense of being, a sense of
> community; you learn that from the womb.
>
> —**Mosôm Danny Musqua**

*M*osôm Danny's words on the earliest stages of life encourage us to recognize our responsibilities for teaching, honouring, and integrating children into all parts of the community, and this process begins during pregnancy. There are some contemporary families and communities who have never lost the principles, ceremonies, and practices I describe in this chapter, and many others (like myself) who are now trying to reclaim this knowledge. The stories here are focused on how the teachings and practices were taking place a few generations ago, and the elders' stories can assist us in strengthening and reclaiming the ways of honouring new life in our families and communities.

If we look at the Anishinaabe teachings of Mosôm Danny, Basil Johnston, and others, it becomes clear that infants and toddlers were seen as bringing hope, happiness, and a sense of potential to families and communities. The teachings tell us that new life was cherished, and at one time pregnant women, infants, and toddlers were nurtured and cared for in that spirit. All community members had roles to play in preparing for new life and ensuring that the proper care was given to the pregnant woman and then the newborn. As Danny points out, this sense of identity and belonging began as early as conception and was fostered through infancy, so that from the youngest age, community members knew their place and developed a sense of trust.

In past times (as in many communities yet today), ceremonies were important in building the relationships (human, animal, and spirit) that would be necessary to maintain a lifetime of good health and well-being. Although ceremonies for new life were not as common by the middle of the century as they had been in earlier generations, some of the historian participants told stories that demonstrated the significance of ceremonies for this first life stage. The joy that new life represented, as well as the care that it involved, is clear from the stories the elders shared. Their stories are supported by what I have been able to learn from the published literature about Algonquian peoples.

Maintaining the Life Line

Among the Nēhiyawak, Michif, and Anishinaabek of the past, there was an unmistakable reverence for life that defined many of their cultural norms and practices. Northern Algonquian hunting societies made great efforts to develop relationships of respect with the animals that they depended on for survival.[1] Life, all life, was understood as being imbued with "spirit," and individuals had the responsibility of demonstrating care for the life forms around them. In keeping with these principles, new life was celebrated because it meant the continuation of the people.

Anthropologist Diamond Jenness witnessed this principle at work among the Wasauksing (Parry Island) Anishinaabek in 1929. Jenness wrote, "The preservation of a strong life-line was the primary concern of every man and woman in the community."[2] Wasauksing community members talked to Jenness about the Milky Way as an "enormous bucket-handle that holds the earth in place." Jenness explained that "if it ever breaks the world will come to an end. The 'life line' (madjimadzuin: 'moving life') is a human Milky Way; it is the chain connecting those who have gone before with those who follow, the line of ancestors and descendants together with all of the inheritance factors they carry with them."[3]

Northern Algonquian peoples knew that life could also be precarious, and so from the beginning they took precautions to ensure a long, healthy existence for new members. This applied not only to what happened in the life of the child, but also that of his or her parents. According to Jenness, the Wasauksing Ojibway considered it important to live "upright" lives, "for a parent who sinned might so shame his infant children that they would refuse to live; or else he might reap some disability that would descend to his children or grandchildren."[4] The health of the young, therefore, was intimately connected to the health of the family and the community.

Midwives, and older women in general, had a significant role in overseeing how new life came to northern Algonquian peoples. Although not as valued as they had once been, midwives carried authority into the 1950s until hospital or doctor-assisted births began to take over in Native communities. All of the historian participants I met with were delivered by a community midwife, in many cases their grandmothers or another female relative. Yet the authority of these women was not simply a question of catching babies. In the greater scheme of things, it was about maintaining *madjimadzuin*, the "moving life" or the human Milky Way, which began with responsibilities around family planning.

Family Planning

There is evidence that Indigenous women have historically used fertility medicines as well as contraceptives and abortifacients, although the extent to which these medicines were used is not as clear.[5] Cree historian Joseph Dion points out that birth control "was not unknown by the Crees," but that it was seldom used "for the simple reason that my people were firm believers in the old adage 'Let nature have its course.'"[6] In the 1930s, American anthropologist Inez Hilger spent time in Wisconsin, Minnesota, and Michigan among the Chippewa. She notes that they used "decoctions" that produced sterility and teas that caused abortions.[7] We don't know if these medicines were widely used and perhaps they weren't since Hilger quoted one participant as having commented, "I don't think there was much of this since Indians liked children too well."[8]

Hilger acknowledged, however, that the Anishinaabek engaged in family planning, quoting women who told her "it was considered a disgrace to have children like steps and stairs," and "if a man had any sense he didn't bother his wife when a child was young."[9] She then posited that "artificial limitation of families was not known to the Chippewa," crediting their slower birth rates to abstinence protocols that were practised among couples who had young children.[10] It is important to note that Hilger, who was also a Catholic nun, and Dion, who was a devoted Catholic, may have been influenced by their faith. Church teachings have made it difficult and at times impossible to discuss family planning openly in some Indigenous communities, so they may have been cognizant of this ethic in their writings.[11]

Because of this secrecy we may never have a full picture of how and when family planning medicines were used. As with all societies, family planning measures would have fluctuated according to the needs of the people, the economic and social stresses of the time, and the cultural and moral values. Prolonged periods of nursing, infant mortality, and polygamy certainly influenced the number of children each woman would raise to adulthood, but smaller or more broadly spaced families also changed as Indigenous people had more contact with settler societies. Historian Nathalie Kermoal notes that nineteenth-century Cree women of the Prairies usually had four children, whereas in mixed-race families there were usually between eight and twelve, a number which had begun to rise as the buffalo hunt years came to an end in the late nineteenth century.[12] These birth rates appear to be connected with the adoption of Christianity as well as an increasingly sedentary lifestyle, and some Métis women claim that these high birth rates were not always so. Maria Campbell, who grew up in northern Saskatchewan, remembers that this wasn't always the case: "The old women I have known said that 'long ago' we never had more children than we could grab and run with if there was a battle."[13] By the 1860s, however, Métis women were having more children on average than the women of the settler populations.[14]

In spite of the influences of settler society, Nēhiyawak, Anishinaabek, and some Michif held on to notions of family planning well into the twentieth century, guarding the knowledge that was necessary to implement it. In cases involving fertility, elderly women were known to administer medicines to women wishing to conceive. Hilger identifies some of these medicines in her book *Chippewa Child Life and Its Cultural Background*, but the information is limited, as those who spoke with her were generally reluctant to speak about specific "recipes."[15] Knowledge related to fertility was usually kept in families or passed on through ceremonies of the Midewiwin. It is interesting to note that in some communities both husband and wife were required to drink the medicine in order to increase fertility of the mother.[16] Among the elders I interviewed, it was Marie who recalled that midwives in her community used a tea to help women become pregnant.

Others I spoke with had memories of older women administering contraceptive medicines within their own families. Maria recalled her grandmother imploring her mother, who was getting frailer with each birth, to take medicine that would prevent another pregnancy. Maria's mother was Catholic and she knew that contraceptive medicines were not condoned by her church:

> My mom had eight children. When she had her fourth child, the doctor told her she would die if she had more, but she did because she was a Catholic and the church said it was a wife's duty to have

babies. My grandmother, who was a traditional healer and midwife, told her she would make her some medicine so she would never get pregnant again. My mom wouldn't take it, and she went on to have three more children. Each one left her weak for months. On her eighth pregnancy my auntie and grandmother pleaded with her to take the medicine. She refused and died, leaving eight children.[17]

Although her mother did not survive, Maria's grandmother was able to help other women who were more open to using traditional medicines: "My grandmother helped many women live to see their grandchildren. She used local plants which were dried and made into tea."[18]

Rebecca spent her childhood in northern Saskatchewan. She wasn't aware of family planning when she was growing up, but as an adult, she asked one of her Elders about how medicines in this realm had been used in the past. The elder told her that "if there was a young woman in the community that was weak after the birth of a child, older women would come together to help her. They would spend the day with her, offering support and wisdom. At the close of the day they would give her a sealer full of medicine and they would tell her how to take it. That medicine would strengthen her until she was ready to have her next child."

These stories demonstrate how older women managed *madjimadzuin*, "the human Milky Way," through their family planning practices. Rebecca's Elder pointed out that special care of the mother was necessary because, as she said, "in those days if a mother died, what happened to her children?" From this Rebecca concluded that "the older women took responsibility to make sure that the health and strength of young mothers was maintained."

According to Mosôm Danny, traditional families looked after the health of their members by planning for births on a seasonal basis. "We went by what the animal world and nature taught us," he said. "Mother Earth taught us and taught the animal world that there are certain seasons that are conducive to healthy offspring." Danny noted, "Over half of my family was born in May and June, and that was on the insistence of my grandmothers!" This allowed for easier care of infants without having to cope with the bitterness of winter. Family planning was undertaken to ensure survival of the people.

Pregnancy: A Sacred Time

In his reflections about new life, Mosôm Danny shared stories about how healthy communities began with care and celebration of each individual from the earliest stages. He pointed out that pregnancy was generally considered a sacred time; a time to honour the spirit that was coming as well as the mother who carried that spirit. Danny learned this from his grandparents, who told stories about a time when communities used to fully invest in the well-being of pregnant women. "In those days, they had a big celebration when a woman got pregnant," he said. "Everybody knew about it. Everybody wanted to be part and parcel of that child within that womb. [The child] had to have a sense of belonging through the mother, and the woman had to have a sense of pride because she was contributing to the life of the community. She was bringing in new life, and she was treated special."

Anishinaabe writer and filmmaker Rebeka Tabobondung has done research on traditional pregnancy and birth practices among the Anishinaabek, and, like me, worked with Wasauksing oral historian Marie Anderson. Tabobondung quotes Marie as saying, "A pregnant woman was a very medicinal woman because she was carrying a new life inside her." Marie added, "If there was a difficult decision coming on the reserve they'd approach this young pregnant woman and they'd ask her for advice … they'd offer her tobacco. It's not that she ever encountered anything like that, but you know the advice that comes out of her really helped those people."[19] A pregnant woman was not only "treated special," she was also honoured as a conduit between spirit life and life on earth. According to Marie, she could be called upon to help the people because of this special status.

Prenatal care was a serious undertaking, with practices and protocols that were common to northern Algonquian peoples. Like Danny, Olive had heard stories about the ceremonial elements of pregnancy, but they were not being practised in her family by the time she was preparing to have her own children. Olive was raised in northwestern Saskatchewan where she eventually married. She related a story that her Cree mother-in-law told her when she was a young bride in 1949, which described an older ceremonial practice:

> With the first movement of the baby, my mother-in-law said that's when the midwife used to get an old lady who was a little pipe carrier and two other elderly ladies; four of them. They would take the girl out to a clean place. They used to put her on the ground, just her and the ground; mother earth, so that she's touching nature. And there, two old ladies would sit on one side and the other ones on the other side. "And then," [my mother-in-law] said, "they used to smoke their little pipe, and then pray, meditate and then talk to the

mother. Then after that they would put their hands on the mother's stomach. It was a bare tummy, they used to put their hands there and pray for the mother and the baby. That's the time they spoke to the baby."

There are likely many ceremonial practices related to pregnancy and prenatal care that have been lost, but other information about pregnancy protocols is abundant both in the literature and in the oral histories. These protocols or practices were based on the understanding that whatever the pregnant mother took in would be ingested by the baby. This applied to what she ate or drank, as well as to what she saw, heard, or experienced in any way. The anthropologist Hilger includes a section on "food taboos and prescriptions" as well as "conduct taboos and prescriptions" for pregnant women in *Chippewa Child Life and Its Cultural Background.*[20] The list of food taboos is long and Hilger itemizes specific consequences for each transgression. For example, Hilger quotes one of the oldest members on the Mille Lacs Reservation as saying, "Both father and mother must not eat turtle. If they do the baby will stretch all the time, and that isn't good for baby. Nor must they eat catfish. I knew a baby who was born with rings of sores encircling its head; the father had eaten catfish."[21] According to the women Hilger spoke with, "the violation of these mores at any time during pregnancy affected the physical nature and/or personality of the unborn child."[22]

Although David G. Mandelbaum did not describe any restrictions for Plains Cree women during their pregnancy in the 1930s, various pregnancy protocols were still being taught up into the mid-1970s to a few of the women I spoke with. (It is important to note that many of the practices I write about in this section are still taught today or are being reclaimed.) Rebecca was taught by her Cree grandmother-in-law in the mid-1970s that "during pregnancy, personal discipline was crucial because everything a woman thinks about and feels would go into the baby." This old lady further advised Rebecca, "Don't fight with your husband or you'll have an angry baby. Walk by water every day and you will have a peaceful child."

During her pregnancies in the 1970s, June was told by her grandmother not to look at animals that were "scary," as this might affect the baby. This story is in keeping with Hilger's research among the Chippewa, who believed that the child could become deformed from such an experience.[23] June also wasn't allowed to eat wild animals; only potatoes and soups. Hilger noted that pregnant Chippewa women "were encouraged to eat venison, wild rice, lake trout and whitefish."[24] Marie learned that a pregnant woman must not let anything startle her; "like if she's walking through the bush she might run across a snake that would startle her, and when she gives birth to her baby, the baby will have a reaction…. The baby could be nicely sound asleep and all of a sudden jump up and scream."[25]

Many of the pregnancy protocols had to do with protecting and enhancing the emotional, spiritual, mental, and physical health of the child. The vigilance that a pregnant woman was expected to observe during pregnancy was part of the training and discipline that both she and her baby would need to live a long and healthy life. In Chapter 4, I discuss the customs and ceremonies that were largely about encouraging children to be productive community members and preparing them to contribute to the survival of their people. Among the James Bay Cree, for example, protocols "connected with success in the food quest were considered of crucial importance in the training of the child."[26]

Another important protocol for pregnant women involved keeping active, which involved physical work.[27] It was believed that active pregnancies would make labour easier. In an oral history book from their region, Hudson Bay Cree elders talked about how pregnant women were encouraged to be active and how early rising during pregnancy was part of training for the work ahead for a new mother.[28] As well, physical activity was related to strengthening the work ethic for the mother-to-be and the child she carried. Rebecca remembered being told by her Cree grandmother-in-law to "work hard while you are pregnant and your child will be a good worker." When June was pregnant, her grandmother, who was also a midwife, brought her all sorts of things to sew. Northern Algonquian peoples had to be good workers, and so this ethic was instilled in the baby from the time of the mother's pregnancy.

Prenatal training included protocols for soon-to-be fathers, although there is less information on this subject. Many of the Chippewa men who spoke with Hilger denied the existence of food prescriptions for the father, although, as described above, one of the interviewees talked about equal transgressions and consequences for the mother and father. In that case, the baby was affected because the *father* had eaten catfish.[29] Hilger's interviewees did note that the "husband was strictly forbidden to strike his wife or to speak roughly to her."[30] There were also stories of bad omens. One such omen was when an animal twitched or jerked while being butchered by the husband of a pregnant woman. When this happened, the bad omen could be offset by feasting and praying, and the father would then refrain from hunting until the birth of his child.[31]

Contemporary elders sometimes talk about how men were once required to restrict their hunting activity or stop altogether while their wives were pregnant. During this time, the community typically pitched in to help with what was necessary for the family. The regulations around hunting were based on an understanding that the partner of an expectant mother was carrying life and so another life could not be taken.[32] Marie did not talk to me about hunting restrictions during pregnancy, but in the oral history work she did with Rebeka Tabobondung, she explained that there were strict protocols around hunting or handling animals that had recently been killed.[33]

Other historian participants talked about general expectations of a father's conduct while his partner was pregnant. As Mosôm Danny said, men were advised to take special care of their pregnant wives. This was supported by a story from Olive. Her Cree mother-in-law told her that prenatal practices in the past used to involve discussions with the men: "The midwife used to talk to the husband, to the man. Like, 'You be kind to your woman. Don't make her haul water or to stretch and lift heavy things. You do that for her.' And also, [her mother-in-law] said, 'You make sure that you help her that she doesn't look at anything that will startle her.'" Olive added that at that time the midwife was highly respected: "No one ever spoke back. You listened to her." Marie told Rebeka Tabobondung that "a long time ago when a girl got pregnant, they considered the man pregnant too."[34] Marie also taught that fathers needed to continue to make sacrifices even after the baby was born. "The father would sleep on the floor or in a place that is uncomfortable so that he would be able to respond and understand that you have to help take care of this baby. When it wakes up during the night and needs to be taken care of they can help do that."[35]

Birth and the Celebration of New Life

According to Mosôm Danny, the birth of children has always been welcomed and celebrated. He described these events: "Birth! The old mosôms and the old kohkoms were all there. They were always available. They were those holy men and women who blessed you with their praise, when they came and saw a new child." Depending on the circumstances and who was available at the time, the birth of the baby involved various members of the community.

Fathers typically did not get involved, although husbands helped their wives if the family was out on the trapline alone.[36] The James Bay Cree believed that fathers "should be on hand" when their partners went into labour because it was thought to make delivery easier.[37] For example, fathers might be called upon to hold up or support their partners when they gave birth.[38] This was also practised among the Chippewa. However, some members of the Chippewa community considered it inappropriate and even dangerous to have men present at a birth, as the man could risk losing "something inside of himself" that would diminish his own life force.[39]

There are stories of women in various hunting and trapping societies giving birth alone when necessary. Among the Chippewa, one woman told about her mother-in-law who "was out trapping with her husband when one of her children was born … she cut the cord herself and continued to work."[40] Glecia Bear heard from Nēhiyawak women in Saskatchewan how they used to "midwife themselves," going off to the bush alone to birth their children.[41] These hearty women told Bear that they made their own birth medicines and that "straight away [we] went back to work; we never used to lie down."[42]

Rebecca shared a story told by her ninety-year-old uncle about his mother (Rebecca's maternal grandmother) from a time when they lived in northern Saskatchewan. During one of his birthdays, his pregnant mother left his birthday meal and went to the bedroom. An hour later she returned with the newborn baby in her arms, having delivered the baby by herself. Rebecca asked her uncle if his mother had given birth to all of his siblings on her own. He said that his grandmother was with his mother for the birth of her first child, but that she delivered the next eight children alone. In many cases, in the absence of others to provide care, women had to deliver their babies on their own out of necessity.

Rose shared a story about her own experience. She married in 1946 and lived with her husband Ernest in Duck Lake, Saskatchewan. When she was pregnant with her fifth child in 1953, she had to deliver the baby herself because she was home alone. It was early May, but there was plenty of snow. Although babies were still being delivered at home in her community at this time, they were usually assisted by a doctor. Rose's husband went to get the doctor but didn't make it back on time. As the baby was evidently going to arrive, Rose remembered thinking *What did Grandma used to do?* She then used the skills she had learned as a child from her midwife grandmother and delivered the baby safely.

In other accounts, there were midwives or female relatives who came to assist the mother with the delivery. Most of the historian participants had midwives in their families, and they remembered people coming to call upon their grandmothers and great-grandmothers for assistance.

When the midwife lived a distance away from where the delivery was to take place, it was often necessary for her to move in with the expectant mother. Living with the mother fostered an extended model of care, something that Olive was familiar with. "People used to come and get [my grandmother] sometimes, and she would be gone for a month, maybe more," she said. "She used to believe in talking to the new mothers about what it is being a mother, about how the baby's born and what to expect." By moving in with families or being in close proximity, the midwives were able to help with prenatal and postnatal care, as well as infant care. In many cases, prenatal care would involve administering medicines to help offset miscarriages or helping to prepare for an easier labour.[43]

In spite of having midwives in their families when they were children, the elders did not have many stories about labour and birth because they were not allowed to be present at the delivery unless they were acting as helpers.[44] Marie's mother was a midwife for her community in central Ontario. Marie explained that she did not attend births with her mother "because it was a sacred thing." It was often her brother who was taken along because he was happy to play outside and wait. Marie noted that he "would play outside all night if you let him. So she'd take him, and if she needed something at home, he would come home and get it for her."

Rose, who delivered one of her babies on her own, had a more active helping role with her midwife grandmother. As a girl she became her grandmother's apprentice and was allowed to attend births and be more closely involved. "I was the gofer," she said. "[I would] get the water and everything. She showed me what to do, put everything ready the way she wanted it. I had to be her assistant, to hand her things. Get the clean water and go dump that, and get the towels, and get the baby blanket and, okay, then you clean the woman, and she was showing me how to do it."

Rosella, who grew up in Molanosa, northern Saskatchewan, went along with her mother on her midwifery work. This was in the 1940s and 1950s. Her mother had learned to be. a midwife from her mother. While Rosella did not become a midwife herself, she learned enough to be able to catch one of her cousin's babies during an emergency situation in 1981. "There was nobody around at that time," she remembered. "There was a dance going on at Montreal Lake Reserve, and everybody took off. I was a widow already and I lived next door. Somebody came running in [to announce my neighbour was in labour]. I said go phone an ambulance, and I'll see what I can do…. [I got] my scissors and rope and whatever I needed because I knew exactly what to do."

Native midwives cared for women within their communities as well as outside of them. They played an important role throughout the Canadian West in assisting women in the settler communities,[45] and this tradition continued after settlement. Olive talked about how her grandmother caught babies in northern Saskatchewan into the 1940s: "Indian babies, Métis babies and French babies…. Even our school teacher—whenever his wife had a baby he used to come and get my grandmother and she used to go and stay there and wait for the baby."

Postnatal Care

The elders had a number of stories about the elements involved in postnatal care for both mother and baby, including the use of medicines. Olive remembered that her grandmother would administer a tonic that would help with recovery. Maria's mother used a similar tonic and remembers that women in her community continued to go to the midwives for a tonic even as they began to be involved in western medical care. Mothers would drink the tonic for about six weeks before going to hospital, and then for about six weeks after the baby was born. Maria remembered the women talking about how it helped them to heal faster. In Chippewyan communities, some women remembered drinking a tea made of the inner bark of oak, maple, or slippery elm, which would be used for ten to fourteen days after a birth.[46]

The extent of postpartum care depended on available resources and the level of assistance a new mother might enjoy. While some women went back to their regular work lives shortly after the birth,[47] Rebecca was told by elder Bella Laliberté of the Flying Dust First Nation that it was best to stay in the house for the first six weeks and be cared for by family members. Bella told her, "Your mother, your grandmother and your aunties [would] always [be] there to help you so that you [could] spend time with your baby." Other elders remembered how women in their childhood communities assisted during the postpartum period, especially with heavy work such as cleaning and laundry. Because Maria's mother was frail and slow to recover from her pregnancies, her grandmother would stay and manage the household while her dad's two younger sisters looked after the children and cooked the meals.

In some cases, the midwife stayed with the family even after the birth. Marie's mother, who was a midwife, told her it was not possible to "just go and deliver and go home. It wasn't like that," she said. "You have to be there for a week." Olive remembered her grandmother being gone "for a month, maybe more," as did Maria. When the midwife was in closer proximity to the family, she would stay for less time but visit frequently. Rose reported that her grandmother would only stay "a day or two to attend to the mother and baby and make sure breastfeeding was on track," and Rosella remembered going "back and forth" with her midwife mother as she attended to women during their postpartum periods.

Care for newborns included customs that began with the treatment of their placentas and umbilical cords. These practices were considered vital in terms of protecting babies and ensuring they had long, healthy, and productive lives. A placenta was not something to be disposed of or left lying around; it held a life force and needed to be disposed of properly. There are stories in the ethnographic literature about Plains and James Bay Cree wrapping the placenta and placing it in a tree out of harm's way.[48] Rose, June, Marie, and Rebecca also had stories about the care of a placenta. Rose talked about how her grandmother would always put it in a paper bag and burn it, saying this was necessary "because it carries life." June reported that her grandmother would give the placentas to her grandfather who would sometimes put them in a tree, or she would bury them in specific locations to help with the work the child could expect to do in his or her lifetime. Burying the placenta by a tree, for example, might ensure that the individual would be a good wood cutter; if it was in the grass, this would ensure a gardener; if by water, a lifetime of fishing.

Sometimes the life force carried by the placenta would be called upon for healing purposes. Marie stressed that "a placenta is very sacred." She remembers having been told that "if some man or some woman [is] suffering with a bad leg or ulcers or something, then the placenta [is] kept. Mom said to put it on a damp cloth and just keep it [on the spot]. Always keep it damp because if there is a person who's really sick comes by, that's what will heal that person. Then you place that right on the sore."

The umbilical cord was also considered sacred, and northern Algonquian peoples had a number of customs related to it. Among the Plains and James Bay Cree, the cord was placed in a small bag that was decorated with beads.[49]

The James Bay Cree would attach it to the moss bag, because "it was believed that if this was not done, the child would become agitated, looking for its 'utisi' (umbilical cord)."[50] Among the Plains Cree, the cord bag was worn around the child's neck, which hung down the child's back: "It had two compartments; in one the cord was stored, the other was filled with tobacco. An old man or woman might call the child and take a pipeful of tobacco from the bag. Before the old person smoked the pipe, he would offer it to his spirit helpers and ask them to grant good fortune to the child. In this way the parents assured a continual round of supplication for their child."[51] These customs ensured a connection between the child and the community and between the child and the elders in particular.

Among the Chippewa, once the baby was finished with the cord, the cord was sometimes left in a place related to the baby's future work. Hilger was told how the cords from baby girls and baby boys were treated. "When a baby boy began to walk, his father took his bag on a hunting trip and dropped it wherever he killed the first animal. That caused the boy to become a good hunter. If it was a bear the father killed, and the bear was in a hole, the cord was thrown into the hole after the bear was out."[52] A girl's cord would be "buried under wood chips in order that she might become a diligent wood gatherer."[53] Among the Anishinaabek in Wisconsin, Minnesota, and Ontario, there was a preference for keeping the umbilical cord and the individual together for life. This would ensure a lifetime of wisdom for the child, and was intended to prevent the restlessness that might ensue if the child felt a need to be constantly looking for her or his cord.[54]

Umbilical cords signified connections that were made between the child and his or her relations. Chippewa scholar Thomas Peacock has written about umbilical cord customs of his people in Minnesota, stating that "the navel cord represents the lifelong connection of mother and baby. In some ancient communities, the mother and baby would take the navel-cord bag into the woods and bury it at the end of the first year of the baby's life. This signified that it was time for the baby to develop as an individual and to someday go off on its own, apart from its mother. In other communities, the mother kept the navel cord and gave it to the child when he or she got older."[55]

Although umbilical cord traditions were not prevalent in the lives of the elders I interviewed, they did have some teachings and stories to share. Marie talked about how the umbilical cord created a connection between the child and the land, based on what she had heard from her Elders:

They put [the cord] into a little piece of hide and they tie it with sinew and then they go and approach this tree. They go down to this clear lake—not a place where there are cottages. This person walks around with this in their hand and when this tree speaks to them, "Ahniin," that's where this person stops. [Then] that tree will converse with the person that's got this umbilical cord in their left hand. It's supposed to be a very young girl or an elder that carries this, and the tree tells this person about the life and the journey of the [baby]. In a lot of cases, it's the tree that gives this person an idea of what the Anishinaabe name of that child will be. I have heard that part too. What they do is they dig down quite a bit and if you can find the root, that's where this [cord] goes. You put it under the root and cover it back up. You put some Sema [tobacco] there.

In this practice, the cord establishes a connection between the lifelong journey of the child, the young and old of the community, and the land.

Rebecca was taught that that the umbilical cord and the placenta should be buried under the roots of a young tree with an offering of tobacco. After the small piece of dried umbilical cord fell off the baby, it was to be placed into the baby's bundle. Rose reported that the umbilical cord was burned as was the placenta, and June recalled some women would keep the umbilical cord for a while and then bury it later. As with the tradition of placing the placenta in a place related to the child's future, June's mother buried her umbilical cord near the house to ensure that she would "be a good woman to look after the house."

Naming the Baby

The period immediately following a birth was when ceremonies and celebrations were held. Elders in the community had a particularly important role in connecting with the new life right from the beginning. One of their most important responsibilities was in giving a "spirit name" to the baby, for this name was considered both sacred and significant. People in Algonquian communities of the past typically carried a variety of names, including "Indian" or "spirit" names, English or "Christian" names, nicknames, and kinship names/terms. In some communities there were six categories of names: "(1) Dream name given ceremonially by a 'namer,' (2) dream name acquired by an individual, (3) 'namesake name' given a child by its parents, (4) common name or nickname, (5) name of gens, and (6) euphonious name without any significance."[56]

The first two categories of names involved what have otherwise been referred to as "spirit" names, or, in more contemporary times, "Indian" names. These names carried a spiritual power that was often transmitted through dreams or visions. The first category of dream name was given shortly after birth, and the second was typically received at puberty or in a vision quest. One could not transmit the power of a name that was given by another, whereas one could pass on the power of a dream name he or she had acquired on his or her own. In later life, for example, a person might name others based on the vision and name they had earned in a fast. "Namesake" names were given by parents, sometimes after a person they admired or through a dream, but these names did not carry spiritual power. Nicknames were often humorous and connected to some element of the person's childhood, and "gens" names were sometimes used by chiefs to identify them with their kinship group.[57]

The giving of spirit names versus other names among the Ojibway of Berens River in Manitoba demonstrates how naming a baby was considered vital to ensuring him or her a lifetime of health, wellness, success and longevity, as the ethnographer Hallowell explained:

> In the Aboriginal systems of nomenclature, each child was given a personal name in a Naming Feast held not long after birth. This custom continued long after the system of surnames and Christian names came into vogue. In the native system, a personal name was derived from a dream of the namer—an old man in the "grandfather" category. The namer transferred "blessings" which he or she had received from other than human persons when they gave a name. Consequently, a personal name had a sacred quality and was seldom used in daily life. In this context, nicknames and kinship terms were sufficient for personal identification.[58]

Hallowell observed that people ensured their safety and well-being by forming relations with "other than human persons," such as animal spirits, and naming was a way to make a connection between the infant and these spiritual beings through the conduit of the namer.

Nēhiyawak also believed that spirit names carried protective qualities. The Plains Cree in the late nineteenth and early twentieth centuries believed that "the Indian was never supposed to repeat his or her name."[59] According to Amelia Paget, "The mentioning of the name, even most solemnly, was supposed to imply disrespect to the powers of guardianship exercised by the name, as well as being an unpardonable slight to the old Indian who gave it."[60] Modesty around the name was also important for the Anishinaabek. According to Thomas Peacock, "It was unusual, even considered *vain* (bragging) for a person to say one's own name."[61]

Because names were considered to be protective, parents could ask an elder for a second name if their child became ill.[62] Among the Chippewa, there are stories about children who were healed after their parents summoned a namer.[63] This relationship between health and naming was not only experienced at an individual level but it also was extended to others in the community. Mosôm Danny talked about how the namer enjoyed the benefits of the health, wellness, and power that a name carried: "Every child that you give a name to adds to your life; it gives you life. That's why [my grandpa] was over 100 years old! He named a lot of children. My grandpa used to call me Neyow because he gave me my name. 'Neyow. My body, come here!' That's what Neyow means."

Naming fostered a connection between elders and infants; those who were closest to the doorways of the spirit world in terms of coming into this world and preparing to leave it. Within this life, the giving of a spirit name by an elder to an infant created bonds along the continuum of life. This can be seen among the Plains Cree communities of the past where female elders were more often called upon to name girls and where the namer and infant established a lifelong relationship through this practice: "The two called each other nikweme, and seem to have maintained something of the grandparent–grandchild relationship."[64]

Among the Nēhiyawak and Anishinaabek, naming typically involved a feast that was attended by family and community.[65] These ceremonies could occur close to the birth or some time later, and they ranged from casual events to much more formal ceremonies. The oral historian Fine Day explained how this worked among the late nineteenth-century Plains Cree people of his childhood. "When a child is born, the parents prepare food, get some cloth, fill a pipe and call in an old man," he said. "Many people come to watch. Old man takes cloth and smokes and talks to spirit, sings, gives it the name and asks spirit to make the name the guardian of the child. Child is passed around until it reaches the mother, and men and women hold the child as they pass it, expressing a wish for the baby."[66]

June recalled naming ceremonies from her childhood in an Anishinaabe community in north central Ontario: "You'd call the old folks and they'd see the baby. And as soon as they [saw] the baby, they'd name it.... Whatever they saw." Marie remembered naming ceremonies that were always attended by a number of elders.[67] She noted that there was always a child from the community who would sit by the doorway where the ceremony was being held. In these ceremonies, the community would witness how a spirit helper would be called upon for the infant. This is how Marie described it: "They would pass the baby around and then the baby would tell the elder what their spirit name was. The baby and the elder would speak the same language, which was a language that no one else could understand. And they would speak this language for maybe five, ten seconds. Then they would go back to their regular language, and the baby's name would come from the spirit that accompanied them."[68]

When I first asked Maria about naming ceremonies in her Road Allowance community in northern Saskatchewan, she replied that "we didn't have elaborate ceremonies like we do today." (Maria was referring to the many ceremonies that are practised today as part of the revival of traditional practices in Algonquian communities.) She said that in some cases, the midwives would name the baby at the birth, or otherwise it was an older person in the family that would name the baby. She talked about a ceremony that she witnessed one summer as a young girl:

> I can remember one of my aunties had a baby and they came to the house. My grandmother delivered the baby out in the tent. When they brought the baby in, we were all sitting around eating supper and I remember this old uncle was holding the baby because he loved babies. Men usually didn't have anything to do with babies and holding them. But he was holding the baby and he gave the baby a name and then he took some food he was eating and I remember him throwing it into the fire.... You don't think about that stuff at the time, but he must have been offering food to the spirits. And that was a feast because everybody had come to see the baby, although nobody called it a feast.

Maria's story demonstrates that communities carried on with their ceremonies in a modified manner despite the government's oppression of traditional ways.

Communities had other ways of celebrating the birth of a child, mostly through support and acknowledgement from the women of the community.

As managers of the life continuum, midwives had lifelong relationships with the babies they caught, and they had various ways of celebrating and honouring those relationships. Marie remembered that her mother always used to crochet clothing for the babies she delivered. Rose talked about the bond that was created between the midwife and child, as witnessed in the practices of her grandmother. For her grandmother, "it was always a special day. She never forgot the days when a baby was born. That was his birthday. And they were always celebrated in a small kind of way. Not like they do today, but she'd always make a little hat, or little pants, or a dress for them; it was always homemade." Rose described how the women in the community would welcome new babies by making care packages that included diapers, quilts, receiving blankets, vests, T-shirts, diaper covers, sweaters, bonnets, dresses, and clothing.

Caring for Infants

Once they had been welcomed and named by their communities, infants settled into a life that was characterized by careful attention to their needs. Among the Wasauksing Ojibway, "a child required the tenderest care even before it saw the light of day."[69] Jenness writes about how both the physical and spiritual needs were attended to:

> Although a baby might appear to learn nothing for several months, the Parry Islanders thought that its soul and shadow were extremely active, conscious of things that were hidden from adult eyes. Objects that its parents could not see caused it to smile or laugh, brought it to pleasure or pain. Shadows (udjibbom) from the world around, especially shadows of animals, visited it continually; and its own shadow, attached to its body by only slender bonds, wandered far and wide over the earth, gathering experience and knowledge. During this early period of its existence the baby needed special protection lest its soul and shadow should permanently disassociate themselves and its body waste away and die.[70]

The concern over the fragility of new life led to the creation of many protocols and customs related to protecting the baby.

Care for the Spirit

Customs around protecting the spirit of the infant continue to be prevalent among Indigenous peoples, for even today, parents in traditional families learn that infancy is a precarious time when the spirit can easily slip back into the other world. I have written about how some of these parenting practices are exercised in contemporary families:

> It is deemed particularly dangerous to take the newborn into environments where she or he might come into contact with negative energy, or where there may be spirits waiting to take the baby back. This is why babies do not attend wakes. Some Aboriginal peoples put holes in a newborn's moccasins as a protective measure. Western Cree say that this gives the baby an excuse not to go if a spirit should come to take them. Some Cree tie a black string around the infant's wrist to ward off malevolent spirits, or set a small stick beside the sleeping infant so they can defend themselves. The soft spot is also a significant reminder of the baby's borderline status. Algonquian and Haudenosaunee peoples say that this opening on the baby's head represents openness to the spirit world. The baby is still connected to that world until that soft spot closes.[71]

These practices stem from long traditions of caring for the spirit of the newborn.

When she first became a mother, Rebecca learned that quiet time in the newborn stage was important because of the precariousness of new life, and this was the reason for staying close to home with the newborn. "My Elder explained that the spirit is pulsing inside the new baby," Rebecca said. "In order for the spirit to become secure, a mother needs to stay at home for six weeks, all the while maintaining a sense of peace. Over the six-week period, the spirit will eventually quiet and fill the child."

Marie's mother taught her that one should always whisper around babies, because if you spoke to them directly they would speak back. She told a story that mirrors a story her father (Francis Pegahmagabow) told Diamond Jenness in 1929. In her father's story, a new baby was asked "Where are you from?" and answered "From far away." Marie's father explained to Jenness that "the Great Spirit saw that this baby was born with too much power and he caused it to die." "So," he cautioned, "you must never ask questions of a baby." Marie had a similar experience with a baby when she was eleven or twelve. "One time I asked my mother, 'How come nobody can speak [around a newborn]?' and she said, 'It's good you asked. There's a ball game on. We'll go down.' So I forgot all about the question and we went down to the ball game. [A new mother] was sitting there with her children. Somebody came along and said, 'Oh, let's see her baby.' She picked up the baby and was playing with the baby's chin. Then she said, 'Where did you come from?' to this baby. And right off the bat the baby said (oh, he was rolling his eyes), 'Waasa' [far away]. So my mother nudged me like that. I'm trying to watch the game and I'm watching the baby. I heard him say three or four words. When we got home, my mother explained, 'Children are born intelligent and each person that's born brings a gift to the world,' and she cautioned me against speaking loudly to babies."

Physical Care

In terms of the physical care provided for babies, Elsie remembered that there was no artificial scheduling; babies were changed when they needed to be changed, and when they were hungry, they were fed. She also commented that "the baby was never alone as far as I know." Infants enjoyed a sense of comfort and security through swaddling and being in close contact with their mothers. Oral historian Glecia Bear has talked about how the Cree believed this was important. In this passage, she reflects on the changes she had seen as a result of taking on "white man's things":

> Today… before the child is born, they already look for a separate room, they put a crib in it and also a bottle, all these white-man's things. In the old days the children were swaddled in a moss bag, warmly swaddled up with the moss, but they now wrap them without anything, and when they bring them home, there they simply dump their baby into that nursery. When the baby cries, they immediately put cow's milk into a bottle and simply give that to the baby, they do not hold the child … in the old days the baby used to be held while suckling, you kissed it and held it and you unbundled it.[72]

Babies were often put in swings to nap or sleep where they could be near their family members. Maria remembers that the new babies would be "strung up inside of the tent or right outside where the old people would look after them," and Elsie remembered the elders singing lullabies to the children while swinging them.

Up into the middle of the twentieth century, cradleboards (or *tikinaagan* as people commonly refer to them in Anishinaabemowin) were widely used by Algonquian peoples across North America. This allowed the mothers to keep in close contact with their babies, and allowed the babies to interact with community members. Frances Densmore offered the following description of the cradleboards used by the Ojibway she worked with around Lake Superior:

> The cradleboard, in which a baby spent most of the first year of its life, consisted of a board about 24 inches long with a curved piece of wood at one end to confine the child's feet and a hoop at right angles above the other end. A light rod was fastened loosely to one side of the cradleboard and to this were attached the two binding bands, about six inches wide, which were pinned or tied over the child. In the old days the upper end of the board was cut in points and painted red or blue, and the entire structure was held together by thongs. Inside the curved wood at the foot of the cradleboard was birch bark of the same shape filled with soft moss. The hoop for the child's head served as a support for a blanket in winter and a thin cloth in summer, thus protecting the child's head from the weather. On this hoop were hung small articles intended as charms for the child's amusement.[73]

Writing about the Anishinaabek in the same area, Thomas Peacock noted that sometimes the cradleboard would have a dreamcatcher hung on it: "a hoop made of willow or the small branches of other softwood trees, and a spider net made of sinew."[74] Peacock explained that "The dreamcatcher was to catch bad dreams and allow only good dreams to come through to the baby."[75]

The mother could carry the cradleboard on her back, with the assistance of a strap that went around her chest or her forehead, or around both. When the mother was not carrying the cradleboard, it could be propped up against a tree so that the child could watch his or her mother and other community members while they worked, which increased the baby's capacity for learning.

The Anishinaabek saw cradleboards as a way of developing the child's physical and mental capacities. "It was the desire of the Chippewa that their children should be straight and vigorous, and to that end the mother began a child's training in early infancy," Densmore wrote. "Two means were employed for this training as well as for convenience in taking care of the child. These were (1) the cradleboard and (2) a custom which arose after the Chippewa obtained cotton cloth and which may be designated as 'pinning up the baby.' With these forms of restraint they alternated periods of freedom when the child was 'let out for exercise.'"[76] Although "the cradleboard afforded warmth and protection, ... it is said that children cried to be put back in the cradleboard after being out of it for a time."[77]

Cradleboards are now making a comeback, but in the particular childhood communities of the historian participants, cradleboards had mostly disappeared. The elders did remember infants being swaddled in "moss bags" that were made of fabric and laced up the front to hold the baby snugly. The moss that lined the bags served as diapers, which was a common practice among northern Algonquian communities at the time.

In 1932, the ethnographer Hallowell made a trip to Lake Pikangikum in northwestern Ontario to visit the Ojibway communities there. What caught his attention was the use of sphagnum moss, which had "highly absorbent and deodorant properties" and which "could be seen drying in the sun in almost every camp."[78] Elders living in York Factory on Hudson Bay described how moss was processed, "If a woman knew she was going to have her baby before the following summer, she would pick the moss during the previous summer and dry it."[79] Among the James Bay Cree, babies spent the first year of their lives in a moss bag.[80]

A number of the elders had stories about how they harvested the moss for diapers. Olive remembered about how the moss was cleaned:

> There was a certain moss that the grannies used to go and gather; it's a moss that's very woolly and spongy. It's kind of a pinkish colour, a very healthy moss. The other mosses are kind of chunky and not good. At times you used to see this moss hanging all over on the branches. They'd pull that and put it all over the branches and they'd leave it there until it was good and dry. That was the old ladies' job. They used to take a canvas or whatever so they could spread it on the ground, take all these down and comb through them. That must've been a days and days work, because they had to stock up for winter. They used to take out all the little twigs and soil.

Madeleine remembered the men in her Cree community at Kehewin First Nation would hook up horses to the wagon and drive the women to collect moss for the babies. Women, especially the older women, had the responsibil-

·ity of drying the moss and then making the moss bags. In some communities, the younger women were recruited to do the work. Rosella remembers that when she was a teenager, she had to make moss bags for her younger siblings. She would harvest the moss from the muskeg around Molanosa. The moss was very soft and light green, and once collected, it was important that she got all the bugs and twigs out so the babies would be comfortable. Comfortable moss bags would prevent the baby from crying while her family was travelling for harvesting activities. In former times, communities had been seasonally migrational, and would have had well-disciplined babies for this lifestyle.

Rebecca talked about how the child learned to self-soothe when snuggled into a moss bag or put onto a cradleboard:

> They like going into the moss bag. It's training for them to quiet themselves and get ready to sleep. And when they wake up and they let you know, you go to them with a smile and they are eager to come out and to be fed. When you take them out, you massage them, and stretch their limbs, and there is this loving gentle massage, coming out of the moss bag or the cradleboard. The child is absolutely adored and cherished and stimulated when they come out. Then they are changed, and they are fed and bathed and played with. And then when they start getting tired, you put them back in. And so they learn this rhythm of being welcomed into awake, and then quieted and put back in to sleep.

Another common practice of caring for infants was breast-feeding, which was valued not just for the nutrition it provided but also for the bonding it allowed between the mother and her infant. In earlier times, children were breast-fed at least until they were two years of age and, in some instances, until they were four or five.[81] The elders in this study remembered that breast-feeding was still widely practised in their childhood communities, but they also talked about conflicting values that had begun to creep in with the mainstream movement towards bottle-feeding in the 1950s. While some Native communities held onto traditional breast-feeding practices during the movement away from breast-feeding, others were being pressured to move to the bottle.[82] Maria remembered when the public health nurse came to her community and told mothers that it was unhealthy to breast-feed: "They were pushing, I think it was Carnation. It was milk with a cow on it."

Olive remembered some old ladies in her community admonishing the younger generations for moving away from breast-feeding. She relayed that "there used to be this old lady who would say that there's a purpose that a woman was given breasts which is to feed the little ones. She and another older lady were coming to the feast and I was standing not too far from there. 'Oh,' she said to the three little girls, 'Look at these three girls.' She said, 'Look at how much they stare. I won't be a bit surprised if these three were brought up with cow's milk because they're staring exactly like the cows do.' In this old lady's thinking, 'when we nurse the babies, they're much stronger.... But now, when they grow up with animal milk, I don't know if they'll even listen to us.'" Glecia Bear was of the opinion that discipline problems were the result of parents not bonding with children in the same ways that they had done in the past.[83] "These young women who give birth to a child today," she said, "they could not claim to be the ones to have the child and to call it their child, the cows have raised the child for them; for the cows have given life to the child which has been born."[84]

"Walking Out": The Toddler Years

As children moved from their infancy into their toddler years, there were ceremonies to mark their transition towards becoming working community members. One such ceremony was known as "walking-out" and took place as soon as the baby took his or her first steps. This was a widespread practice at one time and underlines the importance of teaching children as soon as possible the importance of community responsibility.

There are not many references to the walking-out ceremonies. Regina Flannery witnessed how the James Bay Cree communities celebrated their babies' first steps. The adults did not want the baby to go in or out of the tent alone until he or she could walk, and when the baby did, they would have a feast to celebrate. Flannery framed the walking-out ceremony as "a symbol of success in the food quest."[85] Boys were required to walk where they might find game, and girls were to go where there was firewood. This practice symbolized the roles they would find themselves fulfilling later in life, procuring and cooking the meat, respectively. Flannery describes the ceremony for a little girl:

> When the first walking-out ceremony was for a little girl, she was equipped with a miniature wooden kettle-hook and axe. She walks

towards a pack of firewood in which there was a small amount of meat. Brought this to the oldest woman, who took the pack from her back and the wood was used to cook the meat. The meat was then given to the oldest man who put a bit in the fire with a short informal prayer that the child may have a long life ... then meat from the feast is distributed, the old man eating first and rubbing grease on the child's head.[86]

Although I did not collect any stories about walking-out ceremonies from the elders I interviewed, many of them are involved in walking-out ceremonies today. These ceremonies involve gathering family and community members to celebrate the transition into toddler years, typically around the time of the child's first steps. Participants in the ceremony bring gifts and wishes that pertain to the child's future, as he or she "walks out" in that direction. These things are placed into a bundle that they carry as they walk around the circle of friends and family. They are thus literally and figuratively equipped to move into the life stages that are to come.

Conclusion

The beliefs, practices, and protocols related to this first life stage demonstrate how northern Algonquian peoples valued the sacredness of new life and how they took great measures to foster and protect it. Perhaps because of the precariousness of new life, the utmost care was taken during this life stage. Pregnancy, infant, and toddler care were taken seriously. Food and conduct protocols during pregnancy demanded a discipline from the mother and ideally from other members of the family and community. The care that community members collectively provided during this time was meant to ensure that the newest members learned to trust and depend on the world they had entered.

Ultimately, the health of the baby was connected to the health of the community, and babies also brought communities together through the care that was required and the joy and hope that they represented. Connections between the baby, family, community, the natural world, and the spirit world were ensured through practices related to the care of the placenta and umbilical cord, naming ceremonies, and walking-out ceremonies. These practices of care and ceremony were more than about simply looking after the health of the infant; they were about maintaining the life force. This is evident in considering, for example, that elders might extend their lives by naming infants, as these connections allowed for the movement of energy that sustained the life continuum. Women had the most significant roles in terms of maintaining this life force, although all members of the community partook in responsibilities to ensure the well-being of their babies and preparing them for the next steps that would walk them into their futures.

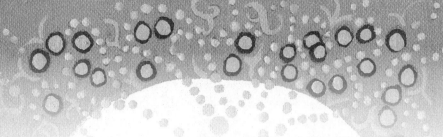

Chapter 4

The "Good Life" and the "Fast Life": Childhood and Youth

Every stage of childhood was a celebration because children needed to develop a sense of belonging; that sense that "You are important to the people." [If] a child doesn't have a sense of belonging and responsibility as part of the whole, that's the weakness that will tear up a community. That's the weakness that the child will have in later years, in times of great need or difficulty. In the old days, they might have even had to put their life [on the line] to save another community member.

There was a selfless bravery that children learned in the past. We needed that sense of togetherness and that sense of belonging to live in "the wilderness." Everybody had to work together to survive. [And children needed to learn] that there was order! There were rules and regulations to everything; there were boundaries, and so as children grew they began to learn family law, and community law.

That's the kind of disciplines that I had to learn, belonging to the community.

—Mosôm Danny Musqua

*M*idewiwin teachings refer to the childhood years as "the good life," for in this life stage, one's needs were ideally provided for in a supportive environment. According to Mosôm Danny, it was critical to treat children well so they could learn trust and enjoy a sense of belonging. As in the first life stage, nurturing was paramount. But in this life stage children also began to learn and practise independence and responsibility. As Mosôm Danny has pointed out, childhood was a time to begin to learn the disciplines of the community in anticipation of becoming a full contributing member. Adolescence was a turning point in which children broke from "the good life" into what Midewiwin teachers refer to as "the fast life," a time of rapid change, introspection, vision, sacrifice, and transition.

Childhood and youth thus involved play as well as preparation towards adult responsibilities, with puberty as the pivotal time for determining the quality of the life ahead. In this chapter I discuss discipline and self-discipline, the work and play of childhood, and how children prepared for the rites of passage upon reaching adolescence and puberty. I also explore how principles of independence and interdependence were fostered during this life stage, demonstrating that children were raised as autonomous individuals who were given a lot of freedom while also being expected to maintain responsibilities to family and community. Through this upbringing, the "good life" fostered a sense of duty and commitment in the child, while the "fast life" shifted them into their adult years and responsibilities.

The "Good Life": Nurturing, Discipline, Self-Reliance, and Interdependence

Algonquian childrearing techniques are evident in the observations of Europeans from the earliest points of contact, as they witnessed "the good life" among Indigenous children. They were often perplexed by Indigenous childrearing styles and approaches, typically interpreting the nurturing as indulgence and a lack of discipline. The Jesuits of New France remarked on the "excessive love of their offspring" among the Algonquian and Iroquoian peoples they encountered, and complained that the children enjoyed "the liberty of wild-assed colts."[1] In the words of historian J.R. Miller, Indigenous childrearing was characterized by an "absence of coercion and routine," which made the Jesuits proposed school regime unpalatable.[2]

Differences between Indigenous childrearing techniques and European approaches were so profound that, two and a half centuries after the Jesuits first made their observations, Eurowestern observers continued to express both curiosity and judgement on this matter. This comes across in the writings of Amelia Paget (1867–1902), who was born and raised in the Northwest and wrote about settlement activity. The daughter of a Scot father and a Métis mother, Paget spoke fluent Saulteaux and Cree, and provided a sympathetic view of Native women's lives. Paget documented the reaction of settlers in late nineteenth-century western Canada to the childrearing practices of the Plains Cree. As she saw it, "the love of their [the Cree's] children was a particularly pathetic trait in their natures. The youngsters were actually adored, and consequently would impress a stranger as being very badly brought up. They were never corrected for any faults, but, up to a certain age, did as they pleased, when, of their own accord, they seemed to realize the respect due to their parents."[3]

Nineteenth-century observers were critical of what they perceived to be the lax childrearing methods of the Métis, according to historian Nathalie Kermoal. Kermoal quotes the Oblate missionary Alexandre Taché, who opined that Métis women on the Prairies sacrificed the overall well-being of their children because of the pleasure they took from them and their apparent fear to correct their behaviour (*la crainte de les reprendre*).[4] Kermoal also refers to French historian Marcel Giraud's remarks about the "affection exagérée" that Métis and "Indien" alike demonstrated towards their young.[5]

From a Eurowestern child's point of view, the childrearing techniques reportedly had an upside. Egerton Ryerson Young II was the son of a missionary and spent his early years among the Cree and Saulteaux in Manitoba. He was cared for by a Cree nanny from 1869 to 1876. In his memoirs, Young reflects on the absence of corporal punishment and coercion, pointing out that his Cree nanny chose to engage in storytelling as a disciplinary measure when he had misbehaved.[6]

Teaching Discipline and Self-Discipline

As Young experienced, discipline was applied—although not in a way he would have expected. Eurowestern observers continued to remark on Indigenous childrearing approaches into the twentieth century. Anthropologists Mandelbaum and Skinner commented on the liberty and indulgence enjoyed by Cree children.[7] Mandelbaum wrote that Plains Cree children "were never beaten and rarely reprimanded," and Skinner observed that the James Bay Cree "taught by example" and "rarely struck."[8] Yet these responses to Indigenous childrearing should not be interpreted as evidence of a lack of discipline for, as historian J.R. Miller has pointed out, Eurowestern observers "usually failed to note that, among Indians, discipline was applied to children, although it was administered in ways unfamiliar to the intruders."[9]

Miller describes the most common elements of traditional Indigenous childrearing, which included positive role modelling, the use of games, storytelling, and rites-of-passage ceremonies. Children were disciplined by "indirect and non-coercive means."[10] Miller links these practices to widespread Indigenous principles that taught how to respect an individual's autonomy:

> among North American indigenous societies in general there was a powerful imperative to avoid imposing one's will on another individual in any but the most extreme situations. This respect for autonomy was extended to young children, permitting them great scope for self-expression and preventing the use of direct, coercive techniques of behaviour modification. Hence, the family and community's efforts to educate the young as to acceptable conduct had to be carried out by the use of sanctions such as embarrassment or ridicule, and the more positive force of story and example.[11]

Métis scholar Leah Dorion has conducted oral history research on traditional parenting practices with contemporary Cree and Métis Elders in Saskatchewan, and writes about Opikinawasowin, "the child rearing way." Dorion's work explains some of the principles behind non-coercive childrearing techniques, as she learned from the Elders that "Cree law means an individual does not have the right to interfere in the sacred path of another by using manipulation or coercion. One is not to interfere with the sacred covenant between the Creator and another being or there will be negative consequences."[12] The principle of non-interference is, thus, grounded in respect for the path of the individual, no matter how young.

Among Indigenous cultures, part of learning the value of independence and autonomy meant that children were not only disciplined but also had to learn *self*-discipline. The ability to be self-disciplined was important because it fed into the survival of both individual and community. Among the Anishinaabek, for example, children needed to know how to be quiet and still, as circumstances often required a composed demeanour. "The ability of a child to keep still when surprised or frightened," wrote ethnologist Frances

Densmore, "was more important to the Indian than to the white race. For example, the scream of a child might cost the lives of many people if an enemy were approaching the village."[13] Chippewa women never allowed a baby to cry for this reason, and "when the children were old enough to listen attentively it was still desired to keep them quiet in the evening." One way of learning this was through a "game of silence" in which "a prize was given to the child who showed the most self-control."[14]

In her book about the life of her great-great-grandmother, Minnesota Ojibway Elder Ignatia Broker talks about how discipline started early. This grandmother grew up in times of great upheaval during the middle of the nineteenth century. Broker notes that being strapped in the cradleboard was the beginning of her grandmother's experience in learning the discipline required to survive. "At certain times when she cried, a brushy stick was scraped across her face and her lips were pinched. These actions would be repeated if the family needed to make a silent journey; then Oona would know she must not cry. It was a matter of survival, especially if there were enemies in the forest."[15] Thomas Peacock has written about historical practices of teaching an infant to be quiet by gently pinching his or her lips shut, a vestige of earlier times when Chippewa villages might have come under attack: "Silence was necessary when the villagers were hiding or fleeing from enemies, and a baby's cry could give away their location."[16]

These examples demonstrate that childrearing was the exercise of what might appear to be contradictory practices of encouraging freedom and autonomy on the one hand, and instilling unwavering responsibility and discipline on the other. Yet, as psychologist Carol A. Markstrom has pointed out, traditional Indigenous societies were grounded in a co-existence between interdependence and individualism,[17] and this was fostered from an early age. Individuals gained status and recognition for their accomplishments, but it was always connected to how well their contributions served the welfare of the group. Markstrom writes of the "profound implications for identity formation" that arise out of this balance between interdependence and individualism, as the child learns his or her own value as well as their place within their community.[18] This analysis corresponds with Mosôm Danny's teaching quoted above, that children needed to develop a sense of esteem and belonging that was connected to family and community responsibility. The values that accompanied identity formation were taught throughout childhood and reinforced in a formal way at coming-of-age ceremonies[19] (discussed below).

Discipline and self-discipline were taught to children in other ways as well, and always within a framework of love and support. Children were raised within a network of extended family and community, with elders playing a key role.

Childrearing: "It Takes a Community"

The current generation of elders were largely residential schooled, and many have described the contrast between what they experienced in their home communities and what they encountered when they were sent to school. The women and men I interviewed did not talk about residential school experiences, as we chose to focus on childhood experiences in the community prior to entering the schools or during time away from the schools. This meant that we spent more time discussing the positive experiences of their childhood as well as the traditional parenting and childrearing techniques they grew up with.

Most of the historian participants spent their early years in an environment of nurturing and what could be called "indulgence." This is in keeping with a lot of the "good life" observations of Eurowestern visitors and ethnographers, as discussed above. Reflecting generally on the position of children in her community of the Kehewin Cree Nation, Madeleine recalled that "no matter how big families were, I always felt that children were very well taken care of and shown a lot of affection." Elsie remarked on how children in her Métis community of Cumberland House were always the "centre of the home." She talked about how "everyone looked after [all the children]," noting that whatever their needs were, somebody would take care of them. As prototypical models of "it takes a community to raise a child," there was a sense of collective care and responsibility for children in traditional Algonquian communities. Rebecca made this point with her memory that children went freely from house to house and were fed by the adults there no matter whose child they were.

The collective responsibility for children is also evident in the relationships that existed between the participants when they were children and the elders of their childhood communities. Madeleine remembered that adults in her community did not distinguish whose child it was. All children belonged, and "everybody had a kind word. Maybe old people called you by an affectionate name or gave you a [nickname] and that's how they would greet you." Elsie told a story about how she confounded the nuns at the boarding school she attended with her fluid and multiple sets of "grandparents":

When I went away to school I had to [stay in] a convent, and I signed away my life. There were only a few times you could go home: when somebody died in your immediate family, at Christmas (if you could) and in the summer. [When elders died] I would want to go home. [I'd tell them] "My grandfather has passed away." Finally the old nun said, "Elsie, you can only have four grandparents!" But I didn't even know the elders' names. They were just nohkom [grand-mother] and mosôm [grandfather], and they [all] called me nososim [grandchild].

All of the old people played a grandparent role to Elsie, and this meant that as the recipient of their care she was accountable to them. She talked about having to pay attention to her conduct as a way of showing respect and responsibility. Elsie was also accountable to them for what happened at her boarding school in Prince Albert. High school was not funded for non-treaty and Métis peoples in her area, and so the community had raised funds through basket socials, sports days, and other activities to send her to a convent school. She laughed as she remembered how frequently people would stop to ask her about school when she was home in the summer: "I would be stopped all along the road as I was walking [in the community because] I had to be accountable for my grades and how I was doing."

Sylvia talked about a similar upbringing as a child of the Red Pheasant Cree Nation in Saskatchewan: "What I remember about being young is that I had a lot of grandmothers and grandfathers, and I felt loved and cared for by all of them. It never dawned on me until much later that I could only have two sets of grandparents." She remembered being nurtured by and "learning about life" from her multiple sets of "grandparents."

While the care of children was a matter for the collective, there were distinct roles in childrearing according to age, gender, and position within the family. Men were less involved in the primary care of young children because of the nature of their work; up to the age of seven or eight, children typically spent time with grandparents, older siblings, and mothers. Mothers and aunts were close to their children, but the requirements of their work also meant that much of the child care fell to elders and older children. Maria described her responsibilities as an older sibling and how this worked in collaboration with her elders:

We had to drag all of our little brothers and sisters with us wherever we went. You didn't take off and go play by yourself without the kids. You had to take the younger kids along for two reasons. One, they needed a babysitter because your mother was busy. The second reason was because you didn't get into trouble when you had a bunch of little kids toddling [after] you. You couldn't go too far. And then your grannies watched out for you. You were still doing the work, but the old ladies were keeping track of you.

According to Mosôm Danny, this kind of care taught children how to be members of an interdependent community. That is, children learned from a young age that they had a responsibility for caring and ensuring the well-being of other family and community members.

Many of the elders I interviewed grew up under the eyes of their grandparents, particularly in their earlier years. In some cases, grandparents became the primary caregivers if the parents were ill, or if they died, or if they had to go away to work. Overall, primary care by grandparents was not seen as unusual as it came from a long tradition among Indigenous peoples. Mandelbaum noticed this in his work with the Plains Cree, and wrote that children "spent a great deal of time with their grandparents and relatively little with their parents who were preoccupied with adult tasks and cares."[20]

Child care on the part of grandparents suited the labour requirements of land-based societies, but this arrangement was also important because it facilitated traditional education. As the most senior and knowledgeable members of the community, elders were the teachers, and the instruction they offered began with the youngest members of the community. Gertie, who grew up as a child of the Nipissing First Nation in central Ontario, explained that elders would typically look after children until they were ready to begin more intense training for adult work. "The elders spent more time with the youngest children because they didn't have to be as focused on learning the value of the work," she said. "The fun and the joy of working, the grandparents could take care of that. But when they became young men and young women, the actual value to the family of the work and the effort that was required could be brought home more clearly by the mother and the father and the aunties and the uncles."

Some participants remembered that it was more pleasant to spend time with their elders because they weren't so stressed about getting the work done. The lessened work demands of the elders meant that they had time to teach the grandchildren, or great-grandchildren, as in Maria's case. Maria remembered that because her grandmother was very active as a midwife, it was her great-grandmother who had the time to answer her questions: "I preferred being with [my great-grandmother] than with my grandmother, because my grandmother was too busy. She was helping my mom, she was tanning hides, she was a worker." She recalled that her great-grandmother was too old to do the heavy work, "but she could take you out berry picking; show you where the medicines and things were.... So we liked being with [great-grandma] because it was always mellow and laid back. If we were lazy and didn't feel like working, well then she would sit and tell us stories!"

Grandparents were the ones who had time to deal with "teachable moments," which came across in Hilary's memories of her grandmother helping her process the racism she experienced as a child. Hilary grew up in Lloydminster, Saskatchewan, but spent a lot of time on the Moosomin reserve where her maternal grandparents and great-grandparents lived. She cherished her time with her "little kokum" Celine Morrisette Wright, who offered her comfort and wisdom while she was growing up in an often hostile environment.

Reciprocity

One of the most important teachings shared between grandparents and their grandchildren was the principle of reciprocity in relationships. Youngsters were not simply passive recipients of care and teaching. They were often helpers to their grandparents and were given tasks and responsibilities that facilitated their learning. Gertie remembered that her grandmother would ask her mother to send the children over when she needed help with physical labour—of all sorts, at all times of the year. She remarked on her grandmother's skills in making the children feel important and proud, while at the same time motivating them to do the work. Her grandmother handled the tanning of hides and had lots of tasks for the kids: "We would stretch the hides for her. At a given point in time, when you are doing hide tanning, you have to stretch that skin. When the hair is all off and all the little fleshy parts are all off and it's nice and clean and it has been doing this soaking business for a while, then you have the take the water out of the hide and you have to stretch it. Well, there's nothing more perfect than five little kids, all stretching this hide that she was preparing!"

Like Gertie, Maria pointed out that her great-grandmother supervised all manner of chores and tasks, but "most of the time it was us that did the work." Maria also often acted as a "runner"/helper to her grandmother, and she learned a lot from this experience.

"I would do all kinds of work for Cheechum [her great-grandmother] and the nohkoms," she said. "I'd run back and forth to the house for whatever they needed when they were working outside smoking and drying meat or tanning hides or making medicine. I hauled wood and water for them and took care of fires. In the case of my Cheechum, I was also her eyes and I sometimes chewed her meat for her. Her name for me was Ni cheechee, which means 'my hand.'"

Rose, who grew up in Duck Lake, Saskatchewan, was a helper to her grandmother who worked as a healer. As a young girl, she would accompany her grandmother on doctoring or midwifery visits, and even help her tend to the dead, as I describe in Chapter 6. This learning relationship as well as a more general discussion of the formal, non-formal, and informal teaching roles of grandparents is also offered in Chapter 6 when I write about the experiences of "old ladies."

Uncles and Aunts

As noted by Gertie, children also had close relationships with aunts and uncles, and these relationships became more significant as they grew older and needed to develop the disciplines required in adult life. There was a transition of care that happened between being seven years old and reaching puberty; what Mosôm Danny calls the "little men and little women" years of moving a child from family circles to community circles. Amelia Paget talked about the "complete alteration" that she witnessed in Cree and Métis children. She saw them move from the life of "doing as they pleased" into the disciplines that were impressed upon them by people other than their parents. At this point in their lives, they needed to become more active and helpful in the work of adults. Paget also wrote that "no disrespect for elders was tolerated, and when the children were supposed to have reached years of discretion they were soon made to understand this, not by their parents but by other relatives and friends. Consequently the parents were spared the pain of correcting their children."[21] According to Gertie, her aunts and uncles took on a bigger role in caring for the older children because they were "a little more energetic in their approach." In her community, disciplining children was a key role for the aunts and uncles.

Mosôm Danny and Maria remembered that there were certain uncles and aunts who took a lead role in instilling discipline and correcting undesired behaviour. Maria talked about the role of *niktâwisis* and *nohtâwisis*: the "little mothers" and "little fathers," stating that "they teach you because your mother and father can't. Maria remembered one great uncle who played this role:

[There was a] really old man, my dad's great uncle; we called him "uncle" and he was the one who would get after us. He'd step in if we were being out of line, but he was also really kind to us. We were never scared of him, but boy, when he got after us we smartened up. He'd take us aside, he'd tell my brothers, "You don't talk like that to your dad." Or, "Don't have that kind of an attitude." And so he'd preach to us, whereas our [parents and] grandfathers, our Mosôms never did that.

Maria's story corresponds to Paget's story written a generation earlier, in which she describes Cree and Métis children being reprimanded by aunts, uncles, and friends when they were being disrespectful of their parents.[22]

In Mosôm Danny's case, it was "Uncle Bill" who was the community judge for the kids in his community of Keeseekoose First Nation. Parents still had a role, but misbehaving children would be referred to others and ultimately to Uncle Bill. Danny explained that "if we were behaving badly, my mother would say, 'All right. If you are going to behave that way, go and talk to your dad.' Then my dad would give us a good lecture. And if we were still misbehaving, he would say, 'Here. (*Motions putting tobacco into the palm of a hand*) Take a little bit of tobacco. Go and see your Uncle Bill.'" Danny further explained that Uncle Bill was "much more of a stranger than your mother or father. He would be very nice, and smile a lot, talk a lot, but he had a serious demeanour about him all the time." In presenting tobacco to Uncle Bill, Danny demonstrated that he was willing to learn from his mistake, for one typically presents tobacco to a teacher.

Danny went on to tell a long and engaging story that demonstrated the type of justice that Uncle Bill would administer. One summer afternoon, Danny had taken his cousin's bike for a ride after being told to leave it alone. As luck would have it, he got in an accident, damaged the bike and got caught. For this Danny was given tobacco and sent to see Uncle Bill. After trying to minimize what he had done, Uncle Bill replied, "When you don't ask to take somebody's stuff, you are stealing. There's no such thing as small things. You stole.... And once you steal, you steal a little bit more, and more, and the next thing you know you want everything for nothing. Just like a small lie to a big lie." The old man then encouraged Danny to give up something of equal value.

Danny used his nine-year-old bargaining skills to try and get away with giving something small, but the old man said, "Your bad decision has brought you to that place of responsibility that you must give up something that carries you around." Through more dialogue Danny was led to the conclusion that the noblest solution was to give his prized horse to his cousin. In the end, Uncle Bill allowed Danny to negotiate this directly with his cousin, who decided to take Danny's dog and new pair of shoes instead.

Upon finishing this story, Danny summed up what this situation had taught him in terms of community responsibility: "There were community laws, and I had to start behaving like a member of the community." It was Uncle Bill's job to deepen Danny's understanding of his responsibilities, including how to handle conflict with another community member.

Discipline and Self-Discipline

Traditional disciplinary techniques included praise for good behaviour, storytelling, and dialogue. Anthropologist Hilger writes that, among the Chippewa, "every attempt was made to make children mind by speaking to them as occasion arose or by teaching them to do so at times of formal instruction."[23] Other common approaches have been noted by Densmore. In describing how children were governed by the Chippewa adults, she comments that "throughout the information given by the older Chippewa, we note the elements of gentleness and tact, combined with an emphasis on such things as were essential to the well-being of the child." She adds that fear "was often used to induce obedience, but not to an extent which injured the child," describing how adults would tell stories that might scare children into staying in the lodge after dark.[24] Fear was generally used to keep children away from situations that were unsafe, and so creatures such as the owl were called upon to deter children from dangerous situations or environments.[25]

There is evidence in the ethnographic literature that corporal punishment was used by some parents. But one Chippewa informant is recorded as telling the ethnographer Inez Hilger that "real Indians don't believe in striking children." According to another informant, one could "knock the spirit out of the child" by engaging in corporal punishment. Still another informant reported that her father had chosen to talk to his children every evening rather than to use corporal punishment.[26] In the research she did on traditional Cree and Métis parenting, Leah Dorion notes that there were stories about using the "willow stick" as a form of punishment. But she points out that one of her historian participants, Elder James Burns, told her that the willow stick "was introduced into traditional parenting through schools, missionaries, [and] churches, and became incorporated into how some families disciplined their children, but it was not an original aspect of traditional Cree parenting which was focused on gentleness."[27]

If the community needed to be reprimanded in some way, a "crier" would address the individual, family, and community at the same time. One such technique among the Ojibway involved the whole community when they would gather in larger camps:

> When everyone had retired and the camp was quiet an old man walked around the camp circle, passing in front of the dark tents. This man was a crier and he made the announcements for the next day, telling whether the people would go hunting or what would be done in the camp. He also gave good advice to the young people who were taught to respect him and obey his words.... He spoke impersonally of the conduct of the young people, describing incidents in such a manner that those concerned in them would know to what he referred. He taught sterling principles of character and gave such advice as he thought was necessary.[28]

The crier would draw attention to undesirable behaviour and in doing so use "shame and ridicule" as a disciplinary technique, similar to what was used among the Plains and Eastern Cree, according to Mandelbaum and Skinner.[29] According to Thomas Peacock, the Elder would also "remind young men who were courting young women that it was time to go home."[30]

Elders in this study remember the use of all of the above-mentioned techniques, though some more than others. One disciplinary technique Elsie recalled was being "lavishly praised" in her childhood, as did Danny and Gertie. Third-person conversations between adults were also used to praise children for good behaviour.[31] Praise often had to do with the quality of a child's contribution to the work of the family, and it reinforced that participatory behaviour. As seen in the earlier example involving help with tanning hides, Gertie's grandmother would get the children to help her with various chores as a way to involve them in community work. Gertie remembered how good this made her and her siblings feel: "For some reason, [helping her] was a big deal to us, because I think she would make you feel good about being able to do some work."

Some of the participants remembered that there were protocols in their families and communities about how praise was to be used. Maria said that praise was typically done by her older sisters or other relatives; praise from a parent was thought to bring bad fortune on a child, perhaps because of an apparent lack of humility. Mosôm Danny also remembered that praise often came from older siblings and cousins.

A few of the elders talked about the use of corporal punishment as a disciplinary technique. Danny's "Uncle Bill" was known as "a switcher," although this reputation was more useful as a threat than as a practice. Danny noted that he "never whipped us, but it was [a threat]. He would take out his pocket knife [to carve the switch]." When asked about corporal punishment, Elsie responded that "it was done in my family, but I didn't see it very often. Where I saw corporal punishment used was in the school that was run by the nuns in my community." Elsie also remarked that corporal punishment came into her family when she was a teenager, at the time her family and community were beginning to move away from traditional customs.

Maria told a story about the time her great-grandmother whipped her with a willow stick.[32] This occurred after nine-year-old Maria had come home feeling wounded from a racist incident at a day school in a nearby community, and had called her father a "good-for-nothing halfbreed." Maria was shocked because her great-grandmother had never hit her before. The beating was accompanied by lots of talk and was never done again.

In Rosella's family, corporal punishment was more common. Rosella grew up in northern Saskatchewan in a small community called Molanosa. She contextualized the use of corporal punishment by saying, "they [her parents] called it discipline, but it was abuse. They didn't know the difference. And because alcohol was involved, well, they had no sense of responsibility." It is important to note that alcohol and the disintegration of community contributed to the use of corporal punishment in these examples. In most cases, discipline was more persuasive, more openly discussed because it was an important step to learning self-discipline.

Self-discipline was a highly valued attribute in children. As seen in the reference above to the "game of silence" that was used to teach children self-control, one way to develop self-discipline was through the practice of becoming a good listener. Mosôm Danny remembered his grandfather explaining to the Indian Agent that his grandmother held significant responsibilities in terms of teaching the children this skill. His grandfather was emphatic that it was the "old lady" who would teach the children how to be attentive and listen, skills that would be vital as they began hunting. Because Danny was being trained as an oral historian, he received extra tutelage in becoming a good listener. Danny's grandmother was constantly teaching and talking to him as they worked and moved about, and she used land and place as a mnemonic device. Danny remembered being told, "Remember this place! Remember what we were doing here. Look around you. This is where you will find what I'm showing you; this is what you will remember if you sit here." She wanted him to acquire a system of memory, "a way to remember things by marking places in my mind."

Leah Dorion has written about the significance of teaching children how to be still and silent in traditional Cree parenting practices. "Getting children to slow down and have quiet time throughout the day is important in Opikinawasowin parenting. The Plains Cree word for silence is Kipihtowewin…. It is taught there needs to be a healthy balance between the amount of stillness, silence, and action in a child's life."[33] Maria remembered her great-grandmother's lessons on the importance of being still and attentive. This was essential to a land-based survival. "[In the spring] we were told to listen to our [animal] relatives," she said. "Frogs had been sleeping, and bears [and so on], and they all had dreams and visions and travels to share with us. By listening to animals in the spring or birds coming home, you learned to recognize the different creatures that lived with you." Maria commented, "Today when we go outside we just say 'frogs are singing.' But we don't know the forty-some species of frogs that live out there." She added, "That was how we learned all of those names, and could distinguish the difference in their voices, or by their songs." She stressed that this was important "because you depended on [the animals] for your life."

Self-discipline and self-reliance were fostered through practices of non-interference. Rene spoke of the self-reliance he was expected to develop as a child. He grew up in the traditional territory of Pagwashing in northwestern Ontario where hunting and trapping were ways of life. Early on he had to engage in harvesting the food he ate. "They taught [me] early," he said. "I learned to skin rabbits and go fishing. I learned to cook scone[s] and stuff. You could go hungry without these skills!"

Gertie talked about the indirect approach practised in her upbringing to teach self-reliance. It was important that she be up early to help with the chores. "I don't recall ever being told to go to bed, or to wake up," she said.

"Somebody might say very loudly in the kitchen, 'If you stay in that bed much longer, you are going to rot.' But they wouldn't say, 'Wake up now.'" There was also a distinction between laissez-faire learning and expectations around family and community responsibility. Gertie had work responsibilities and knew what was expected of her. She talked about the importance of this: "If you are treating and teaching children as they need to be taught, they will know that they have something to do with the future health of the family." She described how they made this distinction as children:

> [As kids] we were under no illusions that if we messed up that deer hide [while helping with tanning] that somebody was going to suffer. We knew that the family would suffer; we knew that the women would suffer, so we did that job right because that's what needed to happen … If you hadn't brought water in for the night, or you hadn't brought wood in and it was your job, you had to do it. No choice, because that affected other people. But if you didn't get your clothes into the wash tub, that was your problem. So that was the difference. If you had something that you were supposed to do that affected the entire family, you did it.

Another of Gertie's responsibilities was to set the fish nets every morning. "If we didn't have the fish to either sell, trade or eat, it could get pretty rough," she said. Staying in bed just wasn't an option.

Work

Gertie's stories demonstrate that work was an important part of childhood experience as it taught children self-discipline and self-reliance and how to be responsible to their community. Children always had plenty of work to do, and these responsibilities increased with age and ability.[34]

Cree oral historian Glecia Bear's stories speak to the qualities that were nurtured through work. She has published an account of how she took care of her sister when they got lost overnight; she was eleven and her sister was eight. This is a remarkable tale of self-reliance as well as community engagement and responsibility for children. At eleven, Bear notes she was given the responsibility for a cow at calving time, and at thirteen she was hauling fish to town and helping her dad on the lake. She stated that, as young girls, "we used to do everything. We used to mud the house and the horse barn; we cut wood in the bush and dragged the firewood home."[35]

As soon as they were able, girls worked alongside their mothers and grandmothers, engaging in domestic, garden and farm work, tanning hides, preparing foods, doing beadwork and sewing, hauling water and wood, berry picking, fishing, trapping, and doing some hunting. These contributions were valuable at the most basic level because of the real contributions they made to their family's well-being. In particular, mothers with many children needed help with the chores and child care that would have been unmanageable otherwise.

Rosella spoke about the multiple responsibilities she carried for the up-keep of her family in Molanosa. Her story indicates the kind of independence that was required of her from an early age. She talked about how she had to collect wood: "I would have a dog and a sleigh of my own, and an axe. I'd go way out in the bush. I could go for a mile and I'd chop logs down and I'd fill up my sleigh and I'd come back. But I had to do that because I was the oldest one in the family. The little boys weren't old enough to help me."

Work was delegated according to age, so that even the youngest children could make a contribution. Gertie reflected on hunting with her father and uncles in her childhood: "I remember hauling moose out of the bush. It didn't matter how old you were; you could carry something." Maria became responsible for food preparation as a youngster: "I started off plucking ducks and skinning rabbits and learning to cut them properly. I picked dandelions and did all that food gathering and learned how to prepare it. At some point people expected me to cook it. You learn that from observation and working with women who are doing it."

Even though several women confessed that the work could be tedious and exacting at times, they still had many positive memories about their experiences. This is likely because the work they did fostered in them a sense of self-esteem and pride. Children were rewarded and praised for contributing to the well-being of the community and for developing skills that would sustain their families in the present and in the future. Maria talked about the pride she experienced in being able to "graduate" from one level of contribution to the next when it came to learning how to cook a duck: "I started out by just whining about how I had to pluck the things in the heat like this, sitting under the shady tree and making sure I got all the good feathers into this bag and the bad feathers in that bag and then having to singe them. Then there came a point when it was time for my sister to do it, and I moved up. I would get the ducks after she plucked them." There was a prestige that went along with this new step. Maria laughed as she commented, "Nobody ever made a big deal when you were sitting back in the bush, plucking."

School

Work was part of a child's land-based education, and was very different from the formal education system Algonquian children eventually encountered. Because residential school experiences were largely negative (much of which has been documented in other literature),[36] I did not ask the participants about their residential school experiences. Some of the participants, however, volunteered information about the value their families placed on education. Negative feelings about school were thus typically a response to the residential school system and not reflective of resistance to western education on the whole. Many families realized that education was a way to succeed in the world that was coming and they wanted their children to have the opportunities that a good education presented.

Olive remembered her father saying that "today everything is changing. You can't afford to be illiterate. It's like being blind." Her parents wanted her to go to school and for this reason, Olive's family moved from their original homestead in northern Saskatchewan so they could be closer to a day school in a town.

The work ethic that applied to land-based education was also applied to formal schooling in many families. Like work, school was valued for the skills it would teach for survival in the future. Sylvia commented on how her family valued education for the girls. "My dad never talked to me about having a husband and having lots of kids," she said. "It was always, 'Get an education, and be something.'" She pointed out that her grandfather drove her by horse and wagon to the elementary school that was five kilometres away from her community, a commitment that did not waver during the harsh prairie winter. Because of the encouragement and support she received, Sylvia was able to complete her high school at a boarding school. She eventually went on to university and saw that her own children did the same.

In the oral history work she did with Leah Dorion, Rose stressed that "Métis families placed a high value on receiving a formal education since they had historically been denied a formal education through government inaction and through their non-recognition policy of the Métis." Dorion added that "Métis children were encouraged by their parents and extended family to work hard at school since formal education was viewed as a privilege."[37]

Rose started school at a convent that was fifteen kilometres away from where she lived with her grandparents outside of Duck Lake, and she was driven by her grandfather every day. Eventually her grandparents paid (with wood) for her to board at the convent. Like that of many of the elders, however, Rose's schooling was limited. She left in her early teens because her family could not afford the tuition any longer and her waged domestic labour was needed as part of the family income.

Play

Although children worked hard and had many responsibilities, play was an important part of growing up, as it is in any culture. Play often involved copying behaviours and the work of adults. In *Chippewa Child Life and Its Cultural Foundations,* Hilger summarizes the play of Chippewa children in noting how "they mimicked their elders in the various occupations of housekeeping, caring for dolls, hunting and fishing and dancing." She points out how "children on several reservations were seen imitating their elders."[38] Densmore as well wrote about a number of toys Chippewa children played with, including (real) stuffed animals, clay or bulrush animals, miniature items such as birch utensils for "playing camp," bows and arrows, and an assortment of dolls. These children made jewellery from berries, miniature snowshoes from pine needles, and baskets from plants, and had particular sports and games, such as the "windigo or cannibal game."[39]

The elders I spoke with did not recollect having toys, but there were some stories of dolls. Maria remembered one time when her mother and aunts got together to make dolls for the girls. She remarked that this could have been an attempt to get the girls more focused on taking care of children. It wasn't long, however, before they were back to playing outside and climbing trees. Most of the memories of play were not of toys, but of spending time on the land and with relatives. For example, Gertie's recollection of play involved going out on Lake Nipissing with her mom to fish, or on berry-picking excursions, or paddling in the canoe with her sister to visit other relatives their own age who lived along the shores.

The "Fast Life": Moving into Adolescence

Basil Johnston's description of "the four hills of life" identifies childhood as a time of preparation and youth as a time of quest. The discipline instilled in children through the ethics of work, self-discipline, self-reliance, and community responsibility helped prepare them to effectively contribute to the well-being of family and community as adults. It was about the physical survival of the people. At the same time, children and youth had to prepare themselves for life's "moral journey."

Both the physical and the moral were tested, strengthened, and celebrated through ceremonial practices and passages. In Chapter 3, I describe a "walking out" ceremony that was a "symbol of success in the food quest"[40] and an example of how some ceremonies focused on a child's potential for contributing to physical survival. These ceremonies lauded the accomplishments of an individual based on what he or she would be able to contribute to the collective. For boys, there were celebrations that marked the first hunt or kill. Experiences like these were described by Mosôm Danny and Rene, who told stories about how proud they felt upon being recognized by their male relatives for killing a moose and catching a fish, respectively. In both cases, their passages were spontaneous or, as Rene pointed out, brought on with the assistance of Mother Earth.

The stories that Danny and Rene told about their entry into the world of "provider" demonstrate that health, well-being, and survival were recognized as a matter of the collective through ceremony, which could be formal or informal. Rene explained how this occurred for him. "There was a whole bunch of uncles standing by the shoreline, fishing for whitefish," he said. "I saw the tail end of a northern pike and I reached in and grabbed it—tossed it right out of the water. And they all said, 'Eehhh!!! Ki sa kin a.' It means, 'You wrestled with him and you beat him and you are a man!' Even that recognition made me feel tall just walking away." According to Rene, it was "the uncles' job" to recognize and celebrate his accomplishment, "but you need a community to do that; not just one or two," he said. "You need a bunch. Maybe ten; ten of them standing there." Collectively, Rene's uncles helped him to feel proud of his changing status in the community. He noted that these feelings of self-confidence, self-esteem, and responsibility were further enhanced at a later point when his uncles invited him to go hunting.

Mosôm Danny talked about how he was awarded a more powerful rifle for his first large animal kill. This happened spontaneously while he was working as a cook on a hunting trip with a number of men. While they were out in the bush, Danny was back minding the base camp alone, and spotted a moose. He successfully shot it and then prepared it for the men to eat upon their return from the day's hunt. In acknowledgement of this, one of the old men took Danny's .22-calibre rifle and gave him his own new .30-30 rifle. "Now you are a man," he said. "You fed us today. You graduated to this rifle. I'll take this .22 and I'll retire. Now you take over." Danny reflected on what this meant, remarking, "It gave me a purpose, you see. As much as I hated to kill animals, I had to [hunt large game] now, to feed the family and to feed the community. That was it. That was the end of my youth. I had entered the world of the adult. Now I was accepted as an equal to the men."

Fasting

Other ceremonies used physical challenges as a way of advancing the spiritual path of boys and girls. Fasting was the most common practice. For land-based cultures, fasting was important because it was a reminder of the tenuous nature of everyone's survival and the necessity of establishing good relationships with animals and the food they provided. As an intense physical and spiritual exercise, fasting cultivated spiritual help towards food security by reinforcing relationships between the youth and the spirit world, while at the same time training the young to withstand periods of hunger.

Religious scholar and historian Christopher Vecsey has noted that, among the Ojibway, fasting in the past "dramatized the Ojibwa dread of starvation and defined the state of hunger as one deserving of pity."[41] This pity then brought about the assistance of the "manitos" (spirits) who could accompany an individual for a lifetime. Drawing on sources from the eighteenth, nineteenth, and early twentieth centuries, Vecsey points out that Ojibway puberty fasts were significant because they helped youth develop his or her identity. Prepubescent children lived with a "borrowed" identity, grounded in the spiritual power they received from the person who named them. Puberty was a time for the child/youth to connect to his or her own source of power, and this was achieved through fasting.[42]

Although fasting among youth—and especially the "vision quest" for pubescent boys—is most commonly known, it is important to note that Anishinaabek of both sexes as young as four or five also fasted up until the early twentieth century. This was likely done to instil training and discipline from an early age. Among the Chippewa, it was critical for children to fast *before* puberty, while they were still "pure" and innocent.[43] Boys and girls entering puberty fasted between one and ten days, depending on their age and their capacity for endurance.[44] Boys and girls had distinct experiences, and while both are equally important, I am only concentrating on the rites of passages for girls, as the focus of this book is on girls and women.

Fasting was an important component of Cree and Ojibway girls' coming-of-age ceremonies, which took place at the onset of menstruation and at which time girls were expected to seclude themselves from their families and communities. The pubescent girl would typically spend four to ten days alone in a lodge specifically constructed for this purpose. This structure was set up for her in the woods or some distance away from the house, although by the early twentieth century some families were isolating girls in make-shift sections of the main lodging. The Chippewa called this time *makwa* or *makwawe*: "turning into a bear" or "the bear lives alone all winter."[45]

It was particularly important to avoid contact with boys and men at this time, as it was believed that the power a girl carried during her first menstruation disrupted male energy and was considered strong enough to kill. A pubescent girl's touch could also wither a plant, kill fish in a lake she entered, kill a tree, or turn soup to water.[46] Among the Ojibway of Parry Island (Wasauksing), a woman's power was considered to be heightened at the time of puberty:

> The Parry Islanders believed that every woman was possessed of a mysterious power that was dangerous to men. This power was latent in them at all times, so that during the hunting season men kept aloof as far as possible lest it should neutralize their hunting medicines and rob them of success in the chase. It was strongest during labour, when any man who inhaled the expectant mother's breath (except the most powerful medicine man) lost all his hunting power; and it was perhaps no less strong at the first blossoming into womanhood. Every month the moon renewed this power, just as it renewed the medicine power of the *wabeno*, *djiskiu*, and *kusabindugeyu*,[47] for it was grandmother moon, by day the oldest and by night the fairest of all women, who brought the first Indian maid to maturity.[48]

Because of this power, a girl on her first menstruation was not to touch, look at, or cross the path of any male.

An Algonquian girl's power also warranted taking precautions about touching herself. Girls were given a scratching stick and were forbidden to touch their own hair, which would be tied back or covered. In some cases, girls' faces were covered with charcoal, which served the purpose of letting others know she was in seclusion while protecting anyone she might gaze upon.

Although it was not a full fast, food was limited and was served by mothers and grandmothers in special serving dishes, which the girl might use during their menstrual periods henceforth. Girls were forbidden to eat food that was coming into season, because of the belief that they could offset the harvest. One Chippewa woman who had gone through this seclusion told Hilger, "If they had given me fish, all the tribe would have had bad luck fishing."[49]

Puberty among Algonquian peoples was considered an optimal time for learning, experiencing spiritual enlightenment, and building commitment. Because of this powerful and liminal state, it was extremely important how a girl conducted herself during this time: her behaviour during seclusion would determine how she would live her life. Girls were to focus on industry, self-reliance, self-restraint, and connection to spirit. Hard work was exemplified by spending their days in seclusion doing sewing and handiwork, preparing hides and chopping wood. Elder women would assist by coming in to talk to girls about the adult responsibilities that lay ahead, and would instruct them in their work and/or give them information about sexuality, courting, and marriage. In some cases, girls would seek a vision and sometimes receive it. Such girls were granted power to heal, act as medicine people, or become other types of leaders. Among the Wasauksing Anishinaabek, girls who had visions were promised a future as great warriors. According to anthropologist Diamond Jenness, "The forefathers of the Parry Islanders [Wasauksing] followed such women leaders with alacrity, believing that they enjoyed a twofold power, the mysterious power inherent in all women and the special supernatural powers they derived from their visions."[50]

When the seclusion period was over, the girl was celebrated with a feast attended by family and community members. Anthropologists Frances Densmore and Ruth Landes wrote that Chippewa and Ojibway girls were then required to observe certain practices for the following year, such as abstaining from berries and seasonal produce.[51] Densmore documented a Midewiwin ceremony in which girls had to show their restraint by refusing to consume berries.[52] She also noted that at each harvest in the following year a girl needed to be introduced to the seasonal food by having it served by someone else or by mixing it with charcoal.[53] Among the Chippewa, during the entire year following a girls' first menses, the pubescent girl "was not to touch babies, or clothes of her father, or brothers, or of any man, for it would cripple them."[54] In her book *Empowerment of North American Indian Girls*, psychologist Carol Markstrom points out that for the girl "these [pubescent] sacrifices were meaningful because they represented those things that would be important to her for the remainder of her life."[55]

Markstrom's work is helpful as she has identified a number of key beliefs about pubescent Indigenous girls that help us to better understand contemporary Native American coming-of-age customs (see Table 4.1). Her study involved Apache, Navajo, Lakota, and Ojibway communities. She learned that puberty ceremonies for girls, as they continue to be practised in these nations, are not simply about acknowledging fertility and reproductive capacity. Rather, they are grounded in Indigenous understandings of menstruation as "an extension of the same power responsible for all creation and annual rejuvenation of the Earth."[56] A girl's first menstruation is considered particularly powerful so it is critical that proper protocols are followed, for as Markstrom writes, "the impacts are not restricted to one component of life (i.e., spiritual or religious) but are pervasive within the person and actually extend to the community and, in some cases, the entire Earth."[57] The continuance of the people, and of life itself, hinges on how this elemental power is respected and managed.

Through her research into this custom, Markstrom found that the Apache, Navajo, and Lakota believe there is a link between the pubescent girl and archetypal female characters from their respective nations' creation stories.[58] This link enabled some girls to channel the power of the archetypal females for the good of their communities: girls in seclusion could be asked to offer favours, blessings, and healing ceremonies to other community members.[59] Although the contemporary Ojibway whom Markstrom consulted did not indicate such a close link between the archetypal female characters and pubescent girls, Markstrom found this link in a story originally captured by ethnologist H.R. Schoolcraft in the mid-1800s. In this account, a girl of twelve or thirteen was told to engage in her vision quest "for the good of all mankind." Six days into her fast, the girl had a vision of Kaugegagbekwa, "Everlasting Woman," who shared her name and gave the girl the ability to bestow it on others. The girl was also granted "long life on Earth and the ability to save life in others."[60]

Table 4.1:
Beliefs about Pubescent Girls Held by North American Indians

1. Menstruation and menstrual fluids are powerful in general, and the first menstrual cycles are particularly powerful.
2. Feminine representations in cosmological constructions, including origin stories, are instructive to the pubescent girl, as well as to women.
3. The special quality of menarche is a necessary (but not sufficient) event for connection of the initiate to the spiritual realm (rituals complete this process).
4. The proper performance of rituals ensures the initiate's successful transition into adulthood and influences her life course.
5. The initiate's performance of tests of endurance will subsequently affect her life course.
6. The malleable state of the initiate at puberty necessitates her subjugation to the instruction and influence of adults, particularly an adult female mentor.
7. Due to her empowered state, the initiate's behaviour at puberty will have an impact on her future; hence, taboos and behavioural restrictions must be followed.
8. Due to her empowered state, the initiate can influence the welfare of others.
9. The coming-of-age event is not only a transition from childhood to adulthood but also a transition into the world of the spiritual.

Source: Carol A. Markstrom, *Empowerment of North American Indian Girls: Ritual Expressions at Puberty* (Lincoln: University of Nebraska Press, 2008), 72.

The women I spoke with had varying experiences with their puberty and coming-of-age ceremonies. For some women, the onset of menstruation was not acknowledged or celebrated in any way, nor did they receive any information about what was happening to their bodies. Some were simply told "now you can have kids," but were unsure about how the process worked. Others had mothers and grandmothers who explained the changes to them. When Rose was nine, for example, her grandmother talked to her about menstruation, "explaining everything."

Rose was lucky to receive this information from her grandmother, as by the 1930s, residential schooling, pressure from the church, and the repression of traditional practices had made it difficult to talk about sexuality or to acknowledge the transition to womanhood.[61] A few participants, however, did undergo fasts or seclusions that were similar to the ceremonies described by Densmore and others. These ceremonies were not as rigorous as they had been in previous generations, and by the 1940s and 1950s, families who maintained these practices often did so in secrecy.[62] The continuation of these ceremonies demonstrates the value that some families placed on marking this life transition, in spite of pressures to abandon their practices.

June reached puberty as a teen growing up in an Ojibway community in central Ontario. Her rite of passage involved being sequestered in a dark room in her house for ten days at the onset of menstruation. Fasting was not part of her seclusion and she was allowed to eat many of her favourite foods: rabbit, partridge, rice, jam, and scones. Yet she was expected to make sacrifices during the year that followed. She explained, "I couldn't go near babies, I couldn't pick berries, haul water, get wood. I couldn't touch trees. If I were to touch a tree they would hurry up and do something with it. I don't know what they did, my grandfather wouldn't tell me." She noted that pubescent girls were not allowed to touch a drum because they could kill it by touching it, as drums are alive and carry spirit power. "That's how powerful a girl is," she said. At the end of her puberty year, June was given a cedar bath and was welcomed into the women's circle. This meant she would take on the responsibilities of an adult woman, which included carrying out adult work responsibilities.

Marie also spent ten days in seclusion when she reached puberty. Her mother took her out of the day school she was attending, and cordoned her off in a separate part of their house, behind a curtain. Her seclusion included some fasting: "[It was] just a little cubbyhole place and all I lived on was a little piece of scone and about a half a glass of water in the morning and at night." She exclaimed, "Oh, I used to really sip that.... But I survived!" Marie also recalled that it was dark and that she was instructed not to touch her teeth, eyes, ears or hair. During the day, she did sewing and darning with the assistance of older women who came to teach her. This was something they did with all the girls going through their seclusion: "They would show you and then they'd leave. And when they came back the next day you had to keep showing what you did. If you didn't do it right, they had another one there ready for you." The activities that Marie engaged in were based on the traditional belief that they would make her a good worker in the future. She talked about the knowledge she acquired from her elders during this time, saying that it was an important "because it was our survival. They taught me how to crochet and how to knit," she said. "And then they talked to me about how to cook wild geese, deer, beaver, whatever."

Unfortunately, Marie's seclusion was cut short when her older brother arrived to visit on the ninth day. Having been told that she had been absent from school due to illness, he insisted on seeing her. When Marie's mother finally conceded and let him visit, he immediately gave her a hug. This broke the protocol about contact with men and consequently broke her fast. Marie lamented that she did not finish her seclusion, as she had just begun to dream and have visions of ancestral visitors. The secrecy of her seclusion and the fact that her mother felt she could not share it is a vivid demonstration of the stress that families were under to curtail these customs.

Like Marie, Rebecca learned self-discipline and the value of hard work in her coming-of-age ceremony. Rebecca had always been a tomboy as a child, but at puberty she learned about the sacred nature of her new feminine identity. She recalled how her first cycle came about. It was summer, and "I was playing at the edge of the lake when suddenly I felt water flowing through my body," she said. "It scared me, so I ran in to tell my mother. She stopped what she was doing and told me that soon I would become a woman." Rebecca's cycle began the following day. She remarked, "I wish that I had my mother with me today, I would like to ask how she knew that my moon-time was about to begin."

During this first cycle, Rebecca's mother taught her how to cleanse herself. Rebecca recalled that her mother taught her to bathe in a special way; to take her time and wash with care when she was in her cycle. "She told me to move softly and think about the work that my body was doing cleaning itself through the cycle of the Moon," Rebecca said. "Today, I realize that the rhythmic movements she taught me followed my body's lymphatic system and cleared the female hormones out of my body."

This teaching was followed by a seclusion that involved staying in the house for a month. During this time Rebecca's mother instilled in her the discipline of work as well as the discipline of caring for the power she had acquired. As Rebecca recalled, "[My mother] gave me new responsibilities. I had to get up at 4:30, to make the coffee and start getting things ready in the kitchen. After the men were gone for the day I washed the floors, did laundry, and cleaned. At the end of the day I used to have to scrub and restock the grub boxes. Sometimes the men would come in late and I would be standing on a box at the sink doing dishes after dark." Rebecca pointed out that "[my mother taught me] devotion to the task: to take pride in my work; to always do my best with the everyday tasks of washing floors, doing laundry and preparing meals." She also received support from her father during this time, recalling that "one night my father came into the kitchen and saw me standing at the sink, silently crying with exhaustion. Without saying a word, he picked up a tea towel and began drying dishes. We worked together until the job was done."

From this coming-of-age experience, Rebecca not only learned that "to be a good worker was a way of life" but also she learned that she had to manage the power that she had been given: "During the month that my mother kept me in the house the task of learning about being a woman absorbed me completely. She taught me the things I could and could not do when I had my menstrual cycle. I was not allowed to cut up meat or pick berries and I could not pick or make medicine. I also learned that if Grandmother Moon comes when a woman is about to prepare feast food, she must humble herself and ask another woman to do it for her."

Some of the other women told me about ceremonies that were variations of the ceremonies described in the ethnographies I have drawn from. Most likely, the ceremonies had been modified to suit the times and the family circumstances. Gertie, for example, engaged in a ceremony of transition and sacrifice that involved both childhood and puberty fasting. One summer, at the age of seven, she was sent by her grandmother to pick berries near their home at Nipissing Fist Nation. She was instructed not to eat any. This was new for Gertie, because up until then she had been allowed to eat as many berries as she wanted. This practice went on for five years, and each time Gertie brought in the berries, her grandmother would make jam. This jam would be put away until winter and then given away. "Making sure that I could see," Gertie recalled, "she would pick up those berries in the jar, hand them to somebody and say, 'My granddaughter picked these berries in the summer and I want you to have them.'"[63] At the end of the five-year period, Gertie's grandmother opened a jar of berries and told her that she could eat some before she gave the rest away. Gertie remarked, "What I learned was that I didn't have to have everything that I saw.... It wasn't a fast [as we know about them now], but I fasted over those berries for a long time. I think she just figured out it took a lot longer for somebody to learn self-discipline in those days than it [had in her generation]."

In some instances, families tried to harness the transformative power of puberty and the power of the pubescent girl for healing purposes. In his ethnography of the Wasauksing/Parry Island Ojibway, Jenness wrote that a pubescent girl's power could be used to heal. He gave the example of a man who suffered from a spine ailment that "rendered him helpless" until he was brought to a pubescent girl's seclusion hut and treated by her. In this case, the girl walked slowly up and down the man's spine and, by transferring her power, "enabled him to rise to his feet with all the vigour of a young man."[64]

Marie told a story in which she was witness to a healing provided by her sister, about twenty years after Jenness had been in their community:

> They brought this man from Deep River and put him in a little shed [outside our house]. I remember they brought my sister out. They had her fasting upstairs. [It was] the last day and they took her in that little shed. Of course, I had to see what was going on.
>
> His legs were bad. This was a returned soldier from the Second World War. I guess he got a spinal injury somewhere and his legs just went. And you know what? They pulled up his pants (like that) and she bit him. They told her to bite him hard. She said, "It's so hot my teeth are going to fall out."
>
> I could see him because I was peeking in the door there. She bit him all the way up and all the way back down. After that, they got her to go like that (*she makes a pulling motion*)—like [she was] pulling something out of him.

Marie finished her story by saying that the healing worked, "because he walked after that."

It was interesting to speak to Rene and Mosôm Danny about what they learned as boys witnessing their sisters and female cousins go through puberty ceremonies. Danny remembered seclusions and ceremonies in which the grandmothers would gather to teach the girls, using pipes, rocks, and drums.[65] He recalled one instance in which he was told to leave the house and go with his grandfather to a tent because one of his sisters had come into her time. "While the ceremony was going on inside," Danny said, "my grandfather lit the pipe outside. He smudged his pipe and then went and smudged the house all around, so no spirits could disturb this girl in her moment of purity. Then we sat outside and we smoked." What Danny learned was that boys and men had a role in supporting the success of a girl's rite of passage.

Rene became aware of the girls' changes in status when they came out of seclusion. "When grandmother took my cousins away, they called it *kitchi kwe we*," he explained. "We wouldn't see them for a while, and would wonder where they went. *Kitchi kwe we*: they were having their first moon. After she came home, she's *kitchi kwe*—she's a woman now." These concepts of *kitche* meaning "great" and *kwe* meaning "woman" delineated a new role for Rene's cousins and changed his relationship with them.[66] He talked about how this grounded his identity as "Anishinaabe," the term used to signify the Ojibway but which translates to "from whence lowered the male of the species."[67] Reflecting on the humility he carried with respect to Mother Earth and to older women in particular, Rene mused, "I often think of what Anishinaabe means. Anish—to lower the man. These names lower us ... [they imply that] women were always here. And us guys, we need to have that balance!" For this reason, when Rene's cousins returned as *kitche kwe*, it implied a new respect and role for him as a boy in relation to them as "great women."

As Rene's story indicates, girls' puberty ceremonies were significant in terms of teaching boys about the respect that was due to the women in their communities. Rene laments the loss of these customs, which in his community occurred when they moved from their traditional homeland onto a reserve. He is aware of how this respect for women has been lost: "You talk about two worlds. When you are on the rez now, that thing is not taught. There is no more *kitchi kwe we*. And I think that's why they get beat up sometimes. There's violence all over the place."[68]

The new status that girls gained after going through their puberty ceremonies traditionally meant that they were welcomed into the women's circle, and with this came new responsibilities. Marie shared her mother's memory of how this rapid change took place in her life experience: "My mother said that you are a mature person when you come out of that; you don't even think like a little girl anymore." Marie recalled that when she was taken out of her ceremony, the first thing she did was to go home and cook a meal, demonstrating a level of expertise that she didn't even know she had. Just as boys were initiated into the role of provider, girls were expected to take on work responsibilities related to sustaining their communities.

Conclusion

The stories told by the women I interviewed correspond to the teachings about children at this life stage: they are to be nurtured and taught the disciplines that they will need to be functioning members of their communities. This is a time of preparation, in which all members of the community have a hand in ensuring that their upcoming members learn what they need to know. Community health and well-being is dependent on this education. Marking the end of childhood, puberty is a time of rapid transition between preparation for and then entering into the world of adult responsibilities. The puberty ceremonies that many of the women described clearly show a shift in expectations, not only in terms of the work that was expected of them but also in learning what sacrifices they would have to make. This may be what Gertie's grandmother was trying to teach her by requiring her to abstain from berries for those five long years. The ethics of hard work, sharing, and sacrifice were built into childrearing practices and into the ceremonies that marked the transition into adult life.

There is not as much information here that demonstrates the spiritual path described in some of the teachings, although the fostering of moral development is certainly evident in the women's stories of disciplinary practices. The quest for vision described by Johnson is more often described with relation to boys fasting, but girls also fasted.[69] Marie's experience in her puberty fast certainly indicates that she was heading in that direction, as she talked about how she was beginning to dream and have visits from ancestral spirits before her fast was interrupted. Perhaps because of the secret nature of the ceremonies during the 1930–1950s, the personal nature of the knowledge, or the secrecy involved, it is difficult to demonstrate how principles of individual identity or spiritual connections worked in the lives of these women or others in their communities. Minnesota Anishinaabe Elder Ignatia Broker wrote that it was the custom of the people "to learn which girls would be Dreamers or Medicine people."[70] How the quest for individual identity and spirit is connected is something that is worthy of further consideration; particularly how the process works for girls and women.

This chapter demonstrates that, up until puberty, gendered identities were not as clearly marked. Rebecca commented, for example, that she was able to be a tomboy until she went into puberty. Her identity as a young girl child was never questioned, but that changed when she began her Moon Time. After puberty, young men and women went separate ways in order to engage in the work that was assigned to them. And it was then that girls entered the circle of adult women.

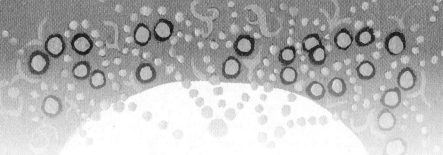

Chapter 5

Adult Years: The Women's Circle

In the adult world you did community work; you worked with the leaders of that community; you worked along with the elders to prepare for winter life, for winter food, clothing, wood and stuff like that. You went to all the meetings, you associated with all the leaders and you participated. You were sworn as a member of your dodem and your community. Now you carried the responsibility for the continuation of the collective as a living, viable community. You had to make sure that you did your fair share to keep the community healthy and well.

—**Mosôm Danny Musqua**

*M*osôm Danny teaches that adulthood was a time to carry responsibilities for providing for family and community, and in Midewiwin teachings this time is referred to as "planning and planting life." During this phase of life, young and middle-aged women had the responsibility of ensuring sustenance for the community and care for the young and old. These responsibilities would have evolved as they went through their adult years, as women took on increasing authority with age, but the stories here demonstrate generally what girls encountered when they entered womanhood, or the "women's circle," as envisioned in the diagram of traditional social organization which I introduce in Figure 5.1 (see explanation below).

With comparison to the other life stages, it is important to note that these years were much more defined by gender. Gertie grew up in central Ontario and remembers puberty as being the beginning of a more distinct separation between male and female; a time when "girls began to spend more time with the older women of their family, and the young men would go off with their fathers, uncles and grandfathers." The divided nature of land-based work lent itself to these distinctions, as men were typically involved in hunting large game while women harvested smaller animals and plant foods and managed family and community affairs. Women also held physical and spiritual responsibilities for maintaining the life force of the community through their ability to give birth. Although childrearing responsibilities fell within the women's circle, I do not spend much time on them in this chapter because pregnancy and childrearing have been discussed in Chapters 3 and 4. Yet all of these responsibilities determined the life course as it was lived during these middle years, and defined the types of authorities that women held.

Entering the Women's Circle

Elders will often say that in the past, men had the responsibility to protect and provide for their communities and that women held the responsibilities of creating and nurturing life. While it is certain that men engaged in hunting outside of the community while women raised children and managed their home territories, it is important to avoid interpreting these teachings from a Western patriarchal framework. In searching for an English word to describe the way in which women and men operated in distinct worlds, Mosôm Danny landed upon the term "jurisdiction." This word is defined as "the power or right to exercise authority" as well as "the limits or territory within which authority may be exercised."[1]

Women had authorities, territories, and even ways of speaking the language that were respected by men, and vice versa, although it is also noteworthy that there was flexibility when it came to work that needed to be done and who was available to do it. According to historian Sarah Carter, the gendered division of First Nations people on the Prairies in the early reserve years "was not always sharply marked and could break down in the face of expediency and individual preference."[2] Women had to know how to take care of everything in terms of survival, for as Rose pointed out, the men in her community of Duck Lake were often out hunting, trapping, or otherwise working, and it was "the fortitude of a Métis woman" to take care of everything in their absence. In the oral history that Elsie provided to her niece Leah Dorion, she noted that during World War II there were no men in her community of Cumberland House, Saskatchewan. Therefore, it was the women who "did all the hunting, fishing, trapping, the gathering of the wood, preparing and all the gathering of berries, and also haying for horse and cows there were in the community." As Elsie remarked, "the women were a hearty breed."[3]

Overall, men and women's "jurisdictions" worked together as part of a system aimed at ensuring balance and well-being in the community. Drawing on her teachings from the Anishinaabe Elder Peter O'Chiese, Maria explained this system by using concentric circles, in which men occupied the outermost circle, women occupied the next circle, followed by elders in the third circle, and the children at the heart (see Figure 5.1).[4] Men protected these inner circles and provided for them by bringing in the resources. It was the women's job to manage and care for these resources in a way that would ensure the well-being of the entire community. Women also looked after social relations within the family and community. Although these responsibilities and duties were not fixed and were often overlapping, the concentric circles visually conceptualize the territories occupied by men and women in traditional societies.[5]

Figure 5.1: Social Organization of "Traditional" Communities

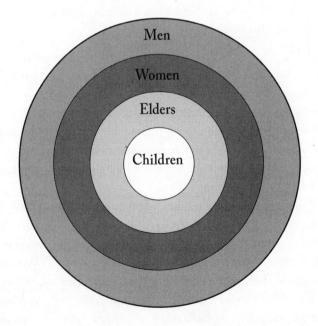

Traditional teachings about the tipi also help us gain an understanding of the spiritual and practical grounding for northern Algonquian women's jurisdiction of the inner circle. Cree Elder Mary Lee teaches that "women were named after that fire in the centre of the tipi, which brought that warmth and comfort."[6] She explains how this understanding is built into the Cree language: "'Woman' in our language is *iskwew*.... We were named after that fire, *iskwuptew*, and that is very powerful, because it honours the sacredness of that fire." These teachings capture how the tipi was equated with the way women traditionally held the home territory, as Lee points out:

> In our language, for old woman, we say, Notegweu. Years ago we used the term Notaygeu, meaning when an old lady covers herself with a shawl. A tipi cover is like that old woman with a shawl. As it comes around the tipi, it embraces all those teachings, the values of community that the women hold. No matter how many children and great grandchildren come into that circle of hers, she always still has room. And if you put it up right, the poles never show on the bottom, and that tipi stands with dignity, just as, years ago, women always covered their legs with the skirt, which also represents the sacred circle of life. When you put the flaps up, it teaches you how we embrace life itself. It's like a woman standing there with her arms out, saying "Thank you" to everything.[7]

Elder Mary Lee, who continues to teach the ceremonies that are part of women's responsibilities for putting up a tipi, concludes her teachings, emphasizing, "That is what the tipi is—it is the spirit and body of woman, because she represents the foundation of family and community. It is through her that we learn the values that bring balance into our lives."[8] Tipis and other types of lodging were thus both the metaphoric and literal terrain of women in the past, as it was the woman who owned the tipi and did the ceremonial work involved in putting it up.[9]

Mosôm Danny learned from his elders that "the tipi, and the contents of it, belonged to the woman." This tradition was familiar to Fine Day, who noted that in the late 1800s, it was typically old women who would make the tipis. He stated, "The woman puts up the tipi and owns it."[10] Writing about what she learned living among Cree and Métis peoples in the Northwest during the late 1800s, Amelia Paget also remarked on the women's relationship with the tipi, writing, "If the buffalo hunt was successful, women would make new tepees or wigwams—many workers would offer their help in sewing it up. Then they would have a feast upon completion, and all the women of the band were bidden to this ceremony, no men ever attended."[11]

While the tipi was the lodging and thus represented the physical home, the woman's place at the centre of it symbolized a tremendous role in the greater community. In our discussions on this subject, Mosôm Danny made a distinction between Western patriarchal notions of "a woman's place in the home" and the jurisdictions and authorities of womanhood in a historical Algonquian context. He remarked that the jurisdiction and authority women held were much greater than they are today. As they became westernized, these powers diminished: "We began to think about only just the house, and around the yard. And on the reserve, that's the way it became. We moved out of our tipis and wigwams into log buildings. The log building was a permanent structure. You didn't tear it down and move it around, where you leave it from one season to go to the next." Danny noted that women had a greater organizational and community management role in migratory life: "In that world, you had places to go each season. And that required a lot of discipline and order to move from one place to the next."

Mosôm Danny's comment draws attention to the fact that "a woman's place" was not confined to the walls of a single household; rather, her place involved maintaining order in the community. He gave the example of a time when his people, of the Keeseekoose First Nation in southeastern Saskatchewan, used to set up camp for their large gatherings in the fall and spring. These camps were organized according to clan, and it was the clan mothers who had what Danny called the "public function" of organizing the spaces community members would occupy according to their particular responsibilities. These roles were necessary to maintain order in the camp community while they were there. He noted "it was the women who set up these things. Today there is not the same level of community planning; we don't know how to plan that way. Such a lot is missing. The old people say, 'We've lost our hearts: our women!'" To this, Danny added, "This damn *Indian Act* and the control they [the government] put upon us, they destroyed our women's place among us." Danny's comment corresponds to what we know about how the *Indian Act* in general stripped First Nations women of their official participation in politics and governance, as explained in Chapter 3.

Families were still moving seasonally up to the 1950s, but they did not have the freedom of mobility they had known in the past. Patriarchy and violence had also moved into these circles and spaces, and so "the woman's place" had become more restricted, as Danny pointed out. Nonetheless, gendered territories and jurisdictions were still operating with the vestiges of tradition to a greater or lesser extent, depending on the family and community.

Maria talked about how space was organized according to gender and age in her home community near Prince Albert, Saskatchewan, where men, women, and elders physically occupied different spaces around the home. She remembered how this worked in the summers during her childhood in particular, when there was more use of outdoor space and larger gatherings of visitors. Tents were set up to accommodate these gatherings. Elders would visit in a tent away from the house, while women would be near the kitchen. Children would move back and forth between the women and elders, with the youngest typically staying close to the elders. Maria pointed out that men never came around the house. They spent time in her father's space, a log cabin that was off a trail in the bush. She explained, "There were a couple of bunks and a stove and that's where my dad kept a lot of his traps and all of his hunting gear. And when the men came to visit him, that's usually where they hung out." Community meeting space consisted of an arbour where everyone would meet to enjoy meals and socialize. When it came time to retire, the men would stay in her father's house while the women and children would stay in the house or in a tent. As Maria remembered, "Those rules were really strict. We never went in that shack of my dad's. That was a men's house. And the men never came into the house for meal time if it was summer. If they were around the house, they were on the side where the arbour was."

As I discuss in the next chapter, some of this spatial organization had to do with protecting women and children from unwanted sexual attention or abuse, as in the case of segregated sleeping arrangements during larger gatherings. But even when they were in smaller extended family groups, women and men held different spaces. These environments were respected to the extent that it was considered inappropriate to go into another group's territory because it could interfere with the authorities and powers within that group.

Some participants talked about how women did not go into men's particular spaces because it would mean a "tangling" of powers.[12] A woman's power, particularly during menstruation, was considered so strong that it could interfere with men's work. Pre-menopausal women therefore did not go around the hunting and trapping equipment that was kept in the "men's houses" away from the main lodging. Rebecca remembered that "when Grandmother Moon came to me for the first time, my mother taught me many things. I was no longer allowed to touch a man's gun or knife, and it was at that time my father gave me my first woman's knife. Although I could clean fish when Grandmother Moon was with me, I was not allowed to cut up meat or pick berries and medicine. I was never to cross between a man and the fire, and I was also not allowed to step over the top of a man's feet or a man who was lying on the floor." Young women thus learned to respect the tools men used to sustain their families; they learned not to tangle with that power. It is important to note that once women had passed through menopause they were able to move into these men's spaces. Maria pointed out, for example, that her grandmother was able to come and go into her dad's house if necessary.

This principle of respecting gendered jurisdictions was significant because it underpinned notions of balance and well-being in the community. Mosôm Danny drew attention to this by recalling a story his grandfather had told him. His grandfather's story is about how he tried to explain jurisdictional issues to their Indian Agent during the 1940s. Danny recalls that the Agent was told by his grandfather not to go to a certain part of the reserve because it was occupied by a bear. When the Agent showed no regard for this advice, the old man admonished him with the following:

> [Don't go there!] That bear's just waking up and she's hungry. She could kill you. And why shouldn't she kill you? That bear's been there for ten, fifteen years. Its mother was there before it. Before I arrived, the bears were there. I let them be and they let me be. I know where they go. It knows there is a boundary there, and there's an authority that I can't go overtake. I will not step into that authority.... Just like over there, you see my wife sitting over there? She's talking to her daughters and some boys. I don't go there. I won't step into that authority base. That's her power. The power to teach the laws of this family. Those laws keep this family held together, and this woman learned them from her mother and my mother. And I'm not going to interfere with that, the same way as I'm not going to interfere with that bear over here.

With his handling of this incident, Danny's grandfather tried to impress on him (and the Indian Agent) that balance and well-being are contingent on respecting boundaries.[13] The following sections in this chapter detail some of the women's world by looking at how they managed the work and social responsibilities that fell within their circle.

Managing the Resources: Work Within the Women's Circle

In her reflections on the teachings she received at puberty, Rebecca summarized one of the core values of Indigenous womanhood: "to be a good worker was a way of life." As demonstrated in previous chapters, hard work was a highly valued attribute, and much of girlhood was spent in preparation for the work responsibilities of adulthood. This Indigenous work ethic is captured by Fine Day, who remarked that a "good woman was never idle" and pointed out that "in the old days the young fellows went after the good worker, not the good looker."[14] In the oral histories of mid-twentieth-century Cree women in Saskatchewan, a high value was placed on "personal competence, self-reliance, and hard work."[15]

Food Management and Security

It is not surprising that Fine Day would have looked for a good worker in a partner, because a woman's abilities in food procurement, preparation, and preservation were critical to the well-being of her family and to its food security. Historian Laura Peers has argued that historians and ethnographers have emphasized large game hunting within Aboriginal cultures at the expense of ignoring women's contributions to community survival.[16] Referring to pre-reserve Saulteaux societies, she writes,

> We are now realizing that the Saulteaux had a much broader, more flexible subsistence base better able to cope with ecological fluctuations, and the role of women in providing food and in making decisions about subsistence and group movements was far greater than previously thought. In fact, what might be called "alternate" or "women's" foods were, for much of the year, the constant in the Saulteaux diet: large game was added to this base when it was available. These "women's" foods included vegetable foods, maple sugar, small game, and, to a certain extent, fish.[17]

Although, as Peers notes, contemporary research has moved on from "Man the Hunter,"[18] it remains important to point out the extent to which Aboriginal women traditionally contributed to the food supply by hunting, trapping, and fishing. Many of the women I spoke with talked about how their grandmothers taught them these skills through their own practices, and while this was commonplace, women's abilities in these areas continually surprised the settler population. Rose remembered how her fishing skills impressed the English owner of a fishing camp in northern Saskatchewan where she worked as a cook when she was fifteen. When he asked her one afternoon if she knew how to use a gun, she replied, "I'm not scared to grab the gun and shoot a deer or something. The only thing I haven't shot is a bear." Rose proved this to be true by shooting an elk and serving it for supper later that season.

Although men typically did the large game hunting, some of the women came from families and communities in which men were scarce or only in the community sporadically. In these environments, women did most of the hunting, trapping, and fishing that fed their families. In other communities, it was considered quite normal that women did the kinds of work that men did. In Elsie's home community of Cumberland House, men would typically go out on traplines in the fall, and the whole community would go to trap together at more remote locations in the spring. During the fall, Elsie's mother also shared a trapline close to the community with another woman to support their families. Like other women in the community, Elsie's mother also went out to do wage labour in the fish plant, or would help in farm labour. A lot of this work required time away from the home, and so when these women went out of the community the children would be cared for by "an aunt or two that stayed behind."

Rosella also grew up in northern Saskatchewan in a family of women who supported their children with trapping and fishing, and who worked their own traplines. In her family, the practice of self-sustaining women began with her grandmother who was "kicked out of the reserve" and subsequently raised her children by herself. Rosella said, "She used to have a dog team to go from Molanosa to Montreal Lake to get groceries for her and others. She hauled wood, she built her own houses, everything." Rosella's mother also raised her children without much assistance from their fathers. Rosella quipped, "My mom was independent; she didn't really need them anyway!" She then qualified this statement by adding, "but there was always somebody who made sure that we had moose meat. Everybody shared; nobody ran out—but that's gone now."

Mosôm Danny talked about how women contributed to community survival through the planning and management of food in his southeastern Saskatchewan community. He asserted that women were particularly responsible for "time and its relation to the ecology of the earth and its seasons." As he noted, "They had a system and a calendar because it was necessary; they had to learn the different growth factors and maturation of plant life around them in order to harvest." He explained that grandmothers in his community had the role of harvesting and sharing the first meats of the spring (young muskrats and beavers), and that it was their job to teach the younger generations about the upcoming seasons in the spirit of preparation and food security:

> In the springtime they would sit down and tell you, "Well, this is where we will pick the Saskatoon berries. The strawberries are going to come to full term at this time. On the eighth moon, we'll get the fish spawning."... And before the leaves came out, there was a walkabout on the land, and teaching about all the different trees and what they produced. [The old ladies] would say, "This is the next moon." They would walk you around and show you what a Seneca root looks like and when it is just coming out of the ground. "[This plant is ready] at the end of this moon" ... that is what they would tell you. And then when September arrived, [they would say,] "Now we have got to start preparing for our move to the winter grounds."

Danny noted that older women concerned themselves with food security by ensuring that men hunted some moose during the month of July so pemmican could be prepared for the winter. It was also their job to ensure that there was enough dry food to go around. "They would make the distribution of the foods in September," he said, "when that fall moon started to come out. They would level out all their dry goods, and make sure that everybody in the community had enough pemmican [for the winter]."

Rebecca remembered that "women knew when meat was needed in the community. The men would go out hunting and women, who were responsible for distribution, made certain that everyone had meat." Danny also talked about how men would bring the food to the women for distribution. Resources belonged to the family and community, and it was up to the women to make sure that these resources were distributed equitably and according to need. According to Danny, men in his community listened to the women, who voiced the needs of the family.

Several of the other historian participants talked about the women's role in food preservation. In their communities, their mothers, aunts, and grandmothers worked with berries that were used for pemmican and dried into cakes. This food lasted well into winter, and could be stored for long periods of time. (Maria recalled finding some edible chokecherry cakes in the cellar of her grandmother's house long after she had passed away.) Women were also in charge of drying meat and fish, which in isolated communities like Rosella's was the only means of preserving food. In other communities, women not only dried but also canned food to prepare for the winter. This was done as a collective activity, and in great quantities. Madeleine remembers this well, growing up on the Kehewin Cree Nation territory northeast of Edmonton: "The women canned everything feasible: vegetables, fish, and even meat. They made pickles; one time my mother said she put up 500 jars!"

Like Madeleine, Maria had memories of the volume of food that needed to be prepared for the winter. This was typically the work of her mother and other women in the community, who worked assembly-line style to get it done, although she noted that "after my mother died, it was nothing for my dad and I to can 400 quarts of meat, vegetables, and berries for the winter" (an example of how gendered work responsibilities were flexible when necessary). Madeleine summarized the important role women played in food preservation: "The women worked extremely hard to make sure there was food. In the winter there were rabbits and deer to be had, but to have a balanced diet the women went out and made sure that all of these other things were preserved."

Olive talked about how resourceful women had to be with food, remarking, "My mother could make a meal out of nothing." She pointed out that her mother could cook equally well whether they were at home in their northern Saskatchewan community or while travelling on berry-picking or other excursions. Olive fondly remembered her mother making bannock and meat on a stick over an open fire. Likewise, Rose remarked on the ability of her mother to make tourtière while they were travelling. Others reminisced about the special-occasion foods that their mothers would make. For Maria, it was blueberry cake on the odd Sunday when blueberries were in season, and Christmas foods such as "boulettes," tourtière, and mincemeat. She described the special significance of boulettes to the Métis:

Bullets (boulettes) are meatballs made from ground wild meat, onions and flour. They are boiled gently in a pot of water and they thicken themselves and make a lovely soup. Dried saskatoon berries are sometimes added for special ceremony or celebration. These boulettes are not the French kind, but rather they represent the round balls (bullets) the men made and stuffed into guns to shoot the buffalo. The long skinny fried breads we dunk in the soup are called bangs and they represent the rod that was used to ram the shot/bullet or ball into the gun. These were carried in the man's gun bag and worn over his shoulder when he was hunting. Bullets and Bangs are a very traditional and special meal.

Maria further described how her mother and the other women of her community worked collectively to make these holiday foods:

> They would start cooking in early November. They'd make the poucin—the Christmas pudding. They would all come together to start getting ready for Christmas baking too, because they didn't have much money. So one family would be responsible for buying all the raisins. [Others would be responsible for something else.] And then you would bring it all together because [in our community we were an extended family] and we would have Christmas together, so the women would do all that kind of baking together.

As girls, the historian participants worked with the women in their community to become skilled at working with food, as it sustained their families and held cultural significance. Working with clothing was another such skill.

Clothing

Traditionally, women provided clothing from furs and hides, cloth and beads. Algonquin scholar and artist Sherry Farrell Racette has written about the sacred within this practice, noting that the preparation of clothing "was not only important in terms of survival and economic pursuits, it was one of the strategies that women employed to maintain balance in the natural world."[19] Clothing was within the women's domain, as it was their responsibility to transform the large game brought in to them and to ensure that the community was properly fed and clothed. Farrrell Racette explains that the artistry employed by women was also important in terms of maintaining respectful relationships with the animals upon which they depended for survival: "Finely tanned and embellished hides were a means of communicating respect to the all-seeing spirits, and sending a hunter into the bush dressed in fine clothing pleased the animals. The practice of embellishing hunters extended onto the animals on which the hunter depended, the dog and the horse, his hunting tools, such as shot pouches, game bags, and gun sleeves."[20] She points out how women played a role in managing the "good fortune" of the community, for "women were charged with the responsibility of visually communicating respect and soliciting the approval of the animals."[21]

By the 1940s and 1950s, when many of the historian participants were growing up, clothing began to take on another important function. A few women talked about how important it was to make families feel and look good because of the overt racism Native people were experiencing during this period when they engaged with the outside world. This was evident in Madeleine's comment that "women made sure that men looked and smelled good when going to town. They dressed [them] nicely and to make sure that they felt every bit as good as the [white people], who rarely saw Indians and vice versa." Maria also pointed out that, after her mother's death, her grandmother stepped in to care for him and saw to it that her dad didn't go anywhere "looking raggy."

Because of scarce resources, clothing was limited. As Maria pointed out, "I didn't know anybody who owned lots of clothes. My mom had the home-made dress she wore on Sunday and then she had two other skirts and two blouses, and I think she had more than most people." She added, "I had one good dress that I wore to church on Sunday or any special day. That one dress was made in the fall and it had to last until spring. The hem was big enough that it could be let down and then used the following year, or [mom] would buy some flour sack material and sew it on to make it longer." She noted that her mother made all their clothing on an old Singer treadle sewing machine, with the help of "Robin Hood":

> She used 100-pound flour sacks which she dyed with plants, and later with dye she bought at the store. The colours were usually red, blue, green or yellow. Sometimes the flour sacks would have a floral design and these were coveted, but it took forever to collect enough to make a dress so usually they were used for trim or traded with other women. [My mother] also trimmed our underclothing with lace she made from store string. These underclothes were only worn for Sundays and special occasions. Panties, or rather bloomers, chemises (undershirts but different from men), and petticoats (slips) were trimmed with lace. Always a big joke among ourselves today is that for every day we wore bloomers [we also wore] Robin Hood across the ass because the dye was so hard to wash off!

Madeleine also talked about the thriftiness of the 1940s and 1950s, re-calling that "women sewed clothes with whatever they had and a lot of time fabrics got recycled. If someone had a big coat, then maybe two jackets were made out of it." Madeleine remembered her mother showing her the Sears catalogue and asking, "Which style do you want?" Her mother would then make the dress by looking at the catalogue. Rose's grandmother also made dresses without patterns; as Rose pointed out, "if she loved a dress, when it wore out, she put it down on [another piece of] cloth and cut one more of it."

Much of the clothing was hand sewn, particularly among the older women. Hilary noted that, in the case of her grandmother, "even her undergarments" were done by hand, and that some of the work, such as pleated blouses, was very fine: "She could put little pleats, from her collarbone all the way straight down the front of her dress, to the waist." The only pieces of apparel that Hilary's grandmother bought were the rubbers that went over her moccasins in winter or during inclement weather. Several women remembered the ex-citement when sewing machines came into their families.

Although there was always mending and repair work to be done, work around clothing tended to be seasonal. Women worked on sewing during winter evenings when there was less gardening and outdoor work. Summers were dedicated to tanning hides, which would then be turned into clothing and moccasins over the fall and winter. In many communities and especially among the older people, moccasins were the only footwear. Women also used the hides to make jackets, and muskrat, rabbit, and beaver pelts were used to make leggings, stockings, and blankets. Winter nights were also occupied by sewing handicrafts, which women could sell or trade at the store for sugar or other special things.

Working for Pay
Women's work also included participation in the cash economy. Many women, like Rosella's and Elsie's mothers, ran their own traplines and sustained their families by selling their furs. Others sold fish. Most women sold berries and, in the West, Seneca root. Maria explained that they replaced the buffalo hunt with berry picking excursions, organizing themselves collectively to get the work done:

> We supplemented our income by picking berries and Seneca root
> and selling them by the pound in the nearest little towns. The roots
> had to be dry, and they shrunk when they dried, so it meant we had
> to pick a lot to make a pound. The store owner then shipped the roots

to Winnipeg and the berries were sold locally. If we were close to a road with lots of traffic such as the highway that went to Prince Albert or to the [Prince Albert] National Park, then one of us kids and the kokums (grannies) would set up shop along the highway and sell berries in birch bark baskets. We also spent our evenings making those baskets because we didn't have anything else to put the berries in. We were lucky to get fifty cents for a basket of berries—and those baskets now sell for a fortune in antique stores! Sometimes we also sold hooked or braided rugs that women had spent the winter making. These also sold cheap and are worth a lot of money today.

Some women worked at wage labour. As noted earlier, Elsie's mother worked for wages at the fish plant. Olive recalled that her mother worked as a domestic for the local doctor. While mothers worked at paid work, it was more common for unmarried girls to take on full-time jobs, as in the case of Rose and Rosella. Rose started working as a chambermaid in a hotel in Prince Albert when she was fifteen and from there she went north where she worked in a fishing camp for two years. Rosella also moved away from her family at the age of fifteen, and worked full time as a clerk in the general store in her community.

One of the strongest themes that came out of the interviews regarding this life stage was the rigour of the work involved. This was coupled with a strong emphasis on the "Indigenous work ethic." As Gertie pointed out, "I don't remember my mother ever being without a job or without work to do. I don't ever remember her saying, 'Oh you guys make me work so hard.' It's just what she did." In addition to the work that she did around the home, Gertie's mother also worked seasonally for the local tourist camp. What Gertie learned from the women in her family was that "if you wanted to have something for your family, then you did the work you had to do. It was never 'Oh, somebody else will come and give that to me,' or 'My husband is going to give that to me.'" Rosella commented on the work ethic as well, "Most of the girls I grew up with were hard workers like me. They had to work hard; we had no choice—we had to survive."

In the women's circle, emphasis was placed on the type of work that was imperative for communities to survive. But other types of work were also learned. These involved cooperative and social activities that were essential to building and maintaining community. Personal and family relationships were paramount, and the women held important responsibilities in these areas.

Keepers of Relationships: Collectivism and Kinship

Land-based communities were by necessity interdependent, and it was a matter of survival that everyone worked well together. Relationship building was thus vital to the well-being of the collective, and as the keepers of relationships, women held important roles. Maria reflected on this role: "When people say it was the women who held culture together, it wasn't 'culture' they held together; it was kinship. They looked after the big, extended family and made sure that nobody fell by the wayside. Culture comes from all of those things—from the way that people live together, the way that people treat each other, the way they interact with one another. That's kinship. In Cree [this concept is captured within] *mino pimatisiwin*. Living a good life."

A strong foundation for the collective came from the relationships women built among themselves, and a lot of this relationship building happened while they were working. Where they could, women worked collectively. There were more opportunities for this in the summer than the winter, as Maria remembered. "All summer long the women would do their work together," she said. "They would dry their meat, do pickling, canning; all those kinds of things. Everything was done outside. All the jars were there and they were divided up equally among the family, depending on how many kids they had." Maria shared other memories of how the women and children used to do their laundry together during the summers of her childhood at a local gravel pit:

> Everybody at home always washed clothes on Mondays and mother would be waiting for the [other women] with all of our laundry and our tubs. She had a huge cast iron pot that she boiled water in, and homemade lye soap and all of the things like scrub boards that we would need for washing.
>
> As kids, we would wake up so excited Monday morning. We'd get all loaded up in the wagon, and about eight or ten wagons of us would go to this big pit about a half a mile up the road from our house. (It had eroded and was full of clean water.) The women would make several fires around the edge of the pit, putting these cast iron pots onto them where there were tripods. They would then sit around and visit while the water was heating up. The kids would strip down to underclothes and swim, and we'd be in the water all day long. As the girls got older, we had to take part in the washing

of the clothes. The boys had other work, like setting snares, or catching food to eat. My mom and the women would cook our lunch out there, usually something warmed up from Sunday supper. They would bring mending out, and in between all of this, while they were waiting for their one batch of clothes to dry, they would sit and do their mending.

It's important to note that the kids bonded over this practice as much as the women did: "It was such an amazing experience for all of the kids; a way for all of us to play together with all our cousins, just to know each other." Maria emphasized the camaraderie and exchanges among the women despite the hard work they had to do: "They laughed and talked and helped each other. If you had just had a baby, you couldn't do all that heavy work, the scrubbing of stuff. So you would come out there with all your laundry, but you might be in charge of cooking while the women did your laundry for you."

When Rose was growing up in Duck Lake, she spent time with the women in her community when they came together to work in quilting bees to sew blankets and bedding, or in knitting bees to make hats, mitts, and scarves for the children who needed them, or to make kits for new babies in the community. This collective work gave women those cherished opportunities for visiting. As Maria noted, "Women used to sit down together and sew blankets. There was a lot of laughter and sharing of personal and intimate things that would go on." She pointed out that there were "healing" benefits that came from women gathering on a regular basis to share their work and their lives. Women could seek comfort and advice from one another, find laughter, and learn, as described by Maria in the foreword to this book. Cooking bees were popular, too, especially for special occasions like Christmas.

Without television, or in many cases radio, visiting was an integral part of the social fabric of northern communities. Rebecca grew up in northwestern Saskatchewan where visiting was integral to community relationships: "Growing up in a small community where children were welcomed into every home, we learned how to relate to one another. When invited to visit 'for tea,' if we made a mistake, adults gently corrected our behaviour."

Where communities did have radio, as they did in Maria's case, women still gathered together to listen to shows like *Ma Perkins* while they did their mending and visiting. *Ma Perkins* was a popular radio soap opera that ran between 1942 and 1960. Its protagonist was a kindly hearted widow who owned and operated a lumber yard in a small southern U.S. town; a sage and brave soul who inspired those who followed her. Maria noted, "Women at home loved her and never missed a show. If they did, a special visit was made by all the women to the person who missed it to tell her what happened."

While the women understood that their collective work was one way of making their work a little less hard and a bit more fun, outsiders didn't always see it this way. When Maria was researching Road Allowance communities in the provincial archives, she found correspondence in which a Member of the Legislative Assembly (MLA) in Saskatchewan complained that Road Allowance people were "always having picnics." As Maria explained, "The MLA sent it to the Municipality who was trying to get rid of us and move us to other places further north." She noted that several documents and letters advocated they had to be moved as they were "diseased and an eyesore in the community." She was appalled to read, "They do little but spend their time having picnics and galloping their horses around."[22]

The underlying message that the Métis were lazy angered Maria because, as she said, "nobody worked harder than we did." Upon reflection, Maria realized that the MLA misinterpreted what they were doing because he saw them laughing and joking while they worked. "So if anybody were driving by and saw a group of women in a sewing circle, they would just think you were a bunch of lazy people, sitting around telling stories all day," she said. "[And] if they drove by [on laundry day] and saw us all laughing and talking and the kids splashing around in the water, the women lolling around [by the gravel pit where we were], they [would have] thought this was a big picnic." Unfortunately, once gas washing machines came into her community, the women no longer had that weekly "ritual" of community building on laundry day. As well, the social and healing benefits of this weekly summer practice were lost.

Another form of work that involved social benefits was berry picking. As noted earlier, northern Algonquian families relied on berries for sustenance and for income. Maria equated berry-picking excursions with the social and community-building function of the buffalo hunt. A number of the other historian participants shared fond memories of berry-picking excursions, as they served this social purpose. During her childhood summers, Marie's family would load up in a boat and travel across the lake for a day trip of berry picking. She remembered that someone might shoot a duck or catch a fish for a shared meal. Some of the historian participants talked about how berry picking was typically done by women and children, although men would sometimes go along to protect them from bears. Rebecca remembered her father sitting in the shade with his rifle, while the women and children picked nearby. Mosôm Danny told a humorous story about one man who was usually sent along on his family's excursions in southeastern Saskatchewan, but was demoted from the job because all he was doing was pacing around the edge of the women's patch, telling boastful stories and flirting.

A number of the historian participants spoke fondly of the longer berry picking excursions they would make with their families. Olive's family would go out for weeks at a time: "It was such a happy time. We used the team [of horses] and wagon. Our wagon used to be full: we had our tent, and we were well equipped." In Maria's family, these excursions occupied most of their summer. "When school was out in June, usually we were on the road," she said. "We'd load up all the wagons and off we'd go, pick berries and pick roots and travel all summer long."

Building relationships through socializing wasn't always about work, however; it also included playing games. In traditional societies, women had had their own games, including the "testicle game," in which they used sticks to throw "a double ball made of two bags of deerskin stuffed with buffalo hair and connected by a strip of hide."[23] This game was played with four to eight women on a side, who passed the double ball down the field towards the opposing team's goal. The women I spoke with had no memories of traditional women's games, but some remembered "hand games" that the elders used to play with bones, sitting in long rows across from one another. Marie had memories of elders playing games using bones and sticks, and Olive talked about a game they used to play with the rabbit's head. She explained, "We used to fight for the head after everything was eaten and there was just the bone left. You'd say, 'Rabbit, who's the ugliest in the family?' And you twisted it around and wherever the nose pointed, that was the ugliest person!"

Gambling was popular, and has historical traditions among women. Fine Day described the gambling that used to go on between women in the late 1800s when people got together in big camps. Some of these gatherings had horse racing, and Fine Day was notable for his skills in these competitions. He reported that "all the Crees from the reserves bet on me." He also provided evidence that the women actively bet on the horses when he said, "The Cree women bet their dishes against the dried meat of the Soto women."

In the historian participants' childhood communities, gambling had been banned by the church, but community members found ways to do it anyway.

Hilary shared a story about being a young child and spending her summers on the Moosomin Reserve, just outside of Cochin, Saskatchewan. She and her grannie would sneak off into the woods to meet others so they could gamble all night. Her story shows community cohesion as well as resistance to the oppressive conditions Aboriginal people were living with in the 1950s. She explained:

> They always had a secret little meeting place in the bush where they would get together.... [Grannie] would wait until it was the dead of night. She would have our blankets that we would be sleeping in, and her gambling stuff and a little bit of food. She was tiny, but she would carry that on her back.
>
> We had to be totally quiet because the priest had spies in the community. And so you had to make like you were just going to visit somebody. I was instructed never to talk. No matter who it was, I wasn't to talk to them—just act shy. I remember sometimes being tired and starting to cry: "Nohkom I'm tired, I don't want to walk any further." So on top of all the stuff she was carrying, she'd throw me up there and carry me.
>
> Pretty soon, there would be young men who came to meet us. One young man would carry me and the other young man would carry her blankets the rest of the way to the gambling site.
>
> [When we got there] she would put out her blankets around where they were sitting and I would curl around her legs and sleep. I'd wake up once in awhile and hear the gambling by bitch lamp,[24] or whatever. There would be laughing and talking and carrying on.... I remember looking forward to the morning time, because there would be kids to play with.

Maria remembered that her mother and aunts played poker with one another for their beadwork or embroidery. She talked about how these goods would circulate around the community as women won and then lost the same goods repeatedly amongst themselves: "It was kind of a joke. My one auntie would have everything tonight, and tomorrow night somebody else would have it. Whatever my mother lost, she would usually win it all back by spring." Hearing this story, Hilary commented, "I think that's where my Nohkom got a lot of her fabric."

Maria made an important distinction about the type of gambling that was done in her childhood and the kind of gambling she sees now. In First Nations communities, casinos have become a source of revenue and entertainment. In her estimation, gambling was historically used as a way to bring people together, and to distribute and redistribute goods. "In those days," she said, "you didn't starve to death because you were gambling. You didn't leave your kids. It's not the same [now]—the *wahkotowin* (kinship/relationship building) is gone from gambling, where it used to be part of it." Hilary and Maria reflected on how gambling had once been a sacred activity among Plains people, and they pondered whether or not it had once been one of the safer "ceremonies" that people could practise in their time. As Maria pointed out, "Even though it was against the law with the church, you wouldn't get punished the same way if you were caught gambling as you would if you were caught in [a Sun Dance] ceremony."

When asked about other forms of recreation, the historian participants from Saskatchewan in particular talked about dances. Dances were held at people's houses, with different families taking turns to host them. Olive, Maria, and Rose talked about a tradition whereby a nickel was planted in a cake, and whoever got the nickel would hold the next dance. Sylvia also had many memories of dances in her community in northern Manitoba because her father was a traditional Métis fiddle player. She recalled that "during Christmas, we would have a dance every night. My dad would play at different houses, and [everyone] would take their kids with them. My aunts and uncles would just push the furniture back [to make space]."

Dances were more frequently held in the winter when men were home from trapping, and they tended to go on all night. In Maria's community, "from New Year's all the way up until Lent people would visit and party and dance. It was just non-stop. And then Lent would come and the Catholics would sacrifice [their dances]. Nobody would have parties any more [after that]." Rosella remembered that dances used to take place in Molanosa's fish plant, and she talked about the dances she attended on the Montreal Lake Reserve as well. "When I was a kid we used to be hauled to Montreal Lake to watch the square dances," she said. "They never had any alcohol there, all they did was dance! So we grew up learning how to dance all these square dances, jigs and everything."

Kids definitely attended dances with their parents, which made this activity an intergenerational exchange of community and relationship building.

Olive pointed out, "When there was a wedding, we went with our parents. It was healthy. It was fun."

Sexuality, Courting, and Marriage

Throughout the 1930s and into the 1950s, when girls passed through puberty and entered the women's circle, they entered into new experiences involving sexuality, courting, and marriage. For some, their relationships with men and boys changed immediately, and they were not allowed to interact or play with boys with the same freedom. Rebecca pointed out that she had been a tomboy prior to puberty, but that afterwards her mother had kept her closer to the house. She noted that girls were chaperoned more closely as soon as they went through puberty. As I describe below, the participants' stories demonstrated that the "traditional" notions of their preceding generations related to sexuality, courtship, and marriage were still being applied. The stories also demonstrate that girls felt caught between these norms and those of mainstream society, particularly as they were coming into more contact with neighbouring white communities during the 1950s.

One important way that young women entered into this world of sexuality, courting, and marriage was by going to community dances. As a teenager, Rose attended these dances with male and female friends. This was a freedom she enjoyed, although she remembered her grandmother waiting up for her and lecturing about the risks of unplanned pregnancy. Other women came from families where courting was more strictly regulated.[25] For example, traditional chaperones were still in place in Maria's childhood community. She told a story about going to her first dance when she was around fourteen, which was held in a neighbouring town. Maria wanted to be like the white girls, but her family held to their strict ideals. She explained:

> When I went to my first dance I had this old lady that came with me.... And she wasn't a pretty old lady! But my dad insisted and she loved me dearly. She was always making a big deal over me. So I just loved her when I was a kid—until I had to take her to my first dance! By that time I was looking through a different lens....
>
> When Dad told me I had to take her, it was the first time that I really looked at her. I thought, *I can't take her!* I mean, I was starting to get into Elvis Presley and all that stuff. To be dragging this old Indian lady around, with her long skirt and her rubbers and moccasins and her funny little beret ... and she had a great big hook

nose! (*laughter*) She was just as homely as a mud fence, but Dad said, "Well, if you want to go dancing you can't go without her."

So I went, thinking, *Well, she'll sit in the corner someplace and I'll just pretend I don't know who she is.* Most of the other kids were white. They were going to think "Who does she belong to?" Nobody else had a chaperone.

If I went outside, she went outside. I then realized that it was her job was to follow me around; she was a traditional chaperone. And if somebody said, "Oh, is that ever a pretty dress," she was just so happy for me. She'd make all these little noises on the side. It was awful! ... She walked behind me, and watched to make sure that I didn't go out with anybody, and that I didn't do anything I wasn't supposed to do.

A few of the other women talked about how they were carefully watched as girls. As June put it, "You couldn't get pregnant because you couldn't get out anyway." Cree oral historian Glecia Bear would agree with June: "In those days the old people used to guard the girls so closely you never went anywhere." [26]

In general, girls reaching puberty were taught to be modest about their bodies. Sylvia remembered being taught by one of the grandmothers in her community "never to wear shorts in front of our brothers." Sylvia said that the main lesson she received from this grandmother was that women were "to respect our bodies." Mosôm Danny reflected on the modesty of the 1940s and 1950s and told a story about how he had asked his grandfather why women in his community wore long skirts. His grandfather referred him to their creation story, in which "the male within God" decided to manifest himself in the physical as Mother Earth. Mother Earth was named for her beauty, he said, and this beauty is equated with women's bodies. It was a modest and reserved beauty that was reflected in the care women took in how they presented themselves publicly.

Modesty in dress and behaviour may have come from traditional teachings, but it was also likely the result of a different set of lessons from residential schools. The women I spoke with are offspring of previous generations who had been indoctrinated with sexual repression from the churches in charge of their schooling. [27] Maria's mother, for example, was raised in a convent and was "prudish," in contrast with her grandmother, who was not residential schooled. Maria commented, "those nuns were sexually repressed and had a sick fascination about sex. They constantly harped on about it. You couldn't wear patent leather shoes because you might see your self (vagina) in the event they were shiny. (As if, when you wore wool bloomers to your knees.) You had to bathe wearing a full petticoat because if you saw your body you might touch it." The intergenerational effects of residential schooling likely stand behind the fact that only a few of the elders in this study received sex education from the women in their families. Under the church, all discussion about sexuality was silenced.

In the case of women who grew up in traditional communities, information about sex was passed on typically by the "aunties" or "other mothers." Maria remembered, "If I wanted to know about boys or stuff like that, I went to my aunties. And sometimes they wouldn't tell me, but they would be talking among themselves and they wouldn't chase me away." Rebecca's mother never talked to her "about creation," but arranged a friend to do it instead:

> When I was ten, while going to school in town, a friend of my mother's came to where I was boarding and invited me for tea. Secretly, I thought that my mother must have told her I had [started] my Moon time, because that would be the only reason that a woman would invite me for tea.
>
> My mother's friend kept me in her house all day. I had tea, but she also taught me everything I would ever need to know about creation…. She talked about how my body would develop and the feelings a girl has when she first likes a boy. When instructing me in the choice of a good man, she said, "If you want to choose a good man, have him take you home for dinner. Watch how he treats his mother, because that's how he'll treat you."

Her mother's friend, Rebecca remembered, was thorough about giving her these teachings:

> I listened to my mother's friend all day. She would talk, stop for awhile, and then start again. When she spoke about being a wife, a mother and a grandmother, I learned the passages in a woman's life, as well as the natural order in caring for self, family, and community. The woman instructed me in caring for and honouring my female being, while at the same time, she spoke at length about the ways that women are respectful of the men in our families. Many years

after my mother's friend gifted me with teachings on how my body would embrace womanhood, her words came alive when I went into labour and delivered a child, and later still, when Grandmother Moon was waning in my life.

It was not until she became a mother herself, that Rebecca realized the wisdom of having had an "auntie" provide the very detailed and specific information about creation that would have caused discomfort for her own mother. This practice was very much in keeping with traditional ways in which the training of older children was undertaken by aunts and uncles.

By their late teens, young women would be thinking about becoming married; a practice that dated to a time when girls were considered marriageable by their ability to contribute to the survival of the community. Looking for a good worker in a partner is one example of how, by the 1950s, marriage still manifested some of the old ways. Marriage had traditionally included arranged, common-law, and polygamous alliances, and it had not been long since these traditions were fully active. Arranged marriages had been very common in the women's parents' and grandparents' generations, and were to some extent still going on. Maria knew that many of her aunts and foremothers had had their marriages arranged. Her grannies, in fact, had picked someone for her when Maria was young, but this did not come to pass as the community was no longer cohesive when she came of age. Mosôm Danny remembers that in his childhood during the 1940s, arranged marriages were still happening, and Rosella and Madeleine mentioned that some of their siblings were also involved in arranged marriages around that time. Some communities did continue to carry on with the tradition of arranged marriages into the 1950s,[28] and Elsie remembered them into the 1960s. Some scholars indicate that fathers were in charge of arranging marriages for their daughters,[29] while others argue that this practice fell within the jurisdiction of older women.[30] In Rosella's case, it was her aunt and uncle who did the matchmaking. In Chapter 6, I discuss examples of how older women still held some of these responsibilities of matchmaking.

The oral histories of some Algonquian women indicate that arranged marriages were not always welcome among the young women who were beholden to them,[31] but, in some cases, the girls were able to resist and exert agency in how they were partnered.[32] There is evidence that some couples in the late nineteenth and early twentieth centuries eloped and were accepted back into their communities without question.[33] In most cases, however, marriage was an arrangement that facilitated survival of the family and well-being of the community; it was not about romantic love. Maria talked about her aunts' experiences, in which arranged marriages were a necessity because there were so few marriageable partners. It was the old ladies' job to match people and ensure there was no mixing of families. Maria was also told that marriage had been a question of economics in the past; a way of ensuring there was a balance of workers in each family unit to ensure sustenance.

Several of the women I spoke with married out of economic necessity, while others demonstrated agency in the choices they made. Rosella explained that in her community of Molanosa, you knew you were old enough to get married when you had all the skills to work and thrive in a traditional lifestyle. She pointed out that "hard workers" were still valued as marriage partners, noting that women in her community attracted men from around the region for this reason.

Rose talked about the way she had managed her husband's attention. Her husband had expressed an interest in her when she was fifteen, but she chose to make him wait, moving north to work in a fish camp instead. She eventually married him three years later. Others spoke about how there were a number of common-law arrangements in their communities. As mentioned earlier, Rosella and Elsie both came from families in which the men were not consistently present, and Maria remembered an aunt who had never married either, although she had male partners who came and went.

Even though some of the older marriage traditions were still active, by the 1950s communities had already experienced a couple of generations of pressure to engage in Christian ideals of what constituted a "proper marriage." This involved "extolling the virtues of a life-long commitment, of a stable home for the children, and of a formal act accompanied by high ritual."[34] Polygamy, which had been practised into the early twentieth century, had particularly come under fire.[35] Values and attitudes towards polygamy did not change overnight, nor did the practices. As late as 1933, Flannery reports that among the Eastern Cree, "young women don't think much of [polygamy but] the older ones even today agree that it was a good thing and did not consider it to have been in any sense degrading."[36] Among the Plains Cree, polygamy had been a way of "reducing the household work"[37] of women, who often came into polygamous marriages with their sisters.[38] Maria remembered polygamous families in her community, and the wives were typically sisters, but there were no other stories of polygamy from the historian participants.

Divorce and separation were also caught up in a mix of traditional and Eurowestern ways, values, and attitudes during this time. The Plains Cree oral historians who worked with the ethnographer Mandelbaum in the 1930s reported that "if a couple proved to be incompatible, either the man or the woman returned to the tipi of his or her parents. The one who remained cared for the children and kept the household effects. After a time, both were free to marry again."[39] Mosôm Danny asserted that traditionally, "when a divorce took place, the man left the tipi. And the grandmother would come and check to see if he cleared more than that." This had to do with Saulteaux men typically coming to live within the woman's family, sometimes for a full year after the marriage, hunting and trapping for his in-laws.[40] If this was the practice, it meant that any property shared by the couple had to be left with the woman's family. Danny asserted that the grandmother would give departing husbands the following lecture:

> You don't own anything [here]. You take your moccasins, your bow, and your hatchet. The tipi was given to you by your grandmother. The blankets were given to you by your cousin over here, and the rugs were given by this family here. The poles were cut by this uncle over here. The community put this up. But, you've still got to bring meat and you've still got to bring food to this family, until your partner finds another partner.

Danny chuckled and said, "It was said sometimes that the men who got divorced would try to find a partner for their wives to take responsibility because they had to continue to feed that family!"

The economies of many twentieth-century unions did not permit as much freedom for divorce or separation. When Maria asked her aunts about their options for divorce, they told her that it wouldn't have been possible for people living in Road Allowance communities, "because there was nowhere to go." In these cases, women needed to stay with their husbands because their families of origin did not have the capacity to support them. Yet some women did leave. Although she doesn't know the circumstance behind it, Sylvia recalled that her grandfather's wife left him and his children when they were very young. Her grandfather was a kind man who went on to raise his family. Maria noted that her one aunt who had never been married would turn her boyfriends out if they became abusive.

As more of the settlers' customs found their way into Aboriginal communities, marriage became more of a union between a man and a woman whereas traditionally it had been more of a community investment. Mosôm Danny pointed out how the community was still involved in marriages when he was still a boy: "When you got married, the whole community got into the preparation of the marriage. Some of the men got together and built you a house, and then they would give you a team of horses. They gave you an axe, a saw and a rifle, and all the blankets you required to be married." The community provided support in material ways, but family and community also had a significant role in helping the young people with their new social and work responsibilities. Among the Moose Cree, "marriage and sustenance were community responsibilities because they were vital to the long-term survival of the whole group."[41] Furthermore, "people expected that a newly married couple would take a few years to work out relations of independence, and community members were available to mediate when problems arose."[42]

Once they were married, young women continued to be mentored by older women. Marriage was as much about strengthening female bonds of kinship and family as it was about a union between a man and a woman.[43] Both matrilocal and patrilocal arrangements have been recorded about the Nēhiyawak, Anishinaabek, and Michif.[44] In arrangements where the man moved in with his wife's kin, it was expected that, as a new husband, he would hunt and provide for her whole family.[45] Girls who moved in with their husbands' families were taken in and taught by the older women among their kin. The most thorough example of this can be found in the story of Plains Cree oral historian Emma Minde, in which she talks about how she moved into her husband's family as a young woman and was taken under the wing of her mother-in-law and husband's aunt. Editor H.C. Wolfart states in the introduction to her story that "the teaching role of the mother-in-law covers the entire range of human life," and that from the day of her marriage onward, "the mother-in-law may well be the most important person in a young woman's life."[46]

Maria recalled how her own mother was required to fall within the "jurisdiction" of her paternal grandmother's authority. Her mother, who had been raised in a convent, found it difficult to adjust to her new husband's community. Maria remembered that "it was kind of hard for my mom when she first came, because she was moving into a different system. My grandmother was very much the boss. My great-grandmother was the ultimate boss, but she was pretty gentle. So my granny was the boss, in everybody's house, in everybody's life, and my mother had to follow that way." In some instances, this situation could have been experienced as oppressive for the younger women, who, like younger wives in polygamous marriages, might find themselves under the authority of the older women who subjected them to a heavy workload. Among the generation of women I spoke with, Rebecca commented on how much she enjoyed the custom of being taught and taken into a welcoming circle of women's kinship when she married and moved to her Cree husband's community in the early 1970s.

Rebecca's experiences demonstrate that, although experiences of sexuality, courting, and marriage were in a period of transition by the 1950s, many of the old ways still held even decades later. In the "traditional" societies of the early twentieth century, marriage had been about establishing strong ties of kinship that would strengthen the community and ensure health, well-being, and community survival. Although this system was starting to break down under pressures to assume the patriarchal, single-family units of European/mainstream society, northern Algonquian communities hung on to some of the extended family culture that marriages had supported in the past.

Conclusion

In the opening epigraph to this chapter, Mosôm Danny asserts that the adult years were about carrying "the responsibility for the continuation of the collective as a living, viable community." It is perhaps not surprising, then, that so much of what the participants shared in relation to these years was about the work that women did for the good of the collective. Women managed material resources and worked as keepers of relationships to ensure family and community well-being.

The training they had received as children in terms of the Indigenous work ethic was now fully applied, and the commitment to family and community that had been fostered in them underpinned their ability to meet the responsibilities of these adult years. In many ways, these middle years were a time of sacrifice, or, as Gertie once said to me, "parenting is the longest fast you will ever do!"

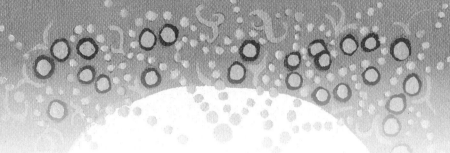

Chapter 6

Grandmothers and Elders

There is a status that comes with old age among First Nations people. In old age, one is considered to have acquired wisdom by virtue of living a long life.... Old age is a very productive stage of life. Old people have much to contribute in that they are the teachers of history, traditions, language and philosophy. They are also keepers of the law, nurturers, advisors and leaders in ceremonial practices.

—Mosôm Danny Musqua, in
The Seven Fires[1]

One cannot overstate the role of elders in traditional Indigenous societies, for once people had reached this "fourth hill," they were revered, respected, and treated with deference. In his book *Honouring Elders: Aging, Authority, and Ojibwe Religion*, Michael D. McNally writes that, among the Anishinaabek, "old age itself marks a kind of religious attainment, and eldership carries a corresponding religious prestige and authority by virtue of the mastery of relatedness."[2] This mastery of relatedness came from having lived a good life and having honoured all of the responsibilities associated with the earlier stages. Life stage ceremonies helped an individual to establish and maintain these good relations with human, plant, and animal life, as well as spirit life.

Once an elder had become a master of these relations, he or she had responsibilities to cycle this power back into the younger generations, to keep the life force and spirit moving. McNally references the work of Jeffrey Anderson, who studied life stage theory or "life movement" among the Arapaho, which he described as "a principle that the cosmos persists in ongoing motion by virtue of an ongoing generational exchange: elder generations pass on power and knowledge toward life to younger generations in return for respect."[3] McNally equates this to the Ojibway understanding of *bimaadiziwin*, explaining that this word, often translated as "life," is a substantive form of a verb that indicates to "move by" or to "move along."[4] Acccording to McNally, the goal is "to live well and to live long in this world."[5]

In the introductory chapter, I referred to Basil Johnston, who noted that "by living through all stages and living out visions, men and women know something of human nature and living and life."[6] Those who did not live a good life or achieve a mastery of relatedness did not achieve the same level of authority as those who did, but all elders were rewarded with some level of respect by virtue of their age. This chapter focuses on how the elders who were present in the childhood lives of the historian participants manifested responsibilities for leadership, teaching, and making connections with the spirit world, as prescribed in the life stage teachings particular to this age.

I begin with a section related to the physical aspects of aging. These first stories demonstrate that, in spite of diminishing physical ability, these elders remained industrious until the end of their lives. Looking at the historian participants' memories of the elders makes it clear that old age was eminently "a very productive stage of life."

I explore four areas in this life stage: leadership and governance; teaching; managing the health of the community; and being doorkeepers to the spirit world. Collectively, these roles and responsibilities demonstrate the powerful position that elderly women held in Algonquian societies. The stories in this chapter give meaning to Mosôm Danny's words that "no nation existed without the fortitude of our grandmothers."

Before analyzing the women's histories, it is worth defining the "community," "ceremonial," and "earth" elder years that I refer to in Chapter 1. This material, along with background teachings on the roles of elderly women in Algonquian societies, provides context for the stories that follow.

General Roles and Responsibilities for the Elder Years

Mosôm Danny's life stage teachings distinguish between community elders, ceremonial elders, and earth elders. In his experience, "You entered the old people's club when you had a grandchild." He outlined the preliminary responsibilities by saying "when you became a grandparent, you would start participating with the old people's council. You sat there as a member. You didn't speak very much, because you didn't know very much. But you listened to the teachings of the old people; how to become an elder, what your responsibility was. You were the keeper of traditions, you were the keeper of your disciplines, you were the keeper of the laws. And you would have to minister the appropriate use of those laws. So you had to know how to do things."

This description frames the community elder role as a beginning for some of the more senior roles elders would adopt in their later years. But Danny went on to say that "the community elder [was] also typically a chief or a councillor. The head man or *chi-ogima*. And the same thing with women, the woman chief. They were there for as long as required." Community elders thus served the community in a leadership capacity, as they increasingly took on responsibilities that had to do with governance.

The next level in elder years was the ceremonial elder. This person carried spiritual responsibilities, such as conducting opening prayers and pipe ceremonies and overseeing council dances in Saulteaux society. Danny talked about how these elders would be the ones doing naming ceremonies, marriage ceremonies, and funerals. Generally speaking, it was the responsibility of these elders to look after the health and well-being of the community, which they did through spiritual practice and engagement. Danny said that a ceremonial elder was responsible for "the circles of healing, the circles of peace, and human justice, when things go wrong." It was the job of the ceremonial elder, he said, "to bring about closure to different things, to mourning, to breakdown in the community."

Danny described earth elders as those who were seventy-five or eighty years old, "the last twenty-five years of life!" This age span and the responsibilities associated with it speak to the lack of such a thing as "retirement" for elders in the world of Danny's childhood. Earth elders in this environment were those who were too infirm to travel, and so it was the learner's responsibility to go to them. He pointed out that they represented "the last phase of the teachings, the philosophy, the in-depth learners of the purest functions of our responsibilities to the Creator."

These teachings about the three phases of elder years correspond to the roles outlined in the Midewiwin and the Aboriginal Healing and Wellness Strategy (AHWS) models presented in Chapter 1. The AHWS model makes a distinction between "grandparents" and "elders," with corresponding responsibilities for "life teacher" and "spirit teacher." Mature adults and elders are distinguished in Midewiwin teachings by the responsibilities of the "doing life" and "elder life," respectively. "Younger" elders may have therefore been more engaged in work related to the life and management of the community, while senior elders provided reflection and teaching on this life, as well as connection to the worlds beyond. The progression from one phase to the next likely had to do with a diminishing physical capacity, which was enhanced by a movement to a more philosophical and spiritual level.

These phases of elderhood applied to both men and women, but the responsibilities of elderly women in particular corresponded to a movement away from the primary function of sustaining communities through physical work and childbearing, and into new authorities and a newfound sense of power. As women aged, they moved gradually from the kind of authority a woman held as a mother to the authority of a "grandmother." To date, I have not found any stories of ceremonies to mark this transition in women's lives in either the written or the oral history, nor is there much information about menopause. It is possible that, given their natural (versus more toxic) environments, and the reverence they would have looked forward to receiving as older women, menopausal symptoms and struggles were not as marked as they are among North American women today. Some elders have indicated to me that menopause wasn't such a big deal in the past. It is also possible that today's generation of elders, those women now in their seventies and eighties, were too young to be included in the knowledge sharing and ceremonies about menopause that might have taken place in the early 1900s. As I pointed out earlier, there is a time and place for stories to make themselves known, and perhaps I have not found the sources because this is not the time or the venue to share them.[7]

Reflecting on the dearth of traditional stories about menopause, Rebecca noted that menopause was likely a much more personal transition, especially when compared to ceremonies that accompanied puberty: "When I asked my mother about the symptoms that might accompany menopause, she said that if women have difficulties when Grandmother Moon is waning, to simply continue to work hard and not complain." In recent years, the women I have interviewed consulted elders about their own menopause and were simply told to go with the physical upheavals, to avoid hormone therapies, and to take the time to know their bodies. Listening to Elder Edna Manitowabi at a Trent University Elders Conference, Rebecca learned that menopause is a time when everything becomes magnified. As she remembered, "Edna told us that menopausal women go through a time of feeling all the things they have not had time to fully experience when they were leading the busy lives of their childbearing years. She said that in her journey to wisdom, a woman must allow herself to acknowledge these feelings."

What is certain is that post-menopausal women in the past had the ability to move into certain jurisdictions that had previously been reserved for men. This applied to everything from the everyday to the ceremonial. In the previous chapter, I pointed out that Maria's grandmother had access to the "men's house" where her dad kept his traps and hunting supplies, whereas the younger women did not. Elderly women were also able to move back and forth in the spiritual arena. As Maria explained, "Once you had reached menopause you were considered both genders; you were both a man and a woman. You could use a man's pipe; you could sit down inside of a circle. Nobody said anything. You could move back and forth between."

The power women had in their grandmother years was not, however, simply about being able to move into men's jurisdictions. Writing about her time spent among the Cree and Saulteaux of the late nineteenth century in northern Saskatchewan, the Scots-Métis author Amelia Paget described how the old ladies used to work as firekeepers. Paget's description provides a good starting point for exploring the greater purpose of "old ladies" in Algonquian societies. She wrote about how difficult it was to start a fire by friction or by flint stone, and pointed out "as the Indians had such difficulty in starting a fire, to the older and more responsible women would be entrusted the task of keeping it alight. And when moving from one place to another these old women would carry a lighted torch of wood, always watching to see that the spark did not die out."[8]

Paget's explanation—that old ladies were given the job of torchbearers because they were trustworthy—is likely not the only explanation as to why they held this responsibility. On a deeper level, it could have been in recognition of the key role they played in keeping their communities alive. Writing about the Cree during the same period as Paget, Cree author Joe Dion described how the old ladies sustained the communities in Big Bear's camp following the 1885 resistance. Dion explained that the elderly women were "an example of industry and thrift" at this time, and that they could always be counted on: "Everything that the elderly ladies gathered and stored away during the summer months was for the enjoyment and benefit of others."[9] Dion extolled the strength and virtue of the old ladies and credited them for getting their communities through the dismal winter of 1885–1886.[10]

The descriptions provided by Paget and Dion demonstrate that it was the spirit of the old ladies that kept their communities alive in the past. This greater purpose as "firekeeper"was an extension of their important position at the centre of the family and community, as described in Chapter 5. A closer look at the similarities for words that describe fire and women in Algonquian languages indicates that women acted as intermediary for spirit connection, a power that grew stronger with age. As noted in Chapter 5, the word for woman in Cree, *iskwew*, is derived from the word for fire, *iskwuptew* (using the spelling from Lee's text). Winona Wheeler notes how fire in this sense is a metaphor for life. She writes, "The taxonomical genealogy of iskwew goes back to the sacred stories of the first woman which explains that women's bodies are links between the spirit and human worlds through which life emerges. The image iskwew elicits is that of a brightly burning fire that nourishes and protects life on its journey to earth."[11]

Mosôm Danny writes that "the word 'fire' in Saulteaux is defined as 'woman's heart.' They say that the love of a woman is so great, so powerful that it caused creation to take place.... Fire is a revered and respected life giver of everything in the universe."[12] Danny stresses that "the foundation of our people is the heart of a woman. When they are strong, we are strong.... The day we begin to recognize this is the day we will become great again."[13]

As the senior lifegivers of their societies, it was the "old ladies" who carried the fires of their nations. They held responsibilities for overseeing the health, well-being, and longevity of their communities; these responsibilities included being "doorkeepers to the spirit world."

Beginning with the Physical: Aging

One of the first impressions in reviewing stories of elderly Algonquian women's lives between the 1930s and the 1950s is how active they were. Gertie, who was a child during the 1950s, shared her lasting impression of her grandmother: "Even from her wheelchair she would go out on the lake every summer to pick berries. She wasn't stuck in the house. She was out and about, she made sure of that. She had to use crutches or canes, but she got out there." Gertie added that "she was never somebody that I would look at and say, 'Oh, poor Grandma.' It was more like, 'Keep up with the old lady!' (*laughs*) 'Keep up with her because she is on the move!'"

Reflecting on the hard work she observed among the elders in her community when she was growing up, Rebecca pointed out that as long as elders had the energy, they continued to contribute in many ways. Elders of all physical abilities were actively engaged with the community. In some cases, elders were still doing physical work such as hauling water, chopping wood, tanning hides, or picking medicines. As they aged, they continued to work on less physically demanding tasks, such as sewing, teaching, or storytelling. Rebecca remarked, "I was taught that as elders grow old and their physical body slows, they move into a new place of quiet where their wisdom becomes even greater." Their purpose and value were recognized until the end.

The vitality of many of the old ladies in the historian participants' childhood communities is evident in that they often lived in their own homes, at least until their very final years. This manner of living demonstrates the balance between principles of autonomy, self-determination, and non-interference on the one hand, and practices of reciprocity and collectivism, on the other. Old ladies were able to live active lives and exercise independence because of the complementary roles of others in the community. Mosôm Danny described how this worked in his youth:

> I was given the job to look after the old people. I was raised up by old people; I knew what their needs were, so they gave me that position. Get water for them, make sure they had enough wood to last them a month, make sure their porches were good. I had to fix all their shacks. I patched up all the walls and the holes and did mud plastering for the winter so the shacks would not be cold. I was also a good bird hunter, so I would go hunting ducks, and give them to these old people all over. That was my job, to feed them, and to cut their wood. And my brother who was raised up by my father and my mother was a pretty good hunter. So he looked after the moose, the deer, and stuff like that for these old people, like widows. That was his job, along with other people. And of course, my sisters were making stockings out of muskrat hide, so the elders always wore moccasins and muskrat socks to keep their feet warm.

Where possible, old ladies carried on with the "women's work" that sustained their households and communities. Hilary remembered her grandmother hauling water from a lake at the bottom of a hill up to the top where she lived on the Moosomin Reserve in Saskatchewan. Others remembered that elderly women were constantly on the move: chopping wood, cleaning and tanning hides, or weeding their gardens. They shared memories of their

grannies picking berries and setting snares for small animals that could contribute to the family food supplies or their personal economies. Maria went
harvesting with her grandmother in the fall when she was growing up in
northern Saskatchewan:

> My grandmother did small trapping and hunting and my brother
> and I would go with her. We would set snares for partridge and rab-
> bits, and we'd have fresh rabbit every day. She would also set snares
> for weasels and all kinds of small fur bearing animals that she would
> sell at the store. There was never any big fur around; we didn't have
> beaver and things like that. She would mostly get weasels and rabbit
> skins which she would tan for our use or else she would sell them.
> Weasels (or ermine skin) used to sell for really good money when
> I was a kid. She would get maybe five or six of them a day, and she
> would hang them in a big round circle. Towards spring they were
> just packed [into that circle], there were all these little skins hang-
> ing that she had trapped. All of that little trapping was extra money
> for women. They were able to buy their beads and their embroidery
> threads and things like that.

The self-sufficient Indigenous work ethic evidently carried on into the
senior years. Rose's grandmother was very independent and had the attitude
to go with it. She couldn't abide someone complaining they couldn't do something: "She was not one to tell a person, 'You can't do this, you can't do that.'
Instead, she'd say, "If you can't do it, well try again....' Grandma would say,
'I'm crippled, and I can do things that you can't do.' (Because she would saw
cord wood and pile it on!)"

Women who were not as physically active still contributed to the work of
the family through supervising the labour of younger women and children.
For example, Maria explained that "when we went to do the laundry [at the
gravel pit], my great-grandmother would sit and sew under a tree. The old
ladies never did any of that heavy work," she said. "If we were smoking meat
or drying meat or drying berries or preparing medicines they would be there.
But they'd only supervise everybody and make sure we did it right. One of the
grandmas was in charge of it, and it was the job of all of us little girls to keep
the fires going. So they stayed there to make sure we did our work properly.
And all of the drying of the meat and everything was right close to where the
old ladies had their arbour or their tent."

Grandmothers who were frail still took on work, finding tasks that were less physically demanding. Many participants recalled that their grandmothers were constantly engaged in sewing and craftwork. Some of the grandmothers made baskets which they could sell. As noted earlier, Olive remembered that it was the old ladies' job to comb out the moss that was harvested for diapers: "That must have been days and days of work, because they had to stock up for winter."

There will be further discussion of other work roles in the following sections, but for now it is important to note that elders were still valued and honoured for contributing to the material needs of the community. As Maria pointed out, "Nobody was to take anything for nothing, so that's why they did things. As pitiful as it seems, my great-granny was still sewing for the family. It made her feel useful. And she was contributing. So whatever she was getting from the family, she was giving back."

Leadership and Governance

If one were to judge by the currently male-dominated arenas of Métis and First Nations' politics, it might be easy to assume that governance was typically "men's business" in Algonquian communities of the past. The history shared by participants about their grandmothers' authorities demonstrates, however, that this was not necessarily the case. Men may have had specific roles that were more visible in terms of politics and governance, but this does not negate the vital role that women—and particularly older women—held in leading and managing their communities.

Reflecting on changes in his childhood community, Rene made a distinction between the type of governance that was happening when they lived in their traditional homeland of Pagwashing in northwestern Ontario and that which ensued after they were forced to move onto the Long Lake #58 Aroland First Nation Reserve in the early 1960s. In his homeland community, Rene explained, it was the old ladies who governed. He knew this because they held certain names or titles that informed the community of each woman's purpose. As a child in the 1950s, Rene was not allowed to use these names; he addressed all the old ladies as *nokomis* (dear, "little," or special grandmother). But he knew their names, and respected the roles and responsibilities that they represented. Rene's biological grandmother, for example, was Kitchi Gabwik, which he translated as "Standing up woman." Rene recalled, "I can see this person standing against the winds of change.

Standing firm, you know. No matter what happened, with all the things that were coming against us; [even during] the encroachment," she stood tall. This grandmother had the responsibilities of protecting the community with her acts of resistance. Rene remembered, "She would mock the Department of Lands and Forests (now the Ministry of Natural Resources), who told her that she must not make a fire to cook her food." He commented, "Our ancestors have been making camp fires for ages, and never burnt the forest down!" Rene also recalled how "Kitchi Gabwik made fishing nets and kept on setting nets when the Department of Lands and Forests told her that it [was] against the law." When Rene's mother was in the tuberculosis sanitarium near Fort William (Thunder Bay), Kitchi Gabwik "insisted that she set up her tent by the sanitarium so that she could visit.... The hospital staff let her make camp." She also resisted life on the reserve and the mainstream school system, as remembered by Rene: "My grandmother only came to Longlac #58 Reserve to visit and let me go to school. The nuns didn't have any power to stop her when she moved back to her traditional homeland to home school me." Rene also remembered that his grandmother put a curse on the Canadian National Railway for the disruption it had caused in their territory.

Kitchi Gabwik had a sister named Wemboma, who held a complementary role. Rene stated that her job was "to arouse, to stir," to get people to act on issues. In fact, she was a "shit disturber, come to think of it! That kind of a woman! She was small, but did those things. She was Wemboma. And when she came to visit, that's who she was." Rene spoke of other ladies such as De chi ka wik: "You look up, and there's a level place. She makes that. Just levels high places, I guess." Like grasses that become too tall, it was De chi ka wik's job to stomp them down; to level the field. Rene commented that sometimes there were people who were "too big for their boots" in the community and it was De chi ka wik's job to bring them back down to earth.

The authority these old ladies held in Rene's homeland community were essential to good governance. They had the strength of character that was reflected in their names: "You get all these grannies with big names like this. And that's how we saw these people. That's how I think our grannies governed our community; because of their names.... What a government!"

Rene attributed the loss of this governing council of grannies to the beginning of social dysfunction in the community. This began to happen because "the grandmothers were dying in the late fifties and early sixties. And then my uncles started to move to the rez and started with the dependency. We were gradually moved off the homeland into this reserve, where my uncles saw their mothers die, and I saw my granny die. And they started drinking and all of a sudden my aunts started getting drunk. Everything seemed to explode around me." Rene remembered feeling *that's not how I was raised!* He talked about the shock of witnessing the changes: "Disrespect set in. I used to go home and see cousins having babies. Whose father is that? All kinds of fathers. And now I had nieces and nephews who had different fathers." This breakdown made him feel a shame that Rene carried well into his adult years, and a big part of his confusion resulted from witnessing the shattering of gender roles in his community. He explained that his understanding of himself as an Anishinaabe, an Ojibway man, was compromised when women lost their respect and authority.

Male-dominated politics in First Nations communities are largely the result of the *Indian Act* of 1876, which crushed First Nations women's official involvement in governance. It did so by replacing the men and women who had participated in the diverse traditional systems of governance with exclusively men as chiefs and councils (until the 1951 revisions of the *Indian Act*).[14] Communities that fell outside of the *Indian Act*, luckily, were more apt to retain the older systems in which women continued to hold power. Such was the case with Rene's community of Pagwashing, and also with many Métis communities. In these instances, governance was rooted in the family, where grandmothers often held sway. This, too, began to change when these grandmothers began to die, as Rene described above. External and internal pressures brought a lot of change to women's status and authority, which at one time could extend across large family networks.

In Maria's family, her great-grandmother was the head of her family network. The Road Allowance community in northern Saskatchewan where Maria grew up was made up of a cluster of extended families and governance was managed through these networks. While Maria's father was "the spokesperson for the head of the family," it was her great-grandmother who held the authority. She explained how this system worked: "My great-grandmother was the one with all the power. Partly, I guess, because she didn't have an axe to grind. Her total and only concern was that everything would be okay with the family. I would think that's why somebody her age would have that kind of power." Maria stressed that "nobody argued with her. She would tell my dad what she thought and he would listen."

In addition to this authority, Maria's great-grandmother was the head of all the extended families of her offspring, which gave her tremendous influence over the community. Maria noted, "If they were going to do something, they made sure it was okay with her first. The people that lived in that community knew that the Campbells wouldn't do anything without that old lady." Important issues would always be discussed among the immediate family first. These family discussions afforded women and children the opportunity to have direct input and participation in decision making. Once a decision was reached, Maria's father would act as the family spokesperson and take the decision to a community meeting, where he would meet with the spokesmen from other families. These men were beholden to the decisions that had been reached at the family level, and the old ladies' attendance at these meetings reminded them of this responsibility. Grandmothers would rarely speak at these meetings, unless they felt that the issues were not being addressed in an adequate fashion.

As a child, Maria used to tag along with her grandmothers, and she remembers a few instances in which her great-grandmother took a public stand. One time was in the 1940s, when the federal government had decided to change Aboriginal traplines and territories. "These were traditional lands the families had harvested for hundreds and hundreds of years, and these lands were passed on to younger generations," Maria explained. "They decided to change them to square blocks and re-assign them, which meant no one would be on their traditional homeland. It caused great turmoil and also meant another death blow to cultural life as well as connection to ancestral land." Maria described how her grandmother took a stand at a trappers' convention:

> Everybody was talking and talking, but they weren't really clear about what they were saying. She listened and listened, and then she got up and really got after the government people that were there. She was really angry, because the trapping block of my dad's had been in our family for who knows how long. It was my grandfather's trapping block and it had been his grandfather's. They were switching everything around and she was really angry about that. And I think it was because the men weren't articulating whatever it was that she felt they should be saying.

Maria remembered how impressed she was "because even the government people shut up and never said a word. They listened to her."

In another instance, Maria remembered her great-grandmother addressing the men at an extended family meeting about an alleged pedophile. This
person lived in another community and was planning to come and work with
some of the men in Maria's family. Maria's uncles were told they could work
with this man if they chose, but that they were to keep him away from their
home community.

Sometimes informal or work gatherings of women would provide the
opportunity for dialogue and action on an issue. American historian Rebecca
Kugel has studied how women engaged in politics among the late nineteenth-
century Ojibway in Minnesota. She writes, "The daily environment of a work
group provided an obvious forum for political debate, and indeed, in the
work group setting, Ojibwe women discussed issues and formulated their
opinions."[15] This was also true of the women in Maria's family. They might,
for example, discuss issues while doing laundry collectively. If during these
times an issue such as domestic abuse came up, the women would decide if the
issue needed to be addressed beyond their circle. If it did, the concern would
be taken by Maria's great-grandmother to the male leaders in the extended
families that made up their community.

Maria remembered an instance which demonstrates how decisions
within the women's jurisdiction were managed and how they held authority in the community overall. This example comes from the time when her
Road Allowance community just outside Prince Albert National Park was
being pressured to move to another Métis settlement in the early 1950s. "The
government told my dad and the men that they should go and look at this
community," she said, "because that's where they were going to try and move
us. They only meant for the men to go, but my mother and a couple of other
women were picked by the rest of the women to go. Those that stayed behind
looked after the kids."

Maria explained that while the men investigated the region's potential
for hunting and procuring resources, it was the women's job to investigate
the water supply, the possibility of setting up a home, and opportunities for
the children. As it turned out, water was problematic: "I remember my mom
telling my aunties that there were no wells. That people were getting water
out of the lake and boiling it." The bottom line, however, were the social relations. "They had moved Métis families from the south and the north and
all over and just dumped them there in one community," Maria said. "Our
family and the people where I come from always lived in family groups. And

so, coming into this place where all of these desperately poor people had been just dropped off, there were tensions. My mother saw that you could not have policed anything like that, because the grandmothers couldn't go and interfere in other people's business."

Maria's mother and the other delegates perceived a lack of discipline within this new community. They were concerned about the fighting that was happening because of the compromised position of the relocated families and the breakdown of traditional family governance systems. In particular, the loss of the grandmothers' ability to manage social relations was more than apparent. In the end, as Maria described, the women decided that they would resist the government directive to move: "When they came back and they had a meeting, the women said, 'No, we're not moving there. We're not taking our kids there.' So we didn't move. And the government was really mad because men wouldn't go. They didn't understand why, because it looked great for the guys. But it didn't look good for the women and their kids, and the men saw that."

What is evident in these stories is that there was often a "head woman" in extended families, and this woman was typically an "old lady" who wielded great authority in terms of community governance. Gertie talked about the significance of a *gii maa kwe* (or *ogi maa kwe*) in Anishinaabe clan governance systems, a head man or head women that each clan would have had in place. Although clans were no longer functioning in such a structured way in her childhood community, there was still a *gii maa kwe* that emerged as the head of the extended families.

Although they did not call her that, it appears that *gii maa kwe* was the role that was played by Maria's Cree/Métis great-grandmother. In Gertie's case, it was her paternal grandmother. "*Gii maa kwe* was the head woman," Gertie explained. "She had earned that from the people who were around her. There wasn't a ceremony or anything like that. But here was an acknowledgement that this person had responsibility. She provided that centre on which to focus. If she wanted to see something done, then that's what would happen. She wasn't bossy, but she took it on herself to do certain things. And so *gii maa kwe* defined her role as the unifier of the family."

In a kin-based society, holding the role as the unifier of the family was significant in terms of governance and maintaining community well-being. Gertie talked about how each time a *gii maa kwe* passed away, an unsettling period would follow until a new head woman emerged. Maria also spoke about what happens to a family in the absence of a head woman, saying that it could represent "the death of a nation." "You see that over and over again," she said, "where there's no matriarch, where there's nobody that's the boss. If that's not there, that's where you see a broken family and all kind of ugly things can happen."

Rene provided some examples of how his grandmother was clearly the boss of his extended family. He shared the following story:

> My granny would say, "Okay, I'm going to pick blueberries today," and my uncle would say, "Mother, we planned on going next week."
>
> "I'm going right now." She just takes the tin down, starts packing and away we went. We paddled along the lakes and rivers to this beautiful lake. And we'd sit down to camp and the next morning I would hear this small little *putt putt putt*—a three horsepower. That's my uncle! (*laughter*)
>
> Eventually everyone is camped on this island, picking blueberries. She just said, "I'm going now." It was that kind of authority, and it worked. Other grannies would also come: "I'm going to go where she is. Pick blueberries, too."

Mosôm Danny commented on the authority of his grandmother in managing the daily activities of their extended family. "It wasn't my grandfather who always talked," he said. "It was my grandmother. She was the one that said, 'You sit here. You go do this. Today, you are going to see this one.'" Danny emphasized, "In her house, she ruled. In her yard, she ruled."

Old ladies also held responsibilities as the ultimate guardians of kinship. As discussed in Chapter 5, grandmothers were often responsible for arranging marriages, a practice that was still going on in some of the participants' communities in the late 1940s. Although they had lost their authority in terms of arranging marriages in many communities, old ladies still held responsibilities for knowing who was related to whom so as to prevent marriages between relatives. Rose remembered her grandmother's careful attention to the boys she was going to dances with as a teenager. Her grandmother would ask, "Do you know who your relatives are?" Danny was taught by his grandmother that, as a bear clan member, he needed to know every bear clan member in the territory of southeastern Saskatchewan.

The responsibility for knowing one's relatives was not only limited to knowing those who were alive. This came out in a story that Maria told about the old ladies' role during their annual cleaning of the graveyard in their community:

> We'd go out to all of the graves, and the old people—two or three old ladies—would be standing at a grave. They would talk to all the little kids there, saying, "This was your great auntie." "She was so and so's sister." They would tell us some stories about her, and then we would go to the next grave. And you would find out, "This was the one that gave us a really bad time; he was a really cranky old man!—and he haunted some people after. That's what happens when you are not kind to people." There would just be all of this stuff, they would be cleaning and making little last minute things on the graves, but you would get all of this history of who were those people in the graveyard, so that you always felt a connection to them.

Old ladies thus ensured that the family members were grounded in their connections to kin, including ancestral kin.

As the heads of their families, grandmothers also administered justice and maintained harmony in the community. Mosôm Danny talked about how elders of both genders managed disputes in his community of Keeseekoose First Nation, but it was "old Kohkom Flora" who would be called upon when tensions would arise over people borrowing possessions that they did not return. Social justice and harmony were also managed through equitable distribution of food. Danny described how the old ladies were in charge of distributing meat at community feasts: "When the food was given out, there were procedures. The women would be the ones who would point out who was in need: 'This one over here. And that one doesn't have very much food at home.' So all the leftovers in the pots, you would take it and give it to her so she could eat for the next few days."

Many of the women talked about the safety they felt with their grandmothers. In their capacity as overseers, the old ladies were instilled with responsibilities to watch out for children's safety in particular. For those communities struggling with alcohol, social breakdown, and sexual abuse, grandmothers could provide some protection and solace. Hilary talked about how her grandmother enhanced her feeling of safety, and about how she had heard of this from other women as well:

> I don't know where all it stems from, but grandmothers were always the protectors of children. They were the ones that maintained

boundaries between parents and their children, or between the relatives.

One time I heard an elderly lady say, "Our kohkom didn't sleep
with us for nothing. There was danger afoot in our house. And when
my kohkom was there, no one came into our bedroom or our bed,
to bother us."

As discussed in Chapter 5, space was organized according to gender and
age in Maria's childhood community, and this enhanced the safety of children.
Maria talked about the spatial organization as a prevention measure against
abuse. "They were very strict when I was a kid about men and children," she
said. "It would have been hard for somebody to molest or bother children as
long as these things were observed." With respect to the role of the old ladies
in ensuring children's safety, Maria pointed out that her grandmother's bed
was always the closest to the door, whereas the children slept furthest from
the door. This ensured that Grandma knew who was coming and going. Maria
noted that elderly people are often light sleepers, and so it was fitting that her
great-grandmother was posted in a place where she would have easily woken
if someone were to go past her in the night.

The role that grandmothers held as protectors against abuse was also
manifest within their role as storytellers. Family and community laws were
embedded within the stories by grandmothers who were also keepers of these
laws. One of the stories that Maria remembered when she was growing up
involved taboos against incest. Every winter, her great-grandmother would
tell the story about the time when Wisakecak (a Trickster figure in Cree
Culture)[16] seduced his own daughter. In this story, Wisakecak is portrayed as
lazy, greedy, and immoral. He gets around the incest taboo by pretending to
die and then disguising himself as a handsome young man who comes to the
village to court his daughter. He is eventually found out and dealt the punishment suitable to someone who had broken the incest taboo.

Maria talked about the importance of the old ladies in her family telling
this story on a regular basis. It was told to remind everyone about the law
against incest and its consequences:

The old ladies used to tell those stories. They would be telling the
kids the stories, but everybody was sitting around because you are all
in the same room. My dad would be working at snowshoes with my
uncles, too, if they were there. They were hearing it over and over; by

repetition, it was really engrained in everybody's head. It reminded us that those things were wrong. And everybody was getting different things from different places. Like the story tells you what a mother is supposed to do if this happens. She didn't do anything when she suspected him for the first time. She could have prevented it. So the story tells you all of this, and when you hear it over and over again you start to think about it.

Maria pointed out that these stories were also intended for outsiders and visitors to establish ground rules: "If you were a strange man coming to visit for the first time, the message was, 'Watch it, young man. This old lady has been around the block and knows what the laws are.'"

Traditional stories are known for having layers of understanding that are intended for different audiences, and they have layers of meaning that unfold over time. Maria talked about how the incest taboo story has continued to teach her throughout her life, providing her with lessons about her own role as a grandmother:

That story taught me how grandmothers are supposed to behave. It taught me that my job is to protect, to make sure that [abuse] doesn't happen to my grandchildren. It's also my responsibility to make sure that my family hears those stories, so that they learn that incest is a taboo and that it's not acceptable behaviour. It teaches the laws about what we are supposed to do [in the case of incest]—and it was really an extreme law.

So all of this works into you as a person getting older. As a kid you are learning something. You know something else when you are a mother; that it is your job to protect—but as an old woman your obligation is to teach others to do the same. All of the obligations and protocols were tied in to the story.

Grandmothers, then, held responsibilities not only to protect but also to guide others with respect to their own responsibilities. Together, these proved that their role as teachers was very significant.

Teaching

Elders are well known for their role as teachers in Indigenous societies. Hudson Bay Cree Elder Abel Chapman described it this way: "A long time ago the youngsters gathered around an elder, like we sit around the TV today. The elder would relate stories about survival. That's how the children learned. Listening to elders. If there was one old man who knew how to play the fiddle, he was the teacher and this was passed on from generation to generation." Flora Beardy and Robert Coutts, who conducted an oral history project with Hudson Bay Cree Elders, point out that "the elders were the teachers in everything."[17]

The women and men I spoke with had many memories about how the elders in their communities fulfilled this role. Although there is typically more information about how elders worked with children, it is important to remember that community members of all ages looked to the elders as their teachers. The previous section demonstrated how elderly women were sought out for their wisdom and advice in matters related to governance. But as Maria noted, it wasn't only her father and other members of her family who looked to her great-grandmother for advice. Other members of the community would also come to her seeking counsel, at which times her great-grandmother "would sit and tell stories" to these members of the community as a way of giving them counsel on the issues they were struggling with.

Elders in Marie's community would hold public forums. As a child, Marie attended community feasts where elders would stand up and speak formally to the community after they had finished eating. She pointed out that the elders took turns in providing these lectures. These experiences correspond to Mosôm Danny's stories of how elders took on a teaching role at feasts: "You would have all your traditional teachings that went along with the feasts. The feasts were like classes; the more you participated in them, the more you learned. After a good scoff of soup and bannock the old people got up each in turn and told something about how they parented, how they looked after their children, how they became good grandparents."

The majority of stories about the teaching role of elders were, however, about how elders worked with children. Given that elders more often than not cared for children, this is understandable. It has been noted that, among the early twentieth-century Plains Cree, "children spent substantial time with their grandparents."[18] Maria remembers being with "old ladies" every day from when she was a baby until she was twelve, the year her family began to break up following the death of her mother. This time with the old ladies provided the foundation for a traditional and lifelong education. As Maria said, "the foundation of all I know comes from this experience. Today, if an elder shares something with me, I understand it without a back story. I can read something and put missing pieces in. I know my language from a woman's place and how to work with it from that place. I know medicines—I never learned how to use all of them but I know them and I know how to look for them. More importantly I learned stories that I can go back and search through when I want to understand something." According to Maria, these old ladies still play a role in her life: "They are the kind of woman I want to be."

As teachers of the youngest children, then, elders taught them to be contributing members of their societies, and they did this through formal, non-formal, and informal education.[19] It is important to make these distinctions because we know too little about the formal structures of education that existed in Aboriginal communities prior to the imposition of formal schooling. Formal education can be that which takes place in institutional or structured environments, or when a teacher is in charge of delivering a set curriculum that fits within a larger educational system. According to this definition, this is precisely what was taking place in Danny's childhood community. He described classes that the elders held on a regular basis:

> It was the elders who were the teachers. When the mothers and fathers would go gathering and hunting, and working during the day, it was the old men and women, the kohkoms past their fifties and sixties and seventies; those were the ones that were holding classes, just like everybody else. We expected that. I remember my brothers and sisters, even the ones who were going to school would come during the summer months. It was at least at the beginning of every moon. It was set—there were time factors! When the moon was ready, that was the day that teachings came in. There was order in the things they did. At the beginning of the moon, we'd know that we had to go sit with kohkom and mosôm.

The structure of these sessions was related to the rhythms of the moon, when elders determined that the children were more open to learning. Of course, there were also protocols and schedules related to storytelling, with winter being the most prolific time for sharing.

Adult individuals who had taken on a key role in the community had to follow specific learning courses within the formal and structured learning systems offered by the elders. The authority to designate and then train these individuals rested with the elders. Traditional healers provide a good example of roles that necessitated structured learning experiences. For healers, there were specific protocols and learning outcomes that were undertaken at an early age, as early as age five.[20] Participants I spoke with referred to the training they received for taking on future roles as historians and traditional knowledge keepers. As noted in Chapter 5, Danny's grandmother taught him to use a system of mnemonic devices that would enable him to fulfill the role he carries today as an Elder and oral historian. Furthermore, because he was often ill when he was growing up, his parents were not able to care for him, and so he spent much of his childhood and youth in the presence of old people from whom he learned their history and traditional ways.

Maria spoke of a knowledge transfer system referred to in Nēhiyawewin as *notokwe opihikeet* (old-lady raised). This specialized system likely emerged in response to the well-founded fears that the fractured knowledge systems that resulted from losing children to residential schools would be too weak to retain the lessons of traditional knowledge. Maria explained that in her community certain children were chosen to remember traditional knowledge so it would not be lost, and they were required to spend more time with their elders. According to Maria, *notokwe opihikeet* "ensures that if [some of the] children are snatched away, then someone in the family will know the language and will have some, if not all of the information." Maria noted that "old-lady raised" children were often the eldest in the family, but they may have also been younger members who were identified as having specific gifts or learning needs.

Another form of specialized learning entailed children spending time as apprentices with the grandmothers to learn roles they were to take on later in life (which is discussed more fully below). For example, Rose worked with her grandmother from a very young age, providing assistance in her work as a community doctor. This work provided experiential training that her grandmother would have parcelled out according to Rose's readiness to learn.

In addition to specialized learning, there would have been general things that all children needed to learn, and much of this would have been managed by their grandmothers. In Danny's story about his grandfather's lecture to the Indian Agent (Chapter 5), we saw that his grandmother had jurisdiction over family law. Danny remembered his grandfather telling the agent that the children were well behaved, obedient, and good at listening. His grandfather credited his wife (Danny's grandmother) for this, and he said, "She's the one that teaches them the fine art of listening, hearing, communicating—all those powers of understanding that I need when I'm out there hunting. I need them to believe that what I'm telling them is right. She does all that for me. She gets those kids ready for me, to take them out into the hunting fields."

This story makes it clear that the grandmother had the job of not only teaching children to be respectful but also teaching them the skills they needed to live in a hunting culture. Maria remembers, too, the specific practice that related to both teaching respect and ensuring survival as a hunting people. *Notokwe maciwin*, "old-lady hunting," was a term used to describe the hunting lessons that young children would receive from their grandmothers. As early as three or four, children would begin to set snares and hunt for small animals under the guidance of their grandmothers. The principle behind this was that the senior lifegivers (grandmothers) should be the first to teach about taking life. This ensured respectful hunting practices and adherence to protocols that both men and women would need to follow later in life. In general, it was the old ladies' job to teach about *pimatisiwin*, life, and it was critical that they began with the very young children.

Much of the learning about *pimatisiwin*, of course, took place through informal learning, as children had plenty of opportunities to tag along with their grandmothers. Informally, grandparents had time to explain things to children and engage in storytelling because they were not labouring at the pace of young and middle-aged adults in the community. Maria attributed much of what she has learned to the time she spent among the elders as a child taking care of them: "I think I was influenced by those old ladies because I was the one who looked after them. I would make their tea, haul their wood, look after their fire…. They would be doing their work, be it sewing, beading, grinding medicine, or playing handgames, and it was my job to be there for them."

That children spent so much time with their elders also exposed them to the types of work they would need to master. In the next section, I discuss the elders' roles in health care of the community, which provided formal, informal, and non-formal education to their apprentices and grandchildren.

Managing the Health of the Community

In general, health care was the women's business among the early to mid-twentieth century Nēhiyawak, Michif, and Anishinaabek. Swampy Cree storyteller Louis Bird has asserted that "the women were the medicine people—the nurses and doctors in the family—because they had all the knowledge about the herbs and plants to cure almost any disease."[21] As Madeleine pointed out, "There were no public health nurses when I was growing up [on the Kehewin Cree Nation], so if we came down with colds or the flu, my mother was our nurse—24/7 if need be."

As mothers, women had to have a certain level of skills and knowledge to look after their families. But when they became grandmothers, they were able to build on these skills and experiences and devote more time to their roles as health care managers and practitioners. Whereas mothers looked after the health of the family, it was grandmothers who looked after the health of the community.

In her book on Métis women in the nineteenth century, Nathalie Kermoal took note of the special roles and status that elder women had as the midwives, doctors, and pharmacists of their communities. She wrote, "They were midwives and doctors without diplomas, pharmacists and herbalists without shops. They went from house to house, village to village, to share their knowledge and care for patients with the healing plants they had carefully harvested from the woods."[22] Kermoal's depiction of the old women going from "house to house, village to village" mirrors what Danny remembers from growing up. He described the old ladies making "rounds," especially with the onset of winter. Moving "from tipi to tipi, from place to place," Danny noted, "it was these grandmothers who went around with their bags of medicine—on their snowshoes." He remembers, too, that the grandmothers even had "hospitals. There was "a big tipi where these kohkoms would work," and these women were referred to as "grandmothers," not nurses. Plus, "there were specialists," he recalled, "who dealt with different illnesses, age groups, and parts of the body."

Grandmothers also provided general doctoring for their home communities as well as for non-Native people in the area. Rosella's grandmother worked in Molanosa but also travelled back and forth to Montreal Lake to doctor people.

Rose's grandmother was also preferred over the Western doctor in Duck Lake where Rose grew up. Her grandmother was called upon to treat both Native and non-Native people. As a young girl, Rose used to assist her grandmother in doctoring, and she recalled a few incidents of going to treat accident-related injuries. One of these involved a young Belgian man who had been burned in a fire at the flour mill on the edge of town. Rose remembered going with her grandmother and being instructed on how to get the shirt off him, which had melted to his body during the accident. For this call, Rose's grandmother received two bags of flour and some oatmeal from the Belgian man's wife. Rose explained that her grandmother was usually paid in a system of exchange where she would "get a piece of meat or something, or sometimes eggs or chickens, stuff like that." This was in accordance with the protocol and tradition of being a healer, particularly when working with traditional healing remedies. Rose explained: "You never sold your herbal medicine. People had to give you something in return. They can't just take it like that, but it could be a shirt, it could be a skirt—whatever you had."

Rosella remembers, too, that sometimes her grandmother had to heal someone suffering from "bad medicine." Rosella explained how her grandmother was involved: "It's like Indian witchcraft. Somebody sends [someone] bad medicine and this person gets sick and something happens to them. She would come along and she would heal them." Rosella never witnessed her grandmother doctoring for bad medicine, nor did Rose, but both had heard that their grandmothers were doing this kind of work. Rose mentioned that her grandmother was very secretive about dealing with it.

Olive's grandmother was also a healer, and she had vivid memories of her grandmother warning her about plants that were used for bad medicine:

> One time we were going to help Grandma pick these tiny yellow leaves and then she stopped. There were two of us following her; me and my cousin. And she said, "Wait. I want to tell you something. Take a good look at this."
>
> It had a very lovely rich purple in the centre. But there were sharp thorns there, even at the bottom of that flower. "I want you to look at this." She said. "Look at the thorns. If you were to ever step on this, you'd be hurt. Those thorns are so sharp they would hurt you." Grandma said, "With this medicine, always, always walk around it. Never have anything to do with it."

When Olive responded that she thought the flowers looked nice, her grandmother told her, "That flower looks nice, but it's for bad purposes. It's as bad as the thorns are sharp."

Olive's story highlights a great strength that elderly women had in terms of managing community wellness: their work as herbalists. Old ladies were known for the relationships they were able to forge with plants and plant medicines. This came through in a story that Sylvia told about how she and other children perceived elderly women when they were growing up. "I remember as a kid we would play old ladies with all these medicines," she said. "We'd pack up all of this stuff and we'd put it beside our beds. Then we would pretend we were real old ladies, and we would wear these long skirts. Because that's how we related to our grannies." Sylvia remembered the grandmothers wrapping medicines in cloth pouches and keeping them under or behind their beds.

The image of old ladies with medicines packed under their beds is a familiar one to many of the women I spoke with. Rebecca had similar memories of her husband's grandmother: "When Grandma invited me into her bedroom, I knew that she wanted to give me something special. She kept new tea towels, jars of berries, and medicines under her bed." Rebecca also remembered that "Grandma hung her medicines outside in the shed. She and I would go out in season to pick medicines. Upon arriving back home, she would instruct me how to clean, dry, and store them until needed."

Elderly women worked with many different kinds of medicines. At the most fundamental level, they were keepers of plant food as medicine, and so often the old ladies were in charge of the community's gardens. Maria described how the old ladies decided when the family gardens would be planted in the springtime:

> My grannies were the ones that got the gardens started. My dad and uncles would get the horses and the ploughs ready in the spring and they would cultivate everybody's garden, but it was my granny who did the planting with the older women. And she never planted the garden until the thunder came and shook the land, and then the rain came. She said those two have to have a meeting first, and then she'd plant her garden. She also planted her stuff in hills because she said that plants were relatives and you had to think about how plants were related.

Maria noted the significance of her grandmother's lead, explaining that, "if the thunder didn't come until June, we didn't do anything until then."

The connection between older women and their gardens was impressed upon Marie during her puberty fast. One of the teachings she received was "when you get older you make gardens so your grandchildren can come and help you." Another thing Marie learned was that, "while the grandchildren are helping you, you teach them. You talk to them and never waste time."

Gardening, then, and work with plant medicines was part of what Mosôm Danny would call the women's jurisdiction. As the "old-lady hunting" teaching tells us, it was the old ladies' job to connect children with this world.

Many of the women had memories of going out with their grandmothers to pick plant medicines. As demonstrated by the story told by Olive about the "bad medicine" plants, grandmothers had a responsibility to instill protocols related to the medicines. Rose talked about the care she learned from her grandmother:

> We would go on a medicine trip, they called it. She'd say, "Okay, you have to pick this." She had a little pointed stick and she would point at the thing. I had to dig away from the bottom. She said, "If you break the root it won't work as strong. Shake it, don't pull on it!" And then we would put it in the little cotton. You couldn't put it in a plastic bag or a paper bag. She always had a little cotton rag and she would tear it into squares. "And don't take the flower off," she would tell me. "Leave it there." It would dry in there and then she would know what kind of medicine it was.

Rose also learned that "you always had to pick the medicines when it was a full moon because the strength is stronger."

Elderly women instilled a sense of respect and reverence for the medicines in children by being clear about the behaviour that was expected of them on excursions. Hilary was a talkative child, but she had to curb her chatter when on medicine-picking trips with her grandmother. Her grandmother would tell her: "Now is the time to keep still; you have to be quiet now." Hilary remembered, "I would hear her singing. She was probably chanting as she was picking things."

Mosôm Danny had a similar memory from when he was a pre-school child:

> I remember one time I was eating a sucker because Grandma was trying to keep me quiet. I was sitting there in the shade and she was looking at this plant. She cleared the grass and she was putting some tobacco down and praying. And I was with my BB Bat, making all kinds of slurping sounds! (*laughter*). All of a sudden she says, "Baby! I'm trying to pray. I'm trying to talk to the spirit of this plant. I need to get some thoughts!" So that was it! I took my blanket and moved it. "Don't move too far away; there might be porcupines," she said.

Danny's grandmother and elderly aunts instructed him that "when you are working on these things they have got to be done right. You have got to be sure that you pray properly." He remembered his grandmothers telling him, "You have got to be able to take some of this medicine and put it aside, along with your tobacco. Maybe just sprinkle some seeds and pass it on." As Danny explained, "You didn't just pick them; you had to spread the life of that plant around."

While they taught children what they knew, grandmothers also shared their knowledge about their plant medicines with other grandmothers. The old ladies would exchange knowledge through dialogue, prayers, and gifts. In Maria's community, the old people would get together "in the spring and the fall to grind medicines and sing the songs that were part of this work." Danny remembered seeing two or three grandmothers working on the open prairie, teaching and conferring with each other. He explained how different grandmothers had specific jurisdictions over territories, plants, and even colours of plants. In spite of the fact that grandmothers might only work with certain plants, they were able to do a substantial amount of work. "Some of these grandmothers would take no more than seven plants," Danny said. "They would mix them in every batch and form for every particular ailment they had—for earaches, nose, sicknesses around the eyes, skin sicknesses … all the parasitic things." Danny asserted that they were "the specialists that we have today: an eye doctor, ear and nose doctor, heart specialist—well they had those kinds of things! They had jurisdictions and practices of certain specialized medicines, those old women."

Grandmothers respected one another's jurisdictions while also generously sharing their knowledge. Danny explained that although they knew their particular medicines well and were able to use them for a variety of purposes, they found it useful to borrow from one another, if they had permission to do so. He remembered that they would say things like, "You have to ask Kohkom Flora for this. I know what it is, but I haven't received her permission to use this yet. But in place of it, I use this one over here. It does pretty much the same thing, but hers is more potent." This gathering and exchange of knowledge between grandmothers was part of the research that they needed to do to build their skills, as Danny pointed out: "You are talking about investigative research? Well that's what these old women did. They did that. They were researching; they were studying the medical properties of these plants, and sharing how that works."

Because of all this work, elderly women were able to offer a variety of remedies. They had medicines for pink eye, scurvy, rheumatism, and the digestive system, pain analgesics, mosquito repellent, medicines for reproductive systems, and tonics for general cleansings. Danny spoke of all this medicine-making as a sacred responsibility of women, which was tied into their relationship with the land. This view is grounded in the creation story as he learned it, in which it was the female who gave life to everything, and who was the great mother. In this world view, as expressed by Danny, "a woman came with all of the knowledge of everything on the earth. *Everything*. She knew all of the plants, all of the medicines, all of the animals ... because she was the mother! She was born with all that knowledge." The connection between women and "Mother Earth," according to Danny, is the reason that "we learned that discipline of checking the animals, checking the things around us, from the wisdom of the grandmothers. Because they were the ones who studied the plants; they were the ones who studied the earth."

The women's power in the community was linked to their role in planning according to the seasons. Danny stated that younger people "learned about herbology, which is associated with time factors." Old ladies had to know which plants were ready to pick and when, as many plants had different uses according to their seasonal lifespan. "These are the things that the women had to learn because they had to have these medicines available," Danny said. "Their responsibility was humungous because they kept the community healthy. They had the responsibility to keep those children alive."

The responsibility for the greater health and well-being of both children and adults of the community clearly belonged to the old women. This is evident in a story that Maria told. She remembered being taken as a child to pick medicine around a lake in a very special place. This lake was called Nōtokēw Sākahikan, "Old Lady Lake." It stands out in her memory because the children were taught to be quiet and reverent when visiting there. Even though there was a beautiful beach, they were not allowed to swim. In speaking to her father many years later, Maria realized that the reason they called it Nōtokēw Sākahikan was because it was a place where the old ladies would pick medicines and, in particular, medicines that they would use in their work with birth and death. Midwives harvested their medicines from this lake, as did those who needed medicines that could "absorb the smell of death." Thinking back, Maria realized that "that whole area had to do with women's medicines. There must have been a lot of women's medicine there." This lake in this special place was where the old ladies connected and worked with the land to support them in what was *their* special medicine: being doorkeepers to the spirit world. As I discuss in the next section, a "grandmother" was always present on the spirit side of the threshold, either to send you into the world through birth or receive you when you returned to the spirit world.

Doorkeepers to the Spirit World

> Men were not part of birth and death—they didn't stay for that. It was the women who took care of the birthing. It was an old lady that brings you in, and an old lady that takes you out. And according to them, on the other [spirit] side, it's an old lady that [welcomes] you; there is a midwife/grandmother on that side [to bring you back to the spirit world].
>
> —Maria Campbell

Elderly women held a role that I am calling "doorkeepers to the spirit world," because they assisted people with the transitions between life and death. In Maria's experience, grandmothers who were midwives caught new life coming into this world, and grandmothers who were healers comforted those leaving it. In death, as Maria learned, "there is always a grandmother on the other side."

Catching New Life

In Michif, Nēhiyawak, and Anishinaabek cultures, elderly women were seen to have the wisdom and authority to safeguard life. Practices of midwifery have already been discussed in Chapter 3, so here I will briefly discuss how and why it was that grandmothers held this role. Grandmothers were given the responsibility to teach about *pimatisiwin*—life—and they were the keepers and teachers of the relationships that we form on this journey. With this understanding, one can see why they were deemed the most suitable people in the communities to catch new life as it entered the world.

There were many practical reasons that led them to this role. Grandmothers had more freedom of mobility and time to devote themselves to the work of midwifery than did mothers. As described in Chapter 3, when the delivery was a distance from where the midwife lived, it was often necessary for her to move in with the expectant mother. By moving in with families or being in close proximity, grandmothers were able to help with prenatal and postnatal care, along with attending to infants. Grandmothers were well suited to catching babies because of the experience they had garnered with age. They could use different levels of experience and energy according to the needs of the birth and were called upon for their special skills. For example, Maria's great-grandmother would be called in to assist only if there was a problem with a birth. Because she was too elderly to do all of the long hours that were required in regular midwifery, she became a specialist and was called upon to assist with extreme situations.

Even when old ladies were not acting as the midwives for a birth, it was important to have them present during the labour. Maria witnessed this as she was growing up. "I used to see all the old ladies go rushing to the house where a baby was being born," she said. "You know ... they weren't there necessarily to help the midwife. But with their experience, all of them being there, it was like, somehow they were holding the energy and helping; just by their telling funny stories and whatever, they were keeping the energy or life force in that place in a good way."

Maria told a story that she had heard from a Métis woman in northern Saskatchewan, which further demonstrates how the presence of older women at a birth was valued:

> This woman said all the old ladies came when she was having her baby. She said they built a fire outside and made a big pot of duck soup, and they laughed and told stories all night and all the next day. And the harder she screamed, the harder they laughed and the more ducks they ate. She was telling me, she just felt like wringing their necks. But what it did was, by them laughing so loud and everything else, she didn't have time to think that much about her pain because she couldn't believe they were doing this to her. And she said it wasn't until she was an old lady that she realized how much they had helped her by doing that; by letting her know that life goes on. It was important for her to know that she wasn't going to die.

On reflection, Maria thought this to be part of a "ceremony of birthing" that was aimed at helping women feel good about the birth, particularly in the Christian environment at the time, where, as Maria remembered, "everything having to do with birthing was associated with evil and death and bad and considered 'unclean.'" She noted that the presence of the old ladies might have helped to communicate to the mother that she was doing something remarkable and full of life.

Closing Life

Elderly women also had an important role to play when it came to death. As with the midwives who would move in with a family when there was a new life coming, grandmothers or elderly aunts would also come to live with families who were coping with the imminent death of a loved one. They administered to the dying through palliative care, but they were also there to look after the living. Maria described the role they played in calming families in crisis over death. "If somebody was dying, then one of them would come and they would stay with you, to take care of the dying person but also to take care of the family," she said. "They would cook things, special things." Maria remembered her auntie being in the kitchen, "and cooking that food that would calm you down." She noted, "She made amazing soup. It wasn't anything that anybody ever talked about, but when you saw her doing that, you knew that everything was okay."

Maria related this to her story about the old ladies who waited outside during a birth. "It was the same thing when somebody was dying," she said. "The old ladies would come in and they would laugh and tell stories. They would tell jokes with the person that was dying, you know, so they could laugh and feel good."

Elderly women often operated as the funeral directors for their communities, doing everything from preparing the body, to instructing the men in building a casket and digging a gravesite, to planning and overseeing the funeral. Medicines used around death were, as Maria described earlier, "old-lady" medicines. With no embalming and the corpse typically lying in wake for four days, the old-lady medicines were necessary for keeping the body and casket fresh. Maria talked about how her grandmother managed the funerals in her community:

> My Grandma was the one who looked after death for community members. My dad and my uncles would make the caskets for our community and the communities close by. I think the reason for that is probably that my dad and my uncles were my grandmother's helpers. That's why so many people came to them, because they came to my grandmother, and my grandmother would delegate work out to her sons.
>
> After Grandma cleaned and dressed the body, my dad and uncles would bring the casket in and they would put the body in there. But before they put it in, my mom and my aunties would come over. We

would put black cloth over top of this board, because the coffin was
made from board. Then they would lay a blanket inside it, and trim
it sometimes with ribbon around the edges to make the casket look
nice. My aunties would make flowers out of crepe paper and then
my dad would come in and they would lift the body inside of that
thing. My grandmother would fix it all up. So she was kind of like
the undertaker.

Rose and Rosella remembered helping their grandmothers with these duties
when they were little girls. Rosella said it was the midwives who often did
this work. She remembered helping her mother wash a body. "I never thought
nothing of it," she said.

Rose helped her grandmother a number of times, and was able to describe
her experiences in detail:

They would come and ask for her. So she would go down there, and
she had to measure the body, then the men would go and get the
lumber to make the casket. She covered the lumber with black cloth
and with white inside, and a straw pillow.

She'd wash the body first, and then she would let it sit and dry off.
And then they were stiff, eh? So she would lift the body, and I would
put the pants on, fully dressed, like a person was going out someplace. And she would say, "Depêche toi. Prends pas toute la journée,"
she'd tell me. So I had to hurry up. Because they get stiff, eh?

Like Rosella, Rose didn't think anything of working with the corpse; this was
part of the work she did as a little girl helper to her grandmother. But she
shared a funny story about how others were not as accustomed to this process:

One day, one of my aunts was with us. She was helping Grandma.
You know, right after death, the air goes out from the body? And
when Grandma moved her, she laid her on the slab there, and she
was turning her over to wash her back. And it was just like air came
out. My aunt fainted right there! (*laughs*) She thought she was coming back to life! (*laughter*)

She grabbed her head and she was crying, "Elmire, she's come
back!" (That's what my grandmother's name was, Elmire).

And Grandma said, "No, no, no. That's just the air coming out
of her." Grandma put her hands right here [on the pulse]. She says,
"No, no, she's dead. Look: put your hand here" (because her hand was

cold and everything). And she says [motioning to the young Rose]: "She does that all the time, she always helps me. She touches a dead body and it doesn't bother her."

Testing for a pulse was a normal procedure. It was Rose's grandmother's job, in the absence of the local doctor, to ensure that the person was dead. As Rose said, "They had to do it because there was nobody else around here."

Rose talked about wakes that would go on for three days after the death, and pointed out that her grandmother had a lead role. "Some would come to sit with the body during the day, some would come during the evening, and some would come during the night," she said. "They would take turns. That way there was always someone with the body. It was never left alone. But most of the time, it was Grandma that stayed there, to see that everything was done right." Rose went on to say that "they don't do like they used to; where they would reminisce of the person's life. They would laugh too." At the wakes, Rose witnessed that, "when it was a man, there were more men. And when it was a woman, there were more women."

Women were in charge of the food at wakes and funerals, which was plentiful, and Marie even had memories of women cooking and sending food up to the site where the men were burying the corpse. In addition to overseeing the cooking, elderly women managed wakes and funerals through the rhythm of keening. Maria described these old-lady roles at wakes she attended:

> There were the old ladies that looked after getting the body ready; getting it all dressed and packing it with medicine, and making sure the casket looked nice. The others would supervise the cooking, and making it into a celebration.

> There were customs that they would bring in that were very old. They would make us cry, for example. The old ladies would come in and they would just wail—do this keening that would make everybody cry. And then, when you finished crying, they would bring out tea, and sit around laughing and telling stories in little groups. Singing songs or whatever. And then it would be time to do the whole thing all over again. You would do that four times during the night for the whole time of the wake.

It was the grandmothers and aunties as well who relayed the protocols of what to do after the burial. "We were told that when the person was buried then we had to turn around," she said. "We turned around clockwise and we would walk out of that graveyard and never look back; we weren't supposed to say that person's name again. We put them out of our mind for a whole year. Because they needed to make their journey, and it was not up to you to make that journey harder for them. And if you cried or talked about them, then you were keeping them there."

Maria added that her great-aunt "was very strict about that; there was no kindness in her voice when she was telling you, 'This is what you have to do: don't be sitting around crying because you're just doing it for yourself.'" At the end of this first year, there would be a feast for the person, at which point it would be acceptable to talk about the person once again. And again, it was the old ladies who governed these processes.

Birth and death were the purview of old ladies and this allowed them to make connections between life in this domain and death in the spirit world. As Maria said, "It's an old lady that brings you in, and an old lady that takes you out."

Conclusion

Elderly women held the fires of their nations in a number of ways. They were often the heads of their families, or the *gii maa kwe* that looked out for the safety and well-being of the community and held everyone together. As storytellers, they acted as keepers of the laws, as demonstrated in the example that Maria provided about the laws around incest. As midwives, doctors, and herbalists, they held responsibilities for the health of the collective. As teachers, they ensured that everyone learned their own responsibilities and was able to live up to them. As keepers of relationships and doorkeepers to the spirit world, they ensured that "all our relations" (human, spirit, and those with the natural world) were intact.

Their authority increased with age, but their leadership was also earned through action. This leadership was recognized by the community; as Gertie said, "There wasn't a ceremony or anything like that. But there was an acknowledgement that [*gii maa kwe*] had responsibility." With age and experience, women also graduated through different stages of elderhood. Although the historian participants did not speak to the categories of "community," "ceremonial," and "earth-elder" provided by Mosôm Danny, some of these distinctions can be seen in the different roles played by the elders in their stories. Younger elders took more active roles in the physical and community work of midwifery, for example, while older great-grandmothers were visited for counsel and called upon for leadership. The clearest example of this distinction comes out in Maria's stories, in which we can see the "doing" work of her grandmothers and the ultimate authority of her great-grandmother, who was the final decision maker.

The elder years were a powerful time of life, in which women were able to move in all circles of the community. The work that old ladies did with plants also points to the strength of their connection with the earth at this stage, and their work as "doorkeepers to the spirit world" is an acknowledgement of their highly evolved spiritual connection. This was no time for retirement, for as Mosôm Danny said, "Old age was a very productive stage of life."[23] Amelia Paget's observation seems to have been true that the old women carried the torch, "always watching to see that the spark did not die out."[24]

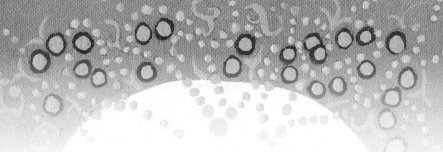

Conclusion

Bundling the Layers:
Building on the Strengths of the Past
to Take Us into the Future

I began this book with intentions of "digging up the medicines" that might further contribute to the healing and decolonization of our communities. As I finish, I can offer some reflections on how I addressed these goals, with the hope that others will be inspired to engage in the dialogue and work through their own reflections and conclusions. In Chapter 2, I referred to the work of Keith Basso, who documented how stories "work like arrows" among the Apache. My hope is that as I launch this book into Indian country and the world beyond, it will work like an arrow, piercing the injustices of our past and slicing open more avenues for change. I encourage each reader to dig out the medicines that suit his or her particular needs, and continue to dig, as there is so much more to learn.

It is important to remember that the period of history that encompasses the stories in this book was a traumatic one for Aboriginal peoples in Canada. The historian participants could have told stories about the disruption, poverty, racism, and abuse that they endured when they were growing up in the 1930s, 1940s, and 1950s. Instead, we documented stories that delineate a world view that can help us shape our current realities. We live with the legacy of our colonial history today, and many of our families and communities continue to be in a state of crisis. In spite of it all, we have avenues of hope and vision; avenues which are cultured and advanced through the oral histories of our elders. In seeking out and listening to these stories, we engage in an act of decolonization; we engage in a way of imagining a stronger way of life, one which belongs to us because it comes from our peoples and our past.

Like any good Indigenous story, there are many different layers of meaning. Some layers may only reveal themselves to me or to readers over time. For now I can briefly speak to what I learned about the power and place of women and girls in these land-based societies; about how the life stage theory of the Anishinaabek is manifest in these histories; and how these social relations contributed to the health and well-being of the individual, family, and community. I conclude with thoughts on how we can apply this knowledge in our communities today and in those of the future. To build on this forward-looking vision, I have incorporated parts of a discussion from an interview with psychologist Jane Middelton-Moz, with whom I visited in the final stages of my writing to talk about the needs of Indian country today.

Layer One: The Power of Women and Girls

When I was in the early stages of researching, Mosôm Danny told me that "women were the centre and core of our community and our nation. No nation ever existed without the fortitude of our grandmothers, and all of those teachings have to be somehow recovered." I discovered there were many ways in which the power of women and girls was honoured during this historical period, in spite of the incursions of patriarchy and violence that were also present. As my sample size of oral historians was relatively small, there is no way of claiming whether their experiences were typical of northern Algonquian communities at the time. Customs and practices can also vary from family to family and from community to community, and the participants I interviewed covered a wide geographic area. The oral histories nonetheless offer some idea about "how it was" for women and girls among the Michif, Nēhiyawak, and Anishinaabek, from the 1930s through to the 1960s, and help us to see that they had some distinct strengths and authorities.

In terms of authorities related to sexual and reproductive health, women during this period had definitely lost some ground, as there was evidence in both the literature and the stories of family planning practices that had existed but had been disrupted over time. Talk about family planning and the use of contraceptive and abortifacient medicines is still difficult in Indigenous communities, in part due to long-standing fears coming out of historical repression on the part of the church. In the case of the oral historians, the large number of children in many of their families demonstrates that family planning was not practised as it might have been in preceding generations. But there were still some "old ladies" who hung onto family planning knowledge and made it available, as it was traditionally their role to manage this area. As in the case of Maria's grandmother, who tried to give her mother some medicines to prevent another life-threatening pregnancy, this work often had to be done in a climate of secrecy and resistance. But it was done—this I know of from other stories that people are still not willing to share in print!

Traditional and women-centred approaches to pregnancy were less controversial, and thus more likely to be openly practised. In traditional ways, pregnancy allowed for the honouring and care of women, and was grounded in a reverence for the power within women to give life. The historian participants talked about how pregnancy was viewed as a sacred time that was supported by all members of the community. Pregnancy was an area that also continued to be managed by women. Until the mid-1950s, when Western male doctors and hospital care began to be more common, pregnancy, birth, and postpartum care were under the authority of "old lady" midwives, some of whom offered extensive attention in the prenatal and postpartum periods. Their significant role in catching incoming life and managing a child's transition into community is a demonstration of a uniquely feminine power; a power that allowed women to be a conduit between the spirit and earthly worlds.

In the infant, toddler, and early childhood years, gender was apparently not a significant factor in terms of identity or experience. Children of both sexes were cared for by grandparents, who taught them their first skills in hunting and harvesting and instructed them in the philosophies and life ways of the people. It is significant that both boys and girls often learned these things from their grannies. Maria's story about "old lady hunting" in which children learned from the senior lifegivers how to take another life speaks to the authority of women to shape the responsible providers of the future. The intent and outcome was to raise children who respected life in all its forms.

Early on, both girls and boys were shown respect as incoming members of the community, and they were celebrated for what they might contribute in the future. During the toddler years, girls were acknowledged for their work in the same manner as boys, through the burying of the placenta and umbilical cord and through walking-out ceremonies. Gender separation began as children started to take on the work tasks of adult life, and the separation became much more pronounced after puberty.

At puberty, youth were traditionally celebrated in ceremonies that recognized the distinct power associated with one's gender.[1] As Carol Markstrom has documented, puberty ceremonies for girls in a number of Indigenous cultures have traditionally been about recognizing the power of the feminine.[2] This is a power that is so strong that the effective management of it was considered important in terms of maintaining health and balance in the universe. I did not capture stories related to this level of power, but Marie's story of her sister's puberty seclusion was a demonstration of the ongoing belief in the healing power of pubescent girls. The story of Marie's own puberty seclusion also demonstrates the unfortunate disruption and the need to hide or alter these practices as a result of the oppression of Indigenous ceremonies by church and state. Marie was kept home from school during her seclusion, but the real reason for this was not shared, even with members of her own family. It was heartening to learn, however, that families like Gertie's created their own new ceremonies to mark this passage where puberty seclusions of previous generations were not possible.

As adults, men and women had distinct responsibilities, authorities, and even spaces that they occupied, but it is important to note that in land-based cultures one was not considered more important than the other. Everyone had work to do, and all work was valid in terms of keeping the community alive. Women were respected for the ways in which they managed material and human resources, and given authority accordingly. The women in the historian participants' families worked at hunting, trapping, and trading, and in some cases lived without husbands, but with the support of the community.

The value placed on their community-centred work meant that women had their own circles or "jurisdictions" in which they were in charge of not only the material resources but also the social relations of the community. As "keepers of relationships," they formed strong bonds among themselves and were responsible for teaching the family laws to the youngsters. This was recognized as a source of authority, for as the first teachers, women held considerable influence. In other areas of power and jurisdiction, women in their childbearing age were also considered so strong that they needed to stay away from the tools of men's labour, lest they "tangle" with the powers that men held. In traditional Algonquian ways, menstruation had the power to heal or to kill, and women were respected and honoured for this power.

As women aged and passed through menopause, they were given a new kind of respect that allowed them to move in and out of male and female jurisdictions, and they were recognized for their leadership. Stories about the grandmothers' leadership positions demonstrate some of the counter-imperial authorities I had been looking for as I set out to write the book. There were a number of elderly women in the participants' stories who were leaders in their extended families; the *gii maa kwe* (head woman) was the final decision maker in many cases.

I believe we have much to gain from holding on to the image of Maria's great-grandmother standing up and having the final word at a meeting in which the government was trying to reorganize traplines. Rene's grannie Kitchi Gabwik standing against the winds of change can help us with a decolonizing vision or with imagining "another state of affairs." We now live with male-dominated politics adopted from the colonizer, and it is liberating to see this was not always our way. Even though there had been half a century of colonial interference in Indigenous traditional governance systems, old ladies often held a significant role in terms of governance because of the respect and authority they maintained in the extended family system. Old ladies were valued for how they looked after the communities through their attention to kinship and by how they managed the health, well-being, and spirit connections of community members. As with the younger women, the old ladies in the participants' stories worked hard to ensure the survival of the community, contributing to the very end.

Layer Two: Connecting the Stories to Life Stage Theory

I have long harboured an interest in how life stage theories of the Anishinaabek played out in the lives of people who lived in land-based communities of the past. The historian participants' stories allowed me to make some of those connections and to continue to wonder about others.

In the physical journey through the "four hills of life," as described by Anishinaabe writer Basil Johnston, young life was supposed to be both cherished and protected. This came through in the participants' stories about the kind of protocols and precautions that were undertaken with pregnant women and infants. When children began to climb the "second hill," the nurturing continued, but there were increasing demands that children acquire the disciplines of adult life, which they learned through work and a spirit of self-reliance. In Johnston's four hills theory, this was a stage of preparation, which culminated at puberty and the vision quest. Stories from the elders in this study demonstrated that children were prepared through nurturing, relationship building, and the expectations that were placed upon them to fulfill age-appropriate duties and responsibilities. As adults climbing the third hill, women were said to be charged with caregiving and providing for their families and communities. This came through in accounts about the tremendous amount of work that the elders witnessed among their mothers, aunts, and grandmothers. Finally, the teaching and leadership roles described in teachings about the fourth hill were evident in the historian participants' stories about the authorities they witnessed among their grandmothers. The three phases of elderhood described by Mosôm Danny were not as clear, but some distinctions could be made between the roles of grandmothers and great-grandmothers in some of the participants' families.

The moral journey that Johnston refers to, involving preparation, quest, vision, and fulfillment of the vision was not as clear in the stories shared by the historian participants. Within the first two stages, there was some evidence of attention to this spiritual trajectory, as naming ceremonies and protocols around the placenta, umbilical cord, and infant care were about connecting infants and children to spirit helpers to ensure their health and longevity. The disciplines that were expected of children could also be seen as part of the preparation that the moral journey required. These disciplines would have certainly helped children to endure the sacrifice and perseverance that would have been required of them during the quest undertaken at puberty. Although some of the participants did a puberty seclusion, it wasn't clear whether they received moral guidance or spiritual direction that was particular to their purpose in life. Likewise, it is not possible to know whether or how the women and elders in the participants' stories fulfilled their personal visions, although there are some glimpses of this in some stories. It is possible, for example, that the grannies who governed Rene's community according to their names were working with visions they had acquired, but there is not enough information about their lifelong spiritual trajectory to say this for certain.

As the moral journey was often a very personal one, it is not surprising that there is little opportunity to track this path as it occurred for individuals. Some of the general material, however, can be linked to Mosôm Danny's teaching about life being a journey in which one's spirit strives to learn about the physical world. As noted in the introduction, Danny teaches that the spirit is more conscious in the earliest stages of life and we spend our lifetimes in pursuit of reawakening the spirit as we journey "home." Within the stories, we find an acknowledgement that infants and elders were closest to the spirit world; there was an understanding that they stood at the doorways that represented entering and then leaving this world. Rebecca shared that infants were thought to have the spirit pulsing inside them, and Marie was taught to take care in how one talked around babies because of the risk that the infant might pass back into the spirit world. In Marie's community, it was also understood that elders and infants could communicate with one another, presumably because they shared an affinity with the "other side." This may be one of the reasons that elders and infants spent so much time together, as depicted in Elsie's and Maria's memories of infants swinging in hammocks above the elders as they sat visiting in tents during the summer. Elders were also charged with naming infants, which not only renewed connection with the spirit world but also affirmed the life force represented by new life meeting with the old. The affinity that elders had with the spirit world also meant that they were charged with catching those coming in from the spirit world and with releasing those who were returning to it. This came out very clearly in stories about the duties of midwives and older women in general.

Layer Three: Contributions to the Health and Well-Being of Native Communities

Health, as it is understood among Algonquian and other Indigenous peoples, includes physical, mental, emotional, and spiritual dimensions, and health is also something that is not individual but collective. We are, thus, only as healthy as are all our relations in all the dimensions. I was interested in finding out how life stage roles and responsibilities factor into the fulfillment of health according to this definition.

Physical health was ideally attended to through care and nurturing, particularly of the young and old, and mentally, there was a respect for the autonomy of the individual as he or she made his or her way through the learning process of life. But it is the social as well as the spiritual components of health that demonstrate some of the more distinct notions of health and well-being among northern Algonquian peoples. The concept of *mino pimatisiwin* ("living a good life") came through in the stories, demonstrating the social and spiritual influences in how health was cultivated and maintained. At one point, for example, Maria commented that "culture" comes from "the way that people live together, the way that people treat each other, the way they interact with one another." Maria then added, "That's kinship; in Cree [this concept is captured within] *mino pimatisiwin*. Living a good life." Health and well-being were contingent on how well one managed relations; all of one's relations, including those with the human community, the land, and the spirit world. Life stage teachings, roles, and responsibilities were set up to facilitate all of these types of relationships.

In terms of human relationship building in the community, Mosôm Danny teaches that belonging was actively fostered from the earliest stages of life. Some of the elders told stories that are fitting with the adage "It takes a community to raise a child." Sylvia, Elsie, and Madeleine noted that they had many "grandparents" in the community, and this created a sense of security and belonging for them. Family and community members used kinship names to address and refer to one another, and this consistently reinforced the relationships, roles, and responsibilities they carried towards each other. Youngsters learned that they could count on being the recipients of care but that they also had a responsibility to contribute to the care of others.

This manifestation of reciprocity is evident when one considers how children were expected to assist their elders. Responsibility was an important part of engendering a sense of purpose, and the milestones of the young in particular were honoured and recognized. Danny's and Rene's stories about their first kill and first catch show how children learned that their contributions to community survival were valued. Girls who underwent traditional puberty ceremonies learned the strength of their power and how it could influence community well-being.

The focus on relationship building demonstrates how individual and community health and well-being were connected: as noted, the health of the individual was understood to be the health of the collective and vice versa. This notion stretched forward and backward in time, for disruptions to the chain of ancestors and the life yet to come could affect community members in the present. Within the human domain, the way in which community members connected across the generations was critical to the health and well-being of the present-day and future community. Relationships between elders and children were considered critical in terms of maintaining the life force and survival of the people. This was beautifully demonstrated in Mandelbaum's description of elders taking and smoking tobacco out of the pouch in which the child's umbilical cord was stored. Elders and children thus worked closely to maintain the circular connection between spirit, new life, and a life fulfilled, and adults in their middle years took care of the old and the young so they could do this work. In the end, everyone had a job to do, and the balance of responsibilities that took place between these stages upheld the order and life force of the people.

Layer Four: Applying Story Medicine, Today, and into the Future

As the primary intention of this book is to assist with decolonizing our communities, and restoring health and healing, it is worth finishing with some thoughts on how these history lessons apply. After I finished writing the life stage chapters, I decided to talk about them with Jane Middelton-Moz, a psychologist who does remarkable community-based intervention and healing work in Indigenous communities all over North America. Jane is internationally known for her work with adult children of alcoholics; multi-generational grief and trauma in individuals, families, and communities; sexual abuse and sexual assault, ethnic and cultural awareness; anger; and cultural self-hate, and has written a number of books in these areas. A person of mixed ancestry that includes the Anishinaabek, Jane has devoted much of her career to Indigenous health and well-being. Her work involves reconnecting the generations within Indigenous communities and helping them to take it upon themselves to rebuild "the circle," as discussed below. As Jane often works with communities who are in crisis, our discussion centred on reinstating the circle among those communities most in need. Yet the lessons I took from talking with Jane can be applied to a broad spectrum of people and situations, as they are about strengthening ourselves through family and community.

The circle, as it took shape in our discussion, encompassed notions of accountability and responsibility, nurturing, and care. Jane talked about how her six-day community intervention workshops are "based on bringing [people] back to the circle" to take up these roles. One vision of this circle can be found in the life stage wheel used by the Ontario Federation of Indian Friendship Centres, which I outlined in the introductory chapter. This wheel demonstrates the valued contributions of everyone in the circle, as everyone has a "job" to do. Another way of reflecting family and community cohesion is the concentric circle diagram I used in Chapter 5 (Figure 5.1), in which children sit at the heart of the community and are surrounded by elders, women, and men, in that order. The balance of this system lies in the interconnected roles and responsibilities of all members of the community.

As I have written in Chapter 4 and elsewhere,[3] the circle was blown apart when residential schools ripped the children—the heart—out of the community. In the preface, Maria writes about the shattering of *wahkotowin*, the system through which we were connected to "all our relations." The removal and abuse of children was one of the worst elements in this shattering. Like a silent bomb that went off in every community, this blow left heartbroken elders without children to teach, men who were traumatized by their inability to protect, and women who were left trying to manage the unmanageable. Alcoholism, depression, and suicide were not long to follow.

In our interview, Jane pointed out that one of the most devastating consequences of intergenerational trauma is "learned helplessness." Over time, many of our people have lost the ability to see how they might change their circumstances for the better. This is a direct result of the powerlessness experienced from watching our lands, children, and cultural ways being taken from us and having no recourse to address the injustice. Learned helplessness begets more trauma, and so the cycle continues, with lateral violence (when those that are oppressed oppress each other)[4] and social dysfunction taking up where colonial policies left off. Pretty soon the oppressor doesn't need to fight us anymore, because we are fighting amongst ourselves.

The learned helplessness response, however, is relatively recent, for according to the stories of the elders in this book, practices of independence and interdependence were still operating within many of their childhood communities only fifty years ago. The parenting styles they described were based on a belief that the autonomy of the individual needed to be respected. Children were thus taught to be self-reliant while learning a sense of responsibility to the community. There was reciprocity in care, for children were expected to help their caregivers, and particularly their elders. Children were also expected to learn the disciplines and work skills that they would need in adult years. This is perhaps not unlike how farm children were raised at the time, although the means of instilling this discipline would have been distinct. As European observers had noted over the centuries, non-coercive and indirect techniques were the hallmark of Indigenous childrearing. Mosôm Danny also pointed out that it was considered vital to treat children well, as the nurturing they received fostered the sense of trust and loyalty that would instill discipline and assist with community survival.

While there are Indigenous families that have held on to elements, practices, and principles of traditional childrearing, Jane sees the loss of these ways in many of the communities she works with. She spoke about this loss in the context of intergenerational trauma and the sense of powerlessness that keeps people trapped:

I think that part of the horrendous effect of colonial oppression is that it kept people helpless, without a voice. People suffered tremendously from the pain of residential school, and frequently came home to parents and extended family who had begun drinking after the heartbreaking experience of having their children taken away. Issues of abandonment, lack of parental contact, and breakdown in the culture were never addressed. The next generation suffered from the alcoholism, addictions, depression, and pain that their parents carried because they did not have the support or validation to resolve their painful experiences in the residential schools or the losses and disconnection they experienced when they returned home. Today, many parents are suffering from generations of pain, and they want to give their children everything. They have difficulty holding their children accountable and responsible in the old way because if the children or youth feel pain or disappointment, it triggers the parents' pain, so they give in to the demands or withdraw the limits. They often overindulge their children in order to give them the things that they were denied instead of holding them responsible and accountable in the traditional way.

When we work with the youth in communities, we frequently find that they, too, are carrying generational shame. The shame stems from growing up with feelings of abandonment in families where there is active addiction and children are frequently taking on the parental role, often raising their brothers and sisters—or from growing up in families where parents are trying to make up for past addiction or pain and not holding their children accountable for anything. Both families produce shame in youth.

Jane talked about the consequences of "rendering youth powerless," going on to say, "We've got some youth bullying community or family members while adults watch and do nothing ... adults not setting or holding on to limits, letting the children and teens run the family by giving in to inappropriate demands. This is happening because the generational pain and cultural oppression has not been addressed and the strength of the old ways has been interrupted and not been passed on."

This loss of independence and interdependence can be seen affecting other areas of community well-being. Jane referred to the "pyramid model" that replaces "the circle" in situations of oppression: in this model, the dispossessed majority at the base of the pyramid look up to the few in positions of power at the top of the pyramid to provide them with solutions. This stands in contrast to the personal stories recounted earlier regarding traditional upbringing, where children learned from the earliest age that they had to take on responsibility for themselves and for others. They also learned to trust that if they contributed to the circle, the circle would look after them. Jane pointed out that when people stop going to each other for support, it renders the community and the people in the circle even more powerless.

Trauma and the resulting addictions have also interrupted the healthy life cycle flow for individuals, which can throw off the balance between care and responsibility in the community. In the introductory chapter, I referred to Elder Liza Mosher's contention that one can get "stuck" at any point along the life cycle continuum. Jane spoke further to how this was one of the outcomes of colonial imposed trauma. In her workshops, she has participants draw a circle that includes each of the four quadrants representing the four hills of life: child, youth, adult, and elder. She tells them:

> If you experience trauma in childhood that is not resolved, you carry that pain into the next stage of your life. Youth often begin drinking and use other addictions in order to make the pain go away. Then, the drinking or addictions begin to cause the pain, a continuous cycle that does not end until the trauma has been addressed. By the time you reach adulthood, the time of giving back, you don't have the tools because you missed lessons of the earlier life stages. And when you move into the Elder stage of life you may have white hair and have grown older but you don't carry the wisdom of the prior life stages because they have been interrupted by the trauma-addiction cycle. Once healing has taken place, an individual can take their rightful place in the life cycle once again.

Jane noted that when she works with people on the life cycle wheel, "they understand right away." She added, "What I find is [that] some old people become powerful 'Elders' once they have worked through their pain."

This picture of communities dispossessed by colonization is bleak, but the good news is that there is incredible strength and knowledge in Aboriginal communities today, especially among those who are taking up a healing path. As Jane pointed out, dispossession and learned helplessness have not been in our communities for long, and the memory and knowledge of how "the circle" works is there. As I have tried to demonstrate with this book, the circle is available to us because it is alive in the memories, experiences, and story medicines of elders living today.

There are also threads and components of the circle that are still active in many families and communities. Although they do not have the same respect, authority, or support for this work that they once had, women still hold a place in terms of managing the social relations of the community. Jane commented that it is typically women who bring her in to do community healing work, although men are becoming more and more engaged in the healing of their communities. As facilitators, Jane's team works to empower the women in this work:

> I think women are really invested in what is happening to their communities, and they are especially concerned with the future of our youth. What I've been saying for a very long time is, "Give me your natural helpers to train, because that's who will change and empower communities. Give me those role models and natural helpers; midwives, healthy elders and respected community members. In fact, sometimes I ask youth to honour an adult in the community by bringing them up and dancing for them. It is often the unseen one or one of the quietest women in the community who is honoured by the youth for her compassion and her welcoming home. She has quietly just taken youth in for years, providing them a safe place and compassionately encouraging them to voice their feelings and concerns.

Training and support for the women in the community thus help them to strengthen the roles they continue to play as leaders in community well-being. Jane's intervention work is valuable because often women take on these roles without proper acknowledgement or support. In communities where men and children have been disempowered with learned helplessness, the result can be that women end up doing it all. This is not a circle.

After considering the power of women and girls as discussed above, I wonder how different our communities might look if we honoured all young girls for their sacredness and their potential, and if we granted the wise "old ladies" the role they once had in governing their families and communities. I was intrigued by Rene's assertion that once the old ladies no longer had control, the violence and dysfunction set in. What would happen if we were to truly reintegrate and value the sacred feminine and, by association, the power of the lifegivers? I believe that change would happen; at the very least, we would see a decrease in the high levels of violence against our women.

In the meantime, Native women continue to play key roles in advancing family and community healing. Jane pointed out that it is often a love for children that brings women to the healing path and the quest for change. This focus on children is a trait that has been observed from the earliest points of contact. As I pointed out in Chapter 4, seventeenth-century Jesuits remarked on "the excessive love of their offspring" when referring to Indigenous child-rearing. Jane commented that of all the cultural groups she works with, it is Native people who consistently tell her they want to heal for their children. She remarked, "Caring for kids is why I am invited into communities," adding, "unfortunately a lot of times people have hit bottom because of the suicides of children and youth." Children thus continue to sit at the heart of Indigenous communities, but this can be buried under layers of oppression, learned helplessness, and addiction.

The power of the circle also still exists, and when needed it shows itself. Speaking of contemporary Indigenous communities that she works with, Jane said, "You may not always see the kind of connectedness that you write about in your book. You may see more lateral violence (people putting down and oppressing each other)—unless there is a crisis. When a crisis occurs, hands down, everybody goes back to that old way." She connected the notion of power to the ability to contribute to the circle once again, stressing that all community members need to have a role in the work that needs to be done. She noted that people have asked her recently, "Jane, how come we can come together when there is a crisis?" Jane's answer: "Because you have power." She explained:

> Oppression has rendered people powerless. Oppression has ren-
> dered the system broken. And even though I believe in counselling
> and health care, and a lot of western healing methods ... when we
> don't empower the silent majority, when we don't empower the
> natural helpers, when we don't empower the Elder men and women,
> we run into trouble. Instead we have brick buildings where people
> are supposed to come for help, and we frequently disempower the
> community. When a crisis like an ice storm, death or illness in the
> community occurs, people return to the circle and offer their help

in a traditional way because they feel empowered in that they have something to offer. This often occurs more rapidly in Indigenous communities because there is still an innate sense of the power of the circle and the community.

In many contemporary Indigenous communities, however, Jane pointed out that "unless there is a crisis, people frequently don't feel empowered to offer help in the old way."

She then told a story that demonstrates how we can begin to empower children and youth by offering them opportunities to contribute. In this story, she took on the disciplinary role of a modern-day "auntie" while conducting a workshop in a Native community:

> I'll never forget two fourteen-year-old girls who were continuously acting out during a community intervention. It was lunch time. No matter what group or race I'm working with, I always ask the Elders to eat first. The girls ignored me, went to the head of the line and began piling food on their plates.
>
> I went up to them and said, "Do you know what an auntie is?" And they said, "No."
>
> I said, "Well I am going to be your auntie this week…. You need to get out of line, now."
>
> They told me to go eff myself, and I said, "Well you know, that's not going to happen."
>
> "Who do you think you are?"
>
> I said, "I'm leading the workshop. Do you want credit this week? Yeah? Okay, then you come with me."
>
> I explained to them, "You and I are going to serve all the people lunch this week and we are going to eat last. Because I'm your auntie, and you have disrespected the circle, you are going to help me."
>
> We served the people lunch for the entire week. We ate lunch together and shared many stories. At the end of the week, the two beautiful young women said they had never felt so proud in their life. It was one of the first times they felt like they had actually contributed to their community. By giving to others, they took their rightful place in the circle.

Jane concluded, "Perhaps if I had made the same intervention in the dominant culture, I would have had to spend time explaining what an auntie was, or the reason why it is important to honour our Elders by feeding them first. These young women knew why we were doing this. They just didn't know how to get to the place of feeling that power inside themselves." This example speaks to the sense of belonging and purpose that can be nurtured and fostered according to life stage theory. Community cohesion and a sense of belonging comes from one's sense of being able to contribute to one's community.

As previously noted, health—and the good life—is not something that belongs to the individual, and so individual solutions will not work. It must come back to the circle, and this is what Jane tries to encourage within her practice. She talked about the need for collective healing in Indigenous communities, based on traditional ways of intergenerational connection:

> When an Indigenous person begins healing from grief and trauma, they are often craving the safety of ceremony, tradition and that web of support that only the circle of community can offer. I often say in communities: if you are going to send youth to alcohol treatment facilities, don't send one, send five. Native people have an innate memory of the power of the circle and a need to belong. It's not every man for himself. It is important when youth come back that they have the support of the circle.
>
> By sending people individually to treatment, we often set them up to fail.... Sending someone from each generation would be the most empowering intervention a community could make. When I work with entire families or the entire community, rather than working with people individually, I have experienced people making dramatic changes in their lives.... Empowerment lies within the support of the circle and the strength of the web.

A lot of Jane's work with Indigenous communities involves reconnecting the generations. In community-intervention workshops, Jane's team brings youth and adults together every morning and afternoon and works with them separately during the day. Their sharing throughout the week fosters communication and connection between generations and empowers the strength of community. She remarked on the hunger that Native youth have for healthy elders in their lives, and for Native culture and tradition:

> One of the games we play with the adults and youth is "Walk Across the Room If...." We ask many questions that participants can begin to answer and thus begin to have a voice. One of the questions that

is always asked is: "Walk across the room if you would like an Elder in your life." I have never been in a Native community where *every* youth, no matter how tough they look, doesn't walk across the room. When we do this exercise and I say, "If you would like to learn more about your culture and tradition …" —every one of them walks. Every single one of them.

Jane and her team work at connecting youth with healthy elders in their communities, a harkening back to intergenerational and life stage roles and responsibilities. In some cases, this involves working with "pro-social consequences" for children who are starting to get into trouble with bullying or other problems in school. They ask children to do things like chop wood for an elder, visit an elder, and inquire about cultural values or ask for stories. "What it really is, is re-entering the circle; feeling a sense of giving and belonging and going back to the way it was before," Jane said. "When communities begin healing, the girls often want to be with the women for women's groups. They have sewing groups, they do beading and talking. And the kids want to continue that as well as the older women."

Jane pointed out that youth want to engage in traditional activities, and they tell this to the adults in their workshops: "Their list of needs always has to do with Indigenous practices and values: 'We love it when you take us hunting. We love it when you take us berry picking.'" Re-establishing relations with the natural world is also significant in terms of connecting with "all our relations." As Jane said, "I find that when people are actually on the land, when they are out in the summer berry picking or hunting, they are in balance the way they used to be. The youth hunger for this return to tradition. They are hungry for connection and belonging."

In their interviews, some of the historian participants told stories about how every elder in their childhood community was a grandmother or grandfather to them. This can be reinstated by building relationships among people who are ready to take up their intergenerational responsibilities. Jane remarked, "I'll never forget this beautiful old man who was living with his adult children who were suffering from addictions and were hitting him frequently. He was often afraid. A youth in the workshop was living with parents who were beating him. The old man and the boy traditionally adopted each other in the community intervention. The boy said, 'I'll take care of you,' and the old man said, 'I'll take care of you.' These connections and traditional adoptions are only an opportunity away."

Through the literature and the historian participants' stories, we learned that ceremony was traditionally significant in terms of managing life stage transitions and in fostering overall health and wellness. Jane commented that when it comes to healing in contemporary Indigenous communities, ceremony "overwhelmingly works." Many families and communities have reintroduced naming ceremonies, walking-out ceremonies, and puberty fasts or seclusions similar to those described in this book. But as Jane pointed out, there can also be new ceremonies, "simple things" that work equally well. In some of the communities she has worked with, for example, they have created a ceremony for welcoming the elders home from residential school: "Going to the place where the planes took them, and just having adults and youth in the community to welcome them home ... the level of grief and sadness and healing that occurs just in a simple welcoming is profound." In other situations, Jane and her team create ceremonies whereby different sectors of the community (men, women, adults, children, youth, elders) create ceremonies to honour one another, or to conduct traditional adoptions. All of this work engages the community in rebuilding the circle.

Although a lot of the work Jane describes takes place in reserve or reservation communities, the principles behind rebuilding the circle, and the lessons of the story medicines, can be applied in urban settings. I have certainly worked at doing this in my own life in a small urban centre in Ontario. As I stated in the acknowledgements, it was the birth of my own children that inspired me to seek out this knowledge, as I wanted to tap into the genius of our peoples and cultures to help me raise strong and responsible community members. I have used my new knowledge about ceremony to honour them as they pass through the milestones of childhood and adolescence; something I was not party to in my upbringing in the 1960s. I have also tried to build families and communities of the heart in the urban settings where we find ourselves, and I am constantly looking for ways to encourage a spirit of self-reliance, independence, and accountability to community. Making connections with the natural world is also critical, and it is important to remember that the natural world is all around us no matter where we live.

As a member of an urban Indigenous community, I also try to find ways that I can be a good "auntie" to the families of the heart that we create in these settings. One way is through mentoring students that I work with in academic settings. I also appreciate how blessed I am to have many grandmothers and grandfathers, aunties and uncles all across the country who can teach and guide me in the ways of our people. And after writing this book, I now have a few more relatives in the greater Turtle Island Indigenous community.

Rebuilding the circle in whatever context we find ourselves in is a work in progress, and we must be creative to find means of reinstating the position of women, connecting with all our relations and picking up those pieces that were left scattered because of colonial interference. But we have tremendous resources, and we have great reason for hope. As Jane said, "It's coming back. As soon as you empower people to take their position where it was [in the circle] and give them the power, then what happens is they will rebuild it. And it happens everywhere I go."

Notes

Introduction

1   I use the term "Elder" with a capital "E" to refer to someone who is a recognized spiritual and cultural leader in an Aboriginal community. I use the term "elder" with a small "e" to refer to community members who are seniors but who do not necessarily hold this type of leadership position.

2   Mosôm is a Cree word meaning "grandfather," and it denotes the role that Danny plays as an Elder to the large community he serves. I prefer it to the term Elder, although the two are interchangeable for the purpose they serve in this book.

3   See Kim Anderson, "Native Women, the Body, Land, and Narratives of Contact and Arrival," in *Storied Communities: The Role of Narratives of Contact and Arrival in Constituting Political Community*, ed. Hester Lessard, Jeremy Webber, and Rebecca Johnson (Vancouver: UBC Press, 2010).

4   There are many terms used to refer to the first peoples of the Americas. I typically use "Native" when referring to first peoples in Canada (simply because this is the term I use the most in community settings) and "Indigenous" when I am speaking more broadly or to indicate an international context.

5   Michif, Nēhiyawak, and Anishinaabek are known as Métis, Cree, and Ojibway or Saulteaux in English. In this work, I use both the English and original language terms, as these terms are also used interchangeably at the community level. I also wish to make the distinction between Ojibway and Saulteaux at times, and use the English terms for this purpose.

6   Numerous Indigenous scholars see work on Indigenous knowledge and history as a project in decolonization. As such, historical research should benefit Indigenous communities and serve as a vehicle for change. See Betty Bastien, *Blackfoot Ways of Knowing: The Worldview of the Siksikaitsitapi* (Calgary: University of Calgary Press, 2004); William J. Ermine, "A Critical Examination of the Ethics of Research Involving Indigenous Peoples" (M.A. thesis, University of Saskatchewan, 2000); Neal McLeod, *Cree Narrative Memory: From Treaties to Contemporary Times* (Saskatoon: Purich Publishing, 2007); Winona Wheeler, "Decolonizing Tribal Histories" (Ph.D. diss., University of California, Berkeley, 2000); and Waziyatawin

Angela Wilson, *Remember This! Dakota Decolonization and the Eli Taylor Narratives* (Lincoln: University of Nebraska Press, 2005).

7　This study is limited in that I did not examine the distinct identities, roles, and responsibilities of two-spirited peoples, those who might be considered in the "third" or "fourth" genders, or trans-gendered peoples. This is important work that remains to be done.

8　The word "teachings" is commonly used among Aboriginal peoples to describe Indigenous knowledge that is passed on through oral tradition. Sto:lo educator Jo-ann Archibald defines teachings as "the cultural values, beliefs, lessons and understandings that are passed from generation to generation." Jo-ann Archibald/ Q'um Q'um Xiiem, *Indigenous Storywork: Educating the Heart, Mind, Body and Spirit* (Vancouver, UBC Press, 2008), 1.

9　I write "traditional" in quotation marks because cultures and societies are constantly changing, as are the traditions that belong to them. This book explores northern Algonquian cultures in which people were still living in close connection to the land. The period covered is that of the storytellers' childhood years, which ranged between the 1930s and the 1960s.

10　Andrea Smith, *Conquest: Sexual Violence and American Indian Genocide* (Cambridge, MA: South End Press, 2005), 15.

11　Kim Anderson, *A Recognition of Being: Reconstructing Native Womanhood* (Toronto: Sumach/Canadian Scholars' Press, 2000).

12　I have modified this phrase from a quote I found in Winona Wheeler's discussion about "the modern historical paradigm." Wheeler quotes the German historian Leopold von Ranke who asserted that "the task of the historian was 'simply to show how it really was.'" See Wheeler, "Decolonizing Tribal Histories," 47.

13　Steven Mintz, "Teaching Family History: An Annotated Bibliography," *OAH Magazine of History* 15, 4 (2001): 11–18.

14　I realize that citizenship is a complicated notion that has attracted the attention of many scholars. In this sense, however, I am simply using it in the way it is defined by Merriam Webster's on-line dictionary, http://www.merriam-webster.com/ dictionary/citizenship.

15　For Cree concepts of *mino-pimatisiwin* as they relate to health, see Michael Hart, *Seeking Mino-Pimatisiwin: An Aboriginal Approach to Helping* (Halifax: Fernwood, 2002); and Naomi Adelson, *"Being Alive Well": Health and the Politics of Cree Well-being* (Toronto: University of Toronto Press, 2000).

16　Basil Johnston, *Ojibway Heritage* (Toronto: McClelland and Stewart, 1976), 112.

17　Ibid., 120.

18　Ibid. 114–115.

19　Ibid., 115.

20　Ibid., 116.

21　Ibid., 112–113.

22　Ibid., 113.

23　Ibid.

24　Ibid., 114–115.

25　Ibid.

26 Ibid., 118.

27 Diane Knight, ed., *The Seven Fires: Teachings of the Bear Clan as Told by Dr. Danny Musqua* (Muskoday First Nation, SK: Many Worlds Publishing, 2001), 55.

28 Ibid., 82.

29 Ibid., 57–58.

30 Ibid., 56–57.

31 Ibid., 62–63.

32 Ibid., 72.

33 Ibid., 84.

34 This framework comes from a popular handout entitled "The Path of Life— Anishinaabe," copyrighted by the Three Fires Midewiwin. The framework is also described by Liza Mosher in her interview entitled "We Have Gone Back to the Original Teachings," in *In the Words of Elders: Aboriginal Cultures in Transition*, ed. Peter Kulchyski, Don McCaskill, and David Newhouse (Toronto: University of Toronto Press, 1999), 141–165.

35 Mosher, "We Have Gone Back to the Original Teachings," 159.

36 Ibid., 159–160.

37 Ontario Federation of Indian Friendship Centres, *For Generations to Come, the Time Is Now: A Strategy for Aboriginal Family Healing* (Toronto: Ontario Federation of Indian Friendship Centres, 1993).

38 Johnston, *Ojibway Heritage*, 112.

39 Advisory Group on Suicide Prevention, *Acting on What We Know: Preventing Youth Suicide in First Nations* (Ottawa: Health Canada, 2002).

Chapter 1: Weaving the Stories

1 See, for example, Jennifer S.H. Brown, *Strangers in Blood: Fur Trade Company Families in Indian Country* (Vancouver: UBC Press, 1980); Jennifer S.H. Brown, "A Cree Nurse in a Cradle of Methodism: Little Mary and the Egerton R. Young Family at Norway House and Berens River," in *First Days, Fighting Days: Women in Manitoba History*, ed. Mary Kinnear (Regina: Canadian Plains Research Center 1987), 19–40; Sarah Carter, *Capturing Women: The Manipulation of Cultural Imagery in Canada's Prairie West* (Montreal: McGill-Queen's University Press, 1997); Sarah Carter, "Categories and Terrains of Exclusion: Constructing the 'Indian Woman' in the Early Settlement Era in Western Canada," in *In the Days of Our Grandmothers: A Reader in Aboriginal Women's History in Canada*, ed. Mary-Ellen Kelm and Laura Townsend (Toronto: University of Toronto Press, 2006), 146–169; Sarah Carter, "First Nations Women of Prairie Canada in the Early Reserve Years, the 1870s to the 1920s: A Preliminary Inquiry," in *Women of the First Nations: Power, Wisdom, and Strength*, ed. Christine Miller and Patricia Chuchryk (Winnipeg: University of Manitoba Press, 1996), 51–75; Nathalie J. Kermoal, *Un passé Métis au féminin* (Quebec: Les Éditions GID, 2006); Rebecca Kugel and Lucy Eldersveld Murphy, *Native Women's History in Eastern North America before 1900: A Guide to Research and Writing* (Lincoln: University of Nebraska Press, 2007); Laura Peers and Jennifer S.H. Brown, "'There is no End to Relationships among the Indians': Ojibway Families and Kinship in Historical Perspective," *The History of the*

Family 4, 4 (1999): 529–555; Susan Sleeper-Smith, *Indian Women and French Men: Rethinking Cultural Encounter in the Western Great Lakes* (Amherst: University of Massachusetts Press, 2001); Sylvia Van Kirk, *"Many Tender Ties": Women in Fur-Trade Society in Western Canada, 1670–1870* (Winnipeg: Watson and Dwyer, 1980).

2   Betty Friedan, *The Feminine Mystique* (New York: Norton, 1963).

3   Edward Ahenakew, *Voices of the Plains Cree* (Toronto: McClelland and Stewart, 1973); Joseph F. Dion, *My Tribe, the Crees* (Calgary: Glenbow Museum, 1979); Fine Day, *My Cree People: A Tribal Handbook* (Invermere, BC: Good Medicine Books, 1973).

4   Maria Campbell, *Halfbreed* (Toronto: McClelland and Stewart, 1973); Jane Willis, *Geniesh: An Indian Girlhood* (Toronto: New Press, 1973); R.M. Vanderburgh, *I am Nokomis Too: The Biography of Verna Patronella Johnston* (Toronto: General Publishing, 1977).

5   Alice Ahenakew, Freda Ahenakew, and H. Christoph Wolfart, *Âh-Âyîtaw Isi ê-kî-Kiskêyihtahkik Maskihkiy. They Knew both Sides of Medicine: Cree Tales of Curing and Cursing* (Winnipeg: University of Manitoba Press, 2000); Emma Minde, Freda Ahenakew, and H. Christoph Wolfart, *Kwayask ê-ki-pê-Kiskinowâpahtihicik. Their Example Showed Me the Way: A Cree Woman's Life Shaped by Two Cultures* (Edmonton: University of Alberta Press, 1997); Glecia Bear, Freda Ahenakew, and H. Christoph Wolfart, *Kohkominawak Otacimowiniwawa: Our Grandmothers' Lives as Told in Their Own Words* (Saskatoon: Fifth House, 1992).

6   Frances Densmore, *Chippewa Customs* (Minneapolis: Ross and Haines, 1970); A. Irving Hallowell, *Ojibwa of Berens River, Manitoba: Ethnography into History*, ed. and with a preface by Jennifer S.H. Brown (Toronto: Harcourt Brace Jovanovich, 1992); M. Inez Hilger, *Chippewa Child Life and Its Cultural Background* (1951; reprint, St. Paul: Minnesota Historical Society Press, 1992); David Goodman Mandelbaum, *Plains Cree: An Ethnographic, Historical, and Comparative Study* (Regina: Canadian Plains Research Center, 1979); Amelia M. Paget, *People of the Plains* (Regina: Canadian Plains Research Center, 2004); Alanson Skinner, *Notes on the Eastern Cree and Northern Saulteaux* (New York: The Trustees, 1911). For later ethnographic work on James Bay Cree women, see Regina Flannery, John S. Long, and Laura L. Peers, *Ellen Smallboy: Glimpses of a Cree Woman's Life* (Montreal: McGill-Queen's University Press, 1995); Regina Flannery, "Infancy and Childhood among the Indians of the East Coast of James Bay," *Anthropos* 57 (1962): 475–482; Regina Flannery, "The Position of Women among the Eastern Cree," *Primitive Man* 8 (1935): 81–86.

7   One must also be aware of the possibility that not all "informants" were respected oral historians in their communities, nor were informants always telling the "truth." As informants were well paid, surely there were some opportunists at work, and the more they talked, the more they got paid!

8   Female ethnographers I referred to in the writing of this book include Densmore, Hilger, Flannery, and Paget. It is worth noting that male bias can still be present in the work of female ethnographers, and that one must always consider the source whether it is male or female. The work of Ruth Landes provides a good example of this. Landes is the only ethnographer of her generation to produce a book-length manuscript exclusively about Algonquian women, a work with the definitive title of *The Ojibwa Woman* (1938; reprint, Lincoln: University of Nebraska Press, 1997). My concerns are with her graphic portrayals of patriarchal

violence, oppression, and abuse among northwestern Ontario Ojibwa in the 1930s, and so I have always found this book hard to read. A product of her time, Landes does not contextualize her depiction of "the Ojibwa woman," nor does she reflect on why her principal informant (a Scots-Cree woman) chose to tell these stories. Rather, the information is presented as definitive of *the* Ojibway woman's experience; patriarchy, violence, and abuse are what Ojibwa culture purportedly had to offer its women. Rayna Green and Eleanor Leacock have criticized *The Ojibwa Woman* as flawed, degrading to women and ethnocentric, the work of an outsider who filtered the information through her own cultural lens and experiences of patriarchy. (See Eleanor Leacock, "Women's Status in Egalitarian Society: Some Implications for Social Evolution," *Current Anthropology* 19, 2 [1978]: 247–276, and Rayna Green, "Review Essay: Native American Women," *Signs* 6 [1980]: 248–267). Sally Cole, Landes's biographer, acknowledges this criticism, but defends the work as valuable because it testifies to "the harsh lives of women in northwestern Ontario in the early years of this century" (Sally Cole, "Dear Ruth: This is the Story of Maggie Wilson, Ojibwa Ethnologist," in *Great Dames*, ed. Elspeth Cameron and Janice Dickin [Toronto: University of Toronto Press, 1997], 75). But as Leacock has demonstrated, *The Ojibwa Woman* warrants a careful read, as it is full of contradictions ("Women's Status in Egalitarian Society," 251). While reviewing *The Ojibwa Woman* for information, I often came to the same conclusion as ethnographer Inez Hilger: that much of the book is not in keeping with information found in other contemporary ethnographies of the Anishinaabek (*Chippewa Child Life and Its Cultural Background*, ix). It does, however, remind one to consider not only historical context but also how experiences can vary between communities and even within families.

9 Winona Wheeler, "Decolonizing Tribal Histories" (Ph.D. diss., University of California, Berkeley, 2000), 79.

10 See Betty Bastien, *Blackfoot Ways of Knowing: The Worldview of the Siksikaitsitapi* (Calgary: University of Calgary Press, 2004), 2; William J. Ermine, "A Critical Examination of the Ethics of Research Involving Indigenous Peoples" (M.A. thesis, University of Saskatchewan, 2000), 83; Neal McLeod, *Cree Narrative Memory: From Treaties to Modern Times* (Saskatoon: Purich Publishing, 2007), 91; Wheeler, "Decolonizing Tribal Histories," 170; Waziyatawin Angela Wilson, *Remember This! Dakota Decolonization and the Eli Taylor Narratives* (Lincoln: University of Nebraska Press, 2005), 1; and Linda Tuhiwai Smith, *Decolonizing Methodologies: Research and Indigenous Peoples* (London: Zed Books, 1999), 29.

11 McLeod, *Cree Narrative Memory*, 91.

12 See Kimberly M. Blaeser, "Writing Voices Speaking: Native Authors and an Oral Aesthetic," in *Talking on the Page: Editing Aboriginal Oral Texts*, ed. Laura J. Murray and Keren Rice (Toronto: University of Toronto Press, 1999), 65; Marlene Brant Castellano, "Updating Aboriginal Traditions of Knowledge," in *Indigenous Knowledges in Global Contexts: Multiple Readings of Our World*, ed. George J. Sefa Dei, Budd L. Hall, and Dorothy Goldin Rosenberg (Toronto: University of Toronto Press, 2000), 23; George L. Cornell, "The Imposition of Western Definitions of Literature on Indian Oral Traditions," in *The Native in Literature: Canadian and Comparative Perspectives*, ed. Thomas King, Cheryl Calver, and Helen Hoy (Toronto: ECW Press, 1987), 176; Kiera Ladner, "Nit-acimonawin oma acimonak ohci: This is My Story About Stories," *Native Studies Review* 11, 2

(1996): 103; and Richard J. Preston, *Cree Narrative: Expressing the Personal Meaning of Events*, 2nd ed. (Montreal: McGill-Queen's University Press, 2002), 64.

13   Raymond D. Fogelson, "The Ethnohistory of Events and Nonevents," *Ethnohistory* 36, 2 (1989): 140.

14   Waziyatawin Angela Wilson, *Remember This!*, 92. See also Harvey Knight's introduction to Saulteaux Elder Alexander Wolfe's collection of stories, which Knight presents as "not merely a presentation of dry material facts of history" but rather "the deep philosophical and spiritual aspects of history." Harvey Knight, introduction to Alexander Wolfe, *Earth Elder Stories: The Pinayzitt Path* (Saskatoon: Fifth House, 1988), ix.

15   Julie Cruikshank, *Life Lived Like a Story: Life Stories of Three Yukon Native Elders* (Lincoln: University of Nebraska Press, 1990), 2, 14.

16   Julie Cruikshank, "The Social Life of Texts: Editing on the Page and in Performance," in *Talking on the Page: Editing Aboriginal Oral Texts*, ed. Laura J. Murray and Keren Rice (Toronto: University of Toronto Press, 1999), 114.

17   Keith H. Basso, *Western Apache Language and Culture: Essays in Linguistic Anthropology* (Tucson: University of Arizona Press, 1990), 100, 117.

18   Ibid., 117, 126, 148.

19   Keith Basso, *Wisdom Sits in Places: Landscape and Language among the Western Apache* (Albuquerque: University of New Mexico Press, 1996), 31.

20   Basso, *Western Apache Language and Culture*, 100.

21   Mcleod, *Cree Narrative Memory*, 98.

22   For resources that speak to the significance of establishing relationships in the research process with Indigenous peoples in general (and from Cree and Anishinaabe perspectives), see Margaret Kovach, *Indigenous Methodologies: Characteristics, Conversations, and Context* (Toronto: University of Toronto Press, 2009), and Shawn Wilson, *Research Is Ceremony: Indigenous Research Methods* (Halifax: Fernwood Publishing, 2008).

23   Wheeler, "Decolonizing Tribal Histories," 242.

24   Although I have concentrated most of my references here to works that deal with Algonquian peoples, it is worth noting that Sto:lo scholar Jo-ann Archibald/Q'um Q'um Xiiem has produced an excellent resource about the nature of working with elders in "storywork." See her *Indigenous Storywork: Educating the Heart, Mind, Body, and Spirit* (Vancouver: UBC Press, 2008).

25   Walter C. Lightening, "Compassionate Mind: Implications of a Text Written by Elder Louis Sunchild," *Canadian Journal of Native Education* 19, 2 (1992): 230.

26   Ibid.

27   Ibid, 229–230.

28   Treaty 7 Elders and Tribal Council, with Walter Hildebrandt, Sarah Carter and Dorothy First Rider, *The True Spirit and Original Intent of Treaty 7* (Montreal: McGill-Queen's University Press, 1996), 328.

29   Ibid.

30   Brant Castellano, "Updating Aboriginal Traditions of Knowledge," 23; McLeod, *Cree Narrative Memory*, 11; Alessandro Portelli, "What Makes Oral History Different?" in *The Oral History Reader*, ed. Robert Perks and Alistair Thomson (London: Routledge, 1998), 69; Preston, *Cree Narrative*, 75.

31 See Cruikshank, *Life Lived Like a Story,* 174.

32 Winona Wheeler, "Indigenous Voices, Indigenous Histories, Part 3: The Social Relations of Oral History," *Saskatchewan History* 51, 1 (1999): 33.

33 Charles E. Trimble, Barbara W. Sommer and Mary Kay Quinlan, *The American Indian Oral History Manual: Making Many Voices Heard* (Walnut Creek, CA: Left Coast Press, 2008), 17; Nora Marks Dauenhauer and Richard Dauenhauer, "The Paradox of Talking on the Page: Some Aspects of the Tlingit and Haida Experience," in *Talking on the Page: Editing Aboriginal Oral Texts,* ed. Laura J. Murray and Keren Rice (Toronto: University of Toronto Press, 1999), 26; Ermine, "A Critical Examination," 118; Wolfe, *Earth Elder Stories,* xiv; Archibald, Ibid.

34 Wheeler, "Decolonizing Tribal Histories," 242.

35 Pauline Shirt spoke at a meeting of the Indigenous Knowledge Network for Infant, Child and Family Health, Toronto, July 30, 2009.

36 We expanded the research to include the Anishinaabek because of the cultural similarity we share and because this is one of the main groups in the Province of Ontario where I live. I also have Saulteaux heritage.

Chapter 2: People and Places

1 I use the word "peoples" in plural to indicate that are distinctions between the groups I am writing about.

2 I have not made much of the distinction between "First Nations" and "Métis" peoples in this work, as is so commonly the practice since Section 25 of the Canadian Constitution defined Aboriginal peoples according to three categories (First Nations, Métis, and Inuit). I have always found these distinctions problematic, as land-based Cree and Métis in northern Saskatchewan certainly have more in common than "First Nations" people who might come from different language families, geographies, and cultures on either side of the country. Further to this, there are many differences between Métis cultures across the country, such that there is a whole school of debate and scholarship around Métis identity—a debate which I am not prepared to engage in here. In this study, the Métis I worked with were for the most part fluent Cree speakers from northern Saskatchewan. The families and communities that they came from were often fluid—one might be "First Nations" but have a Métis mother, or be Métis but married into a First Nations community, and so on. While it is certain that the Cree and Métis in northern Saskatchewan have had different histories because of their ancestral cultures, their legal classification and the policies they were subject to, there are many similarities, and this is what I focus on here.

3 F.L. Barron. "The Indian Pass System in the Canadian West, 1892–1935," *Prairie Forum* 13, 1 (1988): 25–42.

4 This term was first used by Howard Adams in his *Prisons of Grass: Canada from a Native Perspective* (Toronto: New Press, 1975).

5 Olive Patricia Dickason, *Canada's First Nations: A History of the Founding Peoples from Earliest Times* (New York: Oxford University Press, 2002), 303.

6 Ibid., 299.

7 Kim Anderson and Jessica Ball, "Foundations: First Nation and Métis Families," in David Long and Olive Dickason, eds., *Visions of the Heart: Canadian Aboriginal Issues,* 3rd ed. (Toronto: Oxford University Press, 2011), 59.

8   Rose Stremlau, "To Domesticate and Civilize Wild Indians: Allotment and the Campaign to Reform Indian Families, 1875–1887," *Journal of Family History* 30, 3 (2005): 265–286.

9   Anderson and Ball, "Foundations," 61.

10   Marlyn Bennett and Cindy Blackstock, *A Literature Review and Annotated Bibliography Focusing on Aspects of Aboriginal Child Welfare in Canada* (Winnipeg: First Nations Child and Family Caring Society, 2002).

11   Dickason, *Canada's First Nations*, 255–256, 308.

12   Indian and Northern Affairs Canada, *National Assessment of Water and Wastewater Systems in First Nations Communities: Summary Report* (Ottawa: Indian and Northern Affairs Canada, 2003), iii. Note that this figure does not account for Métis communities, Inuit communities, or non-recognized communities (i.e., the Lubicon of Alberta; the Innu of Labrador) that may or may not have basic services. Thanks to Jason McCullough for help with this information.

Chapter 3: The Life Cycle Begins

1   See, for example, Robert Alain Brightman, *Grateful Prey: Rock Cree Human-Animal Relationships* (Berkeley: University of California Press, 1993).

2   Diamond Jenness, *Ojibwa Indians of Parry Island: Their Social and Religious Life* (Ottawa: National Museum of Canada, 1935), 90.

3   Ibid.

4   Ibid.

5   See Michael A. Weiner, *Earth Medicine—Earth Foods; Plant Remedies, Drugs, and Natural Foods of the North American Indians* (New York: Macmillan, 1972); and Virgil J. Vogel, *American Indian Medicine* (Norman: University of Oklahoma Press, 1970).

6   Joseph F. Dion and Hugh Aylmer Dempsey, *My Tribe, the Crees* (Calgary: Glenbow Museum, 1979), 6.

7   M. Inez Hilger, *Chippewa Child Life and Its Cultural Background* (1951; reprint, St. Paul: Minnesota Historical Society Press, 1992), 2, 10.

8   Ibid., 4.

9   Ibid.

10   Ibid., 3.

11   In their book on Métis women in northern Saskatchewan in the late 1970s, Poelzer and Poelzer note the rejection of family planning on religious grounds. Dolores R. Poelzer and Irene A. Poelzer, *In Our Own Words: Northern Saskatchewan Métis Women Speak Out* (Saskatoon: Lindenblatt and Hamonic, 1986), 131.

12   Nathalie J. Kermoal, *Un passé Métis au féminin* (Quebec: Les Éditions GID, 2006), 106.

13   Maria Campbell quoted in Kim Anderson, "Vital Signs: Reading Colonialism in Contemporary Adolescent Family Planning," in *Strong Women Stories: Native Vision and Community Survival*, ed. Kim Anderson and Bonita Lawrence (Toronto: Sumach/Canadian Scholars' Press, 2003), 178.

14   Kermoal, *Un passé Métis au féminin*, 106.

15 Hilger, *Chippewa Child Life and Its Cultural Background*, 3.

16 Ibid.

17 Maria Campbell quoted in Anderson, "Vital Signs," 181.

18 Ibid.

19 Rebeka Tabobondung, "Women Sharing Strength for All Generations: Aboriginal Birth Knowledge and New Media Creation" (M.A. thesis, Ontario Institute for Studies in Education/ University of Toronto, 2008), 128.

20 Hilger, *Chippewa Child Life and Its Cultural Background*, 6–9.

21 Ibid., 6.

22 Ibid.

23 Hilger, *Chippewa Child Life and Its Cultural Background*, 6.

24 Ibid., 7–8.

25 Tabobondung, "Women Sharing Strength for All Generations," 135.

26 Regina Flannery, "Infancy and Childhood among the Indians of the East Coast of James Bay," *Anthropos* 57 (1962), 482.

27 Hilger, *Chippewa Child Life and Its Cultural Background*, 9; Flannery, "Infancy and Childhood," 476.

28 Flora Beardy and Robert Coutts, *Voices from Hudson Bay: Cree Stories from York Factory* (Montreal: McGill-Queen's University Press, 1996), 47.

29 Hilger, *Chippewa Child Life and Its Cultural Background*, 6.

30 Ibid., 8.

31 Ibid.

32 Anishinaabe Elder Mary Elliot, personal communication with author, Sault Ste. Marie, May 2004.

33 Tabobondung, "Women Sharing Strength for All Generations," 137.

34 Ibid., 133.

35 Ibid., 161.

36 Flannery, "Infancy and Childhood," 476; Kermoal, *Un passé Métis au féminin*, 107; Sarah Preston and Alice Jacob, *Let the Past Go: A Life History* (Ottawa: National Museums of Canada, 1986), 35.

37 Flannery, "Infancy and Childhood," 476.

38 Ibid.; Hilger, *Chippewa Child Life and Its Cultural Background*, 13.

39 Hilger, *Chippewa Child Life and Its Cultural Background*, 13.

40 Ibid., 12.

41 Bear quoted in Freda Ahenakew and H. Christoph Wolfart, eds., *Kohkominawak Otacimowiniwawa: Our Grandmothers' Lives as Told in Their Own Words* (Saskatoon: Fifth House, 1992), 73.

42 Ibid., 75.

43 Hilger, *Chippewa Child Life and Its Cultural Background*, 11, 15.

44 Hilger, Flannery, and Mandelbaum have documented labour practices, focusing in particular on the position of the mother during delivery, which often included moving around, kneeling or standing, and using a sapling or rope to brace themselves. See Hilger, *Chippewa Child Life and Its Cultural Backgrounds*, 13–16; David Goodman Mandelbaum, *Plains Cree: An Ethnographic, Historical,*

and Comparative Study (Regina: Canadian Plains Research Center, 1979), 241; and Regina Flannery, John S. Long, and Laura L. Peers, *Ellen Smallboy: Glimpses of a Cree Woman's Life* (Montreal: McGill-Queen's University Press, 1995), 31.

45 Sarah Carter, "First Nations Women of Prairie Canada in the Early Reserve Years, the 1870s to the 1920s: A Preliminary Inquiry," in *Women of the First Nations: Power, Wisdom, and Strength,* ed. Christine Miller and Patricia Chuchryk (Winnipeg: University of Manitoba Press, 1996), 63.

46 Hilger, *Chippewa Child Life and Its Cultural Background,* 16.

47 Ahenakew and Wolfart, eds., *Kohkominawak Otacimowiniwawa,* 75; Flannery, "Infancy and Childhood," 477.

48 Ibid., 477; and Mandelbaum, *Plains Cree,* 139.

49 Flannery, "Infancy and Childhood," 478; Mandelbaum, *Plains Cree,* 139.

50 Flannery, "Infancy and Childhood," 478.

51 Mandelbaum, *Plains Cree,* 139.

52 Hilger, *Chippewa Child Life and Its Cultural Background,* 16.

53 Ibid., 17.

54 See Frances Densmore, *Chippewa Customs* (Minneapolis: Ross and Haines, 1970), 51.

55 Thomas Peacock and Marlene Wisuri, *The Four Hills of Life: Ojibwe Wisdom* (Afton, MN: Minnesota Historical Society Press, 2006), 37.

56 Ibid., 52.

57 Ibid., 52–53.

58 A. Irving Hallowell, *Ojibwa of Berens River, Manitoba: Ethnography into History,* edited and with a preface by Jennifer S.H. Brown (Toronto: Harcourt Brace Jovanovich, 1992), 12–13.

59 Amelia M. Paget, *People of the Plains* (Regina: Canadian Plains Research Center, 2004), 35.

60 Ibid.

61 Peacock and Wisuri, *The Four Hills of Life,* 39.

62 Densmore, *Chippewa Customs,* 56; Mandelbaum, *Plains Cree,* 242.

63 Densmore, *Chippewa Customs.*

64 Mandelbaum, *Plains Cree,* 141. See also Preston, who reported "naming the baby places the person giving the name in a god-parent relationship to the child." Preston and Jacob, *Let the Past Go,* 101.

65 Joseph F. Dion and Hugh A. Dempsey, *My Tribe, the Crees* (Calgary: Glenbow Museum, 1979), 16; Fine Day, *My Cree People: A Tribal Handbook* (Invermere, BC: Good Medicine Books, 1973), 14; Hallowell, *Ojibwa of the Berens Rivers,* 12–13; Mandelbaum, *Plains Cree,* 140; Alanson Skinner, *Notes on the Eastern Cree and Northern Saulteaux* (New York: The Trustees, 1911), 151; Ignatia Broker and Steven Premo, *Night Flying Woman: An Ojibway Narrative* (St. Paul: Minnesota Historical Society Press, 1983), 14–15.

66 Fine Day, *My Cree People,* 14.

67 Marie's memories correspond to the documentation of naming feasts by Diamond Jenness, who did field research in her community of Wasauksing shortly before Marie's birth.

68 For more information from Marie on naming ceremonies, see Tabobondung, "Women Sharing Strength for All Generations," 165.

69 Jenness, *Ojibwa Indians of Parry Island*, 90. Jenness explains that the Wasauksing Ojibway believed that people have both a soul and a shadow. The soul resided in the heart, and was capable of travelling outside the body but only for short periods of time. It was the seat of intelligence and will. The shadow was located in the brain, and was considered the "eyes of the soul," awakening the soul to "perception and knowledge." Unlike the soul, the shadow could travel widely and often went in front of or behind a person who was travelling. See ibid., 18–19.

70 Ibid., 91.

71 Kim Anderson, "New Life Stirring: Mothering, Transformation and Aboriginal Womanhood," in *Until our Hearts Are on the Ground: Aboriginal Mothering, Oppression, Resistance and Rebirth*, ed. D. Memee Lavell-Harvard and Jeannette Corbiere Lavell (Toronto: Demeter Press, 2006), 21.

72 Bear quoted in Ahenakew and Wolfart, eds., *Kohkominawak Otacimowiniwawa*, 223, 225.

73 Densmore, *Chippewa Customs*, 49.

74 Peacock and Wisuri, *The Four Hills of Life*, 37–38.

75 Ibid.

76 Densmore, *Chippewa Customs*, 48.

77 Ibid., 49.

78 Hallowell, *Ojibwa of the Berens Rivers*, 9.

79 Flora Beardy and Robert Coutts, *Voices from Hudson Bay: Cree Stories from York Factory* (Montreal: McGill-Queen's University Press, 1996), 47.

80 Flannery, "Infancy and Childhood," 478.

81 Kermoal, *Un passé Métis au féminin*, 109; Mandelbaum, *Plains Cree*, 143; Skinner, *Notes on the Eastern Cree and Northern Saulteaux*, 151.

82 Tasnim Nathoo and Aleck Ostry, *The One Best Way? Breastfeeding History, Politics and Policy in Canada* (Waterloo: Wilfrid Laurier University Press, 2009), 103.

83 Ibid.

84 Bear quoted in Ahenakew and Wolfart, eds., *Kohkominawak Otacimowiniwawa*, 225.

85 Flannery, "Infancy and Childhood," 478.

86 Ibid., 479.

Chapter 4: The "Good Life" and the "Fast Life"

1 J.R. Miller, *Shingwauk's Vision: A History of Native Residential Schools* (Toronto: University of Toronto Press, 1996), 46, 55.

2 Ibid., 38.

3 Amelia M. Paget, *People of the Plains* (Regina: Canadian Plains Research Center, 2004), 39.

4 Nathalie J. Kermoal, *Un passé Métis au Féminin* (Quebec: Les Éditions GID, 2006), 110.

5 Ibid., 112.

6   See Jennifer S.H. Brown, "A Cree Nurse in a Cradle of Methodism: Little Mary and the Egerton R. Young Family at Norway House and Berens River," in *First Days, Fighting Days: Women in Manitoba History*, ed. Mary Kinnear (Regina: Canadian Plains Research Center, 1987).

7   David Goodman Mandelbaum, *Plains Cree: An Ethnographic, Historical, and Comparative Study* (Regina: Canadian Plains Research Center, 1979), 144; Alanson Skinner, *Notes on the Eastern Cree and Northern Saulteaux* (New York: The Trustees, 1911), 151.

8   Mandelbaum, *Plains Cree*, 144, Skinner, *Notes on the Eastern Cree and Northern Saulteaux*, 151.

9   Miller, *Shingwauk's Vision*, 56.

10 Ibid., 18.

11 Ibid., 19.

12 Leah Marie Dorion, "Opikinawasowin: The Life Long Process of Growing Cree and Metis Children" (M.A. thesis, Athabasca University, 2010), 53.

13 Frances Densmore, *Study of Some Michigan Indians* (Ann Arbor: University of Michigan Press, 1949), 59.

14 Ibid., 51, 59.

15 Ignatia Broker and Steven Premo, *Night Flying Woman: An Ojibway Narrative* (St. Paul: Minnesota Historical Society Press, 1983), 16.

16 Thomas Peacock and Marlene Wisuri, *The Four Hills of Life: Ojibwe Wisdom* (Afton, MN: Afton Historical Society Press, 2006), 38.

17 Carol A. Markstrom, *Empowerment of North American Indian Girls: Ritual Expressions at Puberty* (Lincoln: University of Nebraska Press, 2008), 56–60.

18 Ibid., 59.

19 Ibid.

20 Mandelbaum, *Plains Cree*, 144.

21 Paget, *People of the Plains*, 39.

22 Ibid.

23 M. Inez Hilger, *Chippewa Child Life and Its Cultural Background* (1951; Reprint, St. Paul: Minnesota Historical Society Press, 1992), 58.

24 Frances Densmore, *Chippewa Customs* (Minneapolis: Ross and Haines, 1970), 58–59.

25 See also Hilger, *Chippewa Child Life and Its Cultural Background*, 58.

26 Ibid., 59.

27 Dorion, "Opikinawasowin," 44.

28 Densmore, *Chippewa Customs*, 60.

29 Mandelbaum, *Plains Cree*, 144; Skinner, *Notes on the Eastern Cree and Northern Saulteaux*, 151.

30 Peacock and Wisuri, *The Four Hills of Life*, 48.

31 Dorion, "Opikinawasowin," 68.

32 This story is also documented in her autobiography *Halfbreed* (Toronto: McClelland and Stewart, 1973), 51.

33 Dorion, "Opikinawasowin," 71.

34 See Glecia Bear, "Lost and Found," in *Kohkominawak Otacimowiniwawa: Our Grandmothers' Lives as Told in their Own Words,* ed. Glecia Bear, Freda Ahenakew, and H. Christoph Wolfart (Saskatoon: Fifth House, 1992), 123–145.

35 Ibid., 209.

36 There is an abundance of literature about residential schooling. To find bibliographies and publications about the impact of residential schools, visit the Aboriginal Healing Foundation, www.ahf.ca.

37 Dorion, "Opikinawasowin," 65.

38 Hilger, *Chippewa Child Life and Its Cultural Background,* 110.

39 Densmore, *Chippewa Customs,* 64–72.

40 As described by Regina Flannery, "Infancy and Childhood among the Indians of the East Coast of James Bay," *Anthropos* 57 (1962): 478, and referred to in note 85 of Chapter 3 in this volume.

41 Christopher T. Vecsey, *Traditional Ojibwa Religion and Its Historical Changes* (Evanston: Northwestern University Press, 1983), 135.

42 Ibid., 121–122.

43 Hilger, *Chippewa Child Life,* 43.

44 Ibid., 39.

45 Hilger, *Chippewa Child Life and Its Cultural Background,* 50.

46 Ibid., 52; Jenness, *Ojibwa Indians of Parry Island,* 97.

47 Jenness is referring to medicine men: the "healer and charm-maker,""conjuror," and "seer," respectively. See Jenness, *Ojibwa Indians of Parry Island,* 60.

48 Ibid., 96.

49 Hilger, *Chippewa Child Life and Its Cultural Background,* 51.

50 Jenness, *Ojibwa Indians of Parry Island,* 97.

51 Densmore, *Chippewa Customs,* 70; Ruth Landes, *The Ojibwa Woman* (1938; reprint, Lincoln: University of Nebraska Press, 1997), 6.

52 Densmore, *Chippewa Customs,* 71.

53 Ibid., 53.

54 Hilger, *Chippewa Child Life and Its Cultural Background,* 52.

55 Markstrom, *Empowerment of North American Indian Girls,* 334.

56 Ibid., 73.

57 Ibid., 10.

58 Ibid., 101.

59 Ibid., 81.

60 Ibid., 333, 338.

61 See Barbara Helen Hill, *Shaking the Rattle: Healing the Trauma of Colonization* (Penticton, BC: Theytus Books, 1995), 100; and Kim Anderson, *A Recognition of Being: Reconstructing Native Womanhood* (Sumach/Canadian Scholars' Press, 2000), 91–94.

62 See Kim Anderson, "Honouring the Blood of the People: Berry Fasting in the Twenty-First Century," in *Expressions in Canadian Native Studies,* ed. Ron. F. Laliberte et al. (Saskatoon: University of Saskatchewan Extension Press, 2000), 374–394.

63 Some of these quotes are taken from a previous article on berry fasting, featuring Gertie. See Anderson, "Honouring the Blood."

64 Jenness, *Ojibwa Indians of Parrry Island,* 97.

65 Mosôm provides further accounts of witnessing girls' puberty ceremonies in Diane Knight, ed., *The Seven Fires: Teachings of the Bear Clan as Told by Dr. Danny Musqua* (Muskoday First Nation, SK: Many Worlds Publishing, 2001), 70–73.

66 One of Hilger's informants also referred to the term *kitche kwe,* reporting that when she first menstruated, she was told that she was "old enough": "You are now a "big woman"(kitchekwe, meaning both big woman and first menstruation)." See Hilger, *Chippewa Child Life,* 54.

67 See Edward Benton Banai, *The Mishomis Book: The Voice of the Ojibway* (St. Paul, MN: Red School House, 1988), 3.

68 Carol Markstrom refers to Duran, Duran, and Braveheart's contention that the loss of cultural linkages that were strengthened through coming-of-age ceremonies is a contributing factor in the high level of problematic behaviours in contemporary North American Indian adolescents. See Markstrom, *Empowerment of North American Indian Girls,* 10, 30; and Bonnie Duran, Eduardo Duran, and Maria Yellow Horse Braveheart, "Native Americans and the Trauma of History," in *Studying Native America: Problems and Prospects,* ed. Russell Thornton (Madison: Univerisity of Wisconsin Press, 1998), 60–76. Markstrom also emphasizes the importance of men's involvement in girls' puberty ceremonies. She has documented the revival of supporting roles among the Ojibway men and boys in the contemporary northwestern Ontario community that she consulted. In this community, men and boys carry responsibilities during the year that follows the seclusion. This includes "providing transportation and attending to any of her needs that might arise." Markstrom notes that the "acquisition of respect for and honour of women was a major goal of learning for boys during this year's time." She was told by her informants that "the ceremony was also meaningful for men because it gave them purpose and understanding of their place in the social order of their culture." See Markstrom, *Empowerment of North American Indian Girls,* 334–335.

69 See Jenness, *Ojibwa Indians of Parry Island;* Broker and Premo, *Night Flying Woman;* and Maude Kegg and John D. Nichols, *Portage Lake: Memories of an Ojibwe Childhood* (Edmonton: University of Alberta Press, 1991).

70 Broker and Premo, *Night Flying Woman,* 51.

Chapter 5: Adult Years

1 Taken from *Merriam-Webster Dictionary Online,* www.merriam-webster.com.

2 Sarah Carter, "First Nations Women of Prairie Canada in the Early Reserve Years, the 1870s to the 1920s: A Preliminary Inquiry," in *Women of the First Nations: Power, Wisdom and Strength,* ed. Christine Miller and Patricia Chuchryk (Winnipeg: University of Manitoba Press, 1996), 60.

3 Leah Dorion, "Opikinawasowin: The Life Long Process of Growing Cree and Metis Children" (M.A. thesis, Athabasca University, 2010), 66.

4 I have written more extensively about these teachings in Kim Anderson and Jessica Ball, "Foundations: First Nation and Métis Families," in *Visions of the Heart:*

Canadian Aboriginal Issues, 3rd ed., ed. David Long and Olive Patricia Dickason (Toronto: Oxford University Press, 2011). See also Kim Anderson, *A Recognition of Being: Reconstructing Native Womanhood* (Toronto: Sumach/ Canadian Scholars' Press, 2000), 158–164.

5   Responsibilities that were particular to elderly women are discussed in Chapter 6.

6   Taken from Mary Lee, "Cree (Nehiyawak) Teaching," *Four Directions Teachings.com,* http://www.fourdirectionsteachings.com.

7   Ibid.

8   Ibid.

9   See Fine Day, *My Cree People: A Tribal Handbook* (Invermere, BC: Good Medicine Books, 1973); Amelia Paget, *People of the Plains* (Regina: Canadian Plains Research Center, 2004), and Lee, "Cree (Nehiyawak) Teaching."

10   See Fine Day, *My Cree People,* 53.

11   Paget, *People of the Plain,* 28.

12   Writing about the Lakota, Raymond DeMallie writes that "according to Deloria, the menstrual blood gave a kind of temporary power to a woman, a wakan quality. This was not thought of as polluting but rather as at odds with the wakan power of men; a woman's menstrual power clashed with a medicine man's power. The clash was characterized by the work ohakay, 'to cause to be blocked or tangled.' Hence women were to be secluded from men during their menstrual periods." Raymond J. DeMallie, "Male and Female in Traditional Lakota Culture," in *The Hidden Half: Studies of Plains Indian Women,* ed. Patricia Albers and Beatrice Medicine (Washington, DC: University Press of America, 1983), 257.

13   This lesson was all the more important for the Indian Agent, an active participant in the colonial system that was violating the boundaries of Aboriginal peoples on almost every level: territorial, spiritual, sexual, and so on.

14   Fine Day, *My Cree People,* 13.

15   H.Christoph Wolfart, "Introduction to the Texts," in *Kohkominawak Otacimowini-wawa: Our Grandmothers' Lives as Told in their Own Words,* ed. Bear Glecia, Freda Ahenakew, and H. Christoph Wolfart (Saskatoon: Fifth House, 1992), 26.

16   Laura Peers, "Subsistence, Secondary Literature, and Gender Bias: The Saulteaux," in *Women of the First Nations: Power, Wisdom, and Strength,* ed. Christine Miller and Patricia Chuchryk (Winnipeg: University of Manitoba Press, 1996), 39–50.

17   Ibid., 45.

18   Ibid., 46.

19   Sherry Farrell Racette, "Looking for Stories and Unbroken Threads: Museum Artifacts as Women's History and Cultural Legacy," in *Restoring the Balance: First Nations Women, Community, and Culture,* ed. Gail Valaskakis, Madeleine Dion Stout, and Eric Guimond (Winnipeg: University of Manitoba Press, 2009), 286.

20   Ibid., 287.

21   Ibid.

22   To this, Maria added: "Remember, Tommy Douglas and his [Co-operative Commonwealth Federation] spent a great deal of time chasing us off our lands and burning our homes. The 1940s were a horrific time for our people in Manitoba, Saskatchewan, and Alberta. Many men were away at war and couldn't protect their families and so they would be dispersed—chased out of their houses and have their barns burned."

23 David Goodman Mandelbaum, *Plains Cree: An Ethnographic, Historical, and Comparative Study* (Regina: Canadian Plains Research Center, 1979), 134–135; Fine Day, *My Cree People*, 39. Joseph Dion also makes note of women having their own games in Joseph F. Dion and Hugh A. Dempsey, *My Tribe, the Crees* (Calgary: Glenbow Museum, 1979), 12.

24 A makeshift lamp made out of old rags braided together, soaked in grease and put in a can.

25 Strict supervision around courting, including the use of chaperones, is described in a number of sources, including Alice Ahenakew, Freda Ahenakew, and H. Christoph Wolfart, *Âh-Âyîtaw Isi ê-kî-Kiskêyihtahkik Maskihkiy. They Knew both Sides of Medicine: Cree Tales of Curing and Cursing* (Winnipeg: University of Manitoba Press, 2000), 45; Fine Day, *My Cree People*, 7; Mandelbaum, *Plains Cree*, 147; and Nathalie Kermoal, *Un passé Métis au féminin* (Quebec: Les Éditions GID, 2007), 120.

26 See Glecia Bear, Freda Ahenakew, and H. Christoph Wolfart, eds., *Kohkominawak Otacimowiniwawa: Our Grandmothers' Lives as Told in their Own Words* (Saskatoon: Fifth House, 1992), 215.

27 See Anderson, *A Recognition of Being*, 91–94.

28 James Bay Cree oral historian Alice Jacob tells of getting married in an arranged marriage in 1948, and James Bay Cree author Jane Willis writes about how her family tried to arrange for her to marry in 1958. See Sarah Preston and Alice Jacob, *Let the Past Go: A Life History* (Ottawa: National Museums of Canada, 1986), 49, and Jane Willis, *Geniesh: An Indian Girlhood* (Toronto: New Press, 1973), 182.

29 Fine Day, *My Cree People*, 7; Mandelbaum, *Plains Cree*, 146; Bear, Ahenakew, and Wolfart, eds., *Kohkominawak Otacimowiniwawa*, 211; Emma Minde, Freda Ahenakew, and H. Christoph Wolfart, *Kwayask ê-kî-pê-Kiskinowâpahtihicik. Their Example Showed Me the Way: A Cree Woman's Life Shaped by Two Cultures* (Edmonton: University of Alberta Press, 1997), xxvii. Scholars have cautioned against reading these types of arrangements from the lens applied to them by the earliest European observers; a lens that has turned into the myth that Aboriginal men "sold" their daughters into marriage. This misperception has been addressed by Dion, *My Tribe*, 17, and Rebecca Kugel and Lucy Eldersveld Murphy, eds, *Native Women's History in Eastern North America before 1900: A Guide to Research and Writing* (Lincoln: University of Nebraska Press, 2007), xxix. Katherine Weist has written, "Europeans thought that men bought their wives because they witnessed the giving of horses.... In reality, they were only witnessing one facet of a set of exchanges." See Katherine M. Weist, "Beasts of Burden and Menial Slaves: Nineteenth-Century Observations of Northern Plains Indian Women," in *The Hidden Half: Studies of Plains Indian Women*, ed. Patricia Albers and Beatrice Medicine (Washington, DC: University Press of America, 1983), 44.

30 Laura L. Peers, *Ojibwa of Western Canada, 1780 to 1870* (Winnipeg: University of Manitoba Press, 1994), 57; Preston and Jacob, *Let the Past Go*, 94.

31 Bear in Bear, Ahenakew, and Wolfart, eds., *Kohkominawak Otacimowiniwawa*, 213; Minde, *Kwayask ê-kî-pê-Kiskinowâpahtihicik*, xxxii.

32 Bear in Bear, Ahenakew, and Wolfart, eds., *Kohkominawak Otacimowiniwawa*, 213; Ahenakew, Ahenakew, and Wolfart, eds., *Âh-Âyitaw Isi ê-kî-Kiskêyihtahkik Maskihkiy*, 49; Willis, *Geniesh*, 3; Dion, *My Tribe*, 16–17; Preston and Jacob, *Let the Past Go*, 127.

33 Fine Day, *My Cree People*, 8; Mandelbaum, *Plains Cree*, 148.

34 Minde, *Kwayask ê-kî-pê-Kiskinowâpahtihicik*, xxxi., 13, 57.

35 See Sarah Carter, *The Importance of Being Monogamous: Marriage and Nation Building in Western Canada to 1915* (Edmonton: University of Alberta Press, 2008); Sarah Carter, "Creating 'Semi-Widow' and 'Supernumary Wives': Prohibiting Polygamy in Prairie Canada's Aboriginal Communities to 1900," in *Contact Zones: Aboriginal and Settler Women in Canada's Colonial Past*, ed. Katie Pickles and Myra Rutherdale (Vancouver: UBC Press, 2005), 131–159.

36 Regina Flannery, "The Position of Women among the Eastern Cree," *Primitive Man* 8 (1935): 84.

37 Mandelbaum, *Plains Cree*, 148.

38 Fine Day, *My Cree People*, 8–10; Paget, *People of the Plains*, 40; Peers, *Ojibwe of Western Canada*, 83; Alanson Skinner, *Notes on the Eastern Cree and Northern Saulteaux* (New York: The Trustees, 1911), 57.

39 Mandelbaum, *Plains Cree*, 150.

40 Writing about the Ojibway of western Canada, Laura Peers has stated, "It was the Ojibway custom that after marriage the groom lived with his wife's family for at least a year, hunting and trapping for his in-laws." Peers, *Ojibwa of Western Canada*, 35.

41 Jennifer Blythe and Peggy Martin McGuire, "The Changing Employment of Cree Women in Moosonee and Moose Factory," in *Women of the First Nations: Power, Wisdom and Strength*, ed. Christine Miller and Patricia Chuchryk (Winnipeg: University of Manitoba Press, 1996), 147.

42 Ibid.

43 Kugel and Eldersveld Murphy, eds., *Native Women's History in Eastern North America before 1900*, xxx.

44 Fine Day, *My Cree People*, 8; Peers, *Ojibwa of Western Canada*, 35; Minde, *Kwayask ê-kî-pê-Kiskinowâpahtihicik*, xiii; Skinner, *Notes on the Eastern Cree and Northern Saulteaux*, 151; Flannery, "The Position of Women," 81. Diane Payment has documented a strong female kinship tie among the Métis families that resettled at Batoche in the late nineteenth century. See Diane Payment, ""La vie en rose"? Métis Women at Batoche, 1870 to 1920," in *Women of the First Nations: Power, Wisdom and Strength*, ed. Christine Miller and Patricia Chuchryk (Winnipeg: University of Manitoba Press, 1996), 23.

45 Peers, *Ojibwa of Western Canada*, 35; Fine Day, *My Cree People*, 8.

46 Minde, *Kwayask ê-kî-pê-Kiskinowâpahtihicik*, xi.

Chapter 6: Grandmothers and Elders

1   Quoted in Diane Knight, ed., *The Seven Fires: Teachings of the Bear Clan as Told by Dr. Danny Musqua* (Prince Albert, SK: New World Press, 2000), 82–83.

2   Michael D. McNally, *Honouring Elders: Aging, Authority, and Ojibwe Religion* (New York: Columbia University Press, 2009), 51–52.

3   Ibid., 25. See also Jeffrey Anderson, *The Four Hills of Life: Northern Arapaho Knowledge and Life Movement* (Lincoln: University of Nebraska Press, 2001).

4   Ibid., 49.

5   Ibid.

6   Basil Johnston, *Ojibway Heritage* (Toronto: McClelland and Stewart, 1976), 112.

7   Charlotte Loppie has written a doctoral dissertation about contemporary Mi'kmaw women and menopause, but there is little else out there on Aboriginal women and menopause. See Charlotte Loppie, "Grandmothers' Voices: Mik'maq Women and Menopause" (Ph.D. diss., Dalhousie University, 2004).

8   Amelia M. Paget, *People of the Plains* (Regina: Canadian Plains Research Center, 2004), 33.

9   Joseph F. Dion and Hugh A. Dempsey, *My Tribe the Cree* (Calgary: Glenbow Museum, 1979), 115–116.

10 Ibid., 116.

11 Winona Wheeler, "Decolonizing Tribal Histories" (Ph.D. diss., University of California, Berkeley 2000), 16.

12 Quoted in Knight, *The Seven Fires*, 16, back cover.

13 Ibid.

14 For discussion and analysis on how the Indian Act has interfered with First Nations women's involvement in governance, see Judith F. Sayers et al., *First Nations Women, Governance and the Indian Act: A Collection of Policy Research Reports* (Ottawa: Status of Women Canada, 2001).

15 Rebecca Kugel, "Leadership within the Women's Community: Susie Bonga Wright of the Leech Lake Ojibwe," in *Native Women's History in Eastern North America Before 1900: A Guide to Research and Writing*, ed. Rebecca Kugel and Lucy Eldersveld Murphy (Lincoln: University of Nebraska Press, 2007), 171.

16 Wisakecak is a Trickster figure in Cree Culture, and there are countless stories about him that are both entertaining and educational. As Omushkego Cree Elder Louis Bird says, "This guy plays many parts, fills in the answer where there is no explanation. In a way he plays a part that makes us laugh, and the mystery then can be just sort of eased away from your mind." See Louis Bird and Susan Elaine Grey, *The Spirit Lives in the Mind: Omushkego Stories, Lives and Dreams* (Montreal: McGill-Queen's University Press, 2007), 175.

17 Flora Beardy and Robert Coutts, *Voices from Hudson Bay: Cree Stories from York Factory* (Montreal: McGill-Queen's University Press, 1996), 90.

18 David Goodman Mandelbaum, *Plains Cree: An Ethnographic, Historical, and Comparative Study* (Regina: Canadian Plains Research Center, 1979), 144.

19 David Livingstone defines these types of learning as follows: "When a teacher has the authority to determine that people designated as requiring knowledge effectively learn a curriculum taken from a pre-established body of knowledge, the form of learning is formal education, whether in the form of age-graded and bureaucratic modern school systems or elders initiating youths into traditional bodies of knowledge. When learners opt to acquire further knowledge or skill by studying voluntarily with a teacher who assists their self-determined interests by using an organized curriculum, as is the case in many adult education courses and workshops, the form of learning is non-formal education or further education. When teachers or mentors take responsibility for instructing others without sustained reference to an intentionally-organized body of knowledge in more incidental and spontaneous learning situations, such as guiding them in acquiring job skills or in community development activities, the form of learning

is informal education or informal training." See D.W. Livingstone, "Adults Informal Learning: Definitions, Findings, Gaps and Future Research," SSHRC Research Network, New Appproaches to Lifelong Learning Papers (Toronto: Centre for the Study of Education and Work, OISE/University of Toronto, 2001), 2.

20 For example, Dene healer Be'sha Blondin talks about her training that began at age five in Kim Anderson, "Notokwe Ophihikeet—'Old-Lady Raised': Aboriginal Women's Reflections on Ethics and Methodologies in Health," *Canadian Woman Studies/les cahiers de la femme* 26, 3/4 (2008): 6–12.

21 Bird and Gray, *The Spirit Lives in the Mind*, 182.

22 "Elles étaient sages femmes et medicins sans diplômes, pharmaciennes et herboristes sans échoppes. Elles allaient de maison en maison, de village en village, pour partager leur savoir et soigner les patients avec des plantes salvatrices soigneureusement récoltée dans les bois." Nathalie Kermoal, *Un passé Métis au féminin* (Quebec: Les Éditions GID, 2006), 144. Translation mine.

23 See the epigraph to this chapter.

24 Paget, *People of the Plains*, 33.

Conclusion: Bundling the Layers

1 Once again, I acknowledge the limitations of my work in not exploring the implications of gender roles for two-spirited or other gendered identities. There is work to be done!

2 Carol A. Markstrom, *Empowerment of North American Indian Girls: Ritual Expressions at Puberty* (Lincoln: University of Nebraska Press, 2008).

3 Kim Anderson and Jessica Ball, "Foundations: First Nation and Métis Families," in *Visions of the Heart: Canadian Aboriginal Issues,* 3rd ed., ed. David Long and Olive Patricia Dickason (Toronto: Oxford University Press, 2011).

4 Jane Middelton-Moz, *Boiling Point: The High Cost of Unhealthy Anger to Individuals and Society* (Deerfield Beach, FL: Health Communications, 1999).

Bibliography

Adams, Howard. *Prisons of Grass: Canada from a Native Perspective.* Toronto: New Press, 1975.

Adelson, Naomi. *"Being Alive Well": Health and the Politics of Cree Well-being.* Toronto: University of Toronto Press, 2000.

Advisory Group on Suicide Prevention. *Acting on What We Know: Preventing Youth Suicide in First Nations.* Ottawa: Health Canada, 2002.

Ahenakew, Alice, Freda Ahenakew, and H. Christoph Wolfart. *Âh-Âyitaw Isi ê-ki-Kiskêyi-htahkik Maskihkiy. They Knew Both Sides of Medicine: Cree Tales of Curing and Cursing.* Winnipeg: University of Manitoba Press, 2000.

Ahenakew, Edward. *Voices of the Plains Cree.* Toronto: McClelland and Stewart, 1973.

Albers, Patricia, and Beatrice Medicine, eds. *The Hidden Half: Studies of Plains Indian Women.* Washington, DC: University Press of America, 1983.

Anderson, Jeffrey. *The Four Hills of Life: Northern Arapaho Knowledge and Life Movement.* Lincoln: University of Nebraska Press, 2001.

Anderson, Kim. *A Recognition of Being: Reconstructing Native Womanhood.* Toronto: Sumach/Canadian Scholars' Press, 2000.

_____. "Honouring the Blood of the People: Berry Fasting in the Twenty-First Century." In *Expressions in Canadian Native Studies,* edited by Ron. F. Laliberte et al. Saskatoon: University of Saskatchewan Extension Press, 2000.

_____. "Vital Signs: Reading Colonialism in Contemporary Adolescent Family Planning." In *Strong Women Stories: Native Vision and Community Survival,* edited by Kim Anderson and Bonita Lawrence. Toronto: Sumach/Canadian Scholars' Press, 2003.

_____. "New Life Stirring: Mothering, Transformation and Aboriginal Womanhood." In *Until Our Hearts Are on the Ground: Aboriginal Mothering, Oppression, Resistance and Rebirth,* edited by D. Memee Lavell-Harvard and Jeannette Corbiere Lavell. Toronto: Demeter Press, 2006.

_____. "Notokwe Ophihikeet—'Old-Lady Raised': Aboriginal Women's Reflections on Ethics and Methodologies in Health." *Canadian Woman Studies/les cahiers de la femme* 26, 3/4 (2008): 6–12.

_____. "Affirmations of an Indigenous Feminist." In *Indigenous Women and Feminism: Politics, Activism, Culture,* edited by Jean Barman, Shari Hundorf, Cheryl Suzack, and Jeanne Perreault. Vancouver: UBC Press, 2010.

_____. "Native Women, the Body, Land, and Narratives of Contact and Arrival." In *Storied Communities: The Role of Narratives of Contact and Arrival in Constituting Political Community,* edited by Hester Lessard, Jeremy Webber, and Rebecca Johnson. Vancouver: UBC Press, 2010.

Anderson, Kim, and Jessica Ball. "Foundations: First Nation and Métis Families." In *Visions of the Heart: Canadian Aboriginal Issues,* 3rd ed., edited by David Long and Olive Patricia Dickason. Toronto: Oxford University Press, 2011.

Archibald, Jo-ann/Q'um Q'um Xiiem. *Indigenous Storywork: Educating the Mind, Body, and Spirit.* Vancouver: UBC Press, 2008.

Barron, F.L. "The Indian Pass System in the Canadian West, 1892–1935." *Prairie Forum* 13, 1 (1988): 25–42.

Basso, Keith. *Western Apache Language and Culture: Essays in Linguistic Anthropology.* Tucson: University of Arizona Press, 1990.

_____. *Wisdom Sits in Places: Landscape and Language among the Western Apache.* Albuquerque: University of New Mexico Press, 1996.

Bastien, Betty. *Blackfoot Ways of Knowing: The Worldview of the Siksikaitsitapi.* Calgary: University of Calgary Press, 2004.

Bear, Glecia, Freda Ahenakew, and H. Christoph Wolfart, eds. *Kohkominawak Otacimowiniwawa: Our Grandmothers' Lives as Told in Their Own Words.* Saskatoon: Fifth House, 1992.

Beardy, Flora, and Robert Coutts. *Voices from Hudson Bay: Cree Stories from York Factory.* Montreal: McGill-Queen's University Press, 1996.

Bennett, Marilyn, and Cindy Blackstock. *A Literature Review and Annotated Bibliography Focusing on Aspects of Aboriginal Child Welfare in Canada.* Winnipeg: First Nations Child and Family Caring Society, 2002.

Benton Banai, Edward. *The Mishomis Book: The Voice of the Ojibway.* St. Paul, MN: Red School House, 1988.

Bird, Louis, and Susan Elaine Gray. *The Spirit Lives in the Mind: Omushkego Stories, Lives and Dreams.* Montreal: McGill-Queen's University Press, 2007.

Blaeser, Kimberly M. "Writing Voices Speaking: Native Authors and an Oral Aesthetic." In *Talking on the Page: Editing Aboriginal Oral Texts,* edited by Laura J. Murray and Keren Rice. Toronto: University of Toronto Press, 1999.

Blythe, Jennifer, and Peggy Martin McGuire. "The Changing Employment of Cree Women in Moosonee and Moose Factory." In *Women of the First Nations: Power, Wisdom and Strength,* edited by Christine Miller and Patricia Chuchryk. Winnipeg: University of Manitoba Press, 1996.

Brant Castellano, Marlene. "Updating Aboriginal Traditions of Knowledge." In *Indigenous Knowledges in Global Contexts: Multiple Readings of Our World,* edited by George J. Sefa Dei, Budd L. Hall, and Dorothy Goldin Rosenberg. Toronto: University of Toronto Press, 2000.

Brightman, Robert Alain. *Grateful Prey: Rock Cree Human-Animal Relationships.* Berkeley: University of California Press, 1993.

Broker, Ignatia, and Steven Premo. *Night Flying Woman: An Ojibway Narrative.* St. Paul: Minnesota Historical Society Press, 1983.

Brown, Jennifer S.H. *Strangers in Blood: Fur Trade Company Families in Indian Country.* Vancouver: UBC Press, 1980.

_____. "A Cree Nurse in a Cradle of Methodism: Little Mary and the Egerton R. Young Family at Norway House and Berens River." In *First Days, Fighting Days: Women in Manitoba History*, edited by Mary Kinnear. Regina, SK: Canadian Plains Research Center, 1987.

_____. "Doing Aboriginal History: A View from Winnipeg." *Canadian Historical Review*, 84, 4 (2003): 613–615.

_____. "Older Persons in Some Cree and Ojibwe Stories: Gender, Power, and Survival." In *Papers of the 37th Algonquian Conference*, edited by H. Christoph Wolfart. Winnipeg: University of Manitoba Press, 2006.

Brown, Jennifer S.H., and Elizabeth Vibert, eds. *Reading Beyond Words: Contexts for Native History*, 2nd ed. Peterborough: Broadview Press, 2003.

Campbell, Maria. *Halfbreed.* Toronto: McClelland and Stewart, 1973.

Carter, Sarah. "First Nations Women of Prairie Canada in the Early Reserve Years, the 1870s to the 1920s: A Preliminary Inquiry." In *Women of the First Nations: Power, Wisdom, and Strength*, edited by Christine Miller and Patricia Chuchryk. Winnipeg: University of Manitoba Press, 1996.

_____. *Capturing Women: The Manipulation of Cultural Imagery in Canada's Prairie West.* Montreal: McGill-Queen's University Press, 1997.

_____. "Creating 'Semi-Widow' and 'Supernumary Wives': Prohibiting Polygamy in Prairie Canada's Aboriginal Communities to 1900." In *Contact Zones: Aboriginal and Settler Women in Canada's Colonial Past*, edited by Katie Pickles and Myra Rutherdale. Vancouver: UBC Press, 2005.

_____. "Categories and Terrains of Exclusion: Constructing the 'Indian Woman' in the Early Settlement Era in Western Canada." In *In the Days of our Grandmothers: A Reader in Aboriginal Women's History in Canada*, edited by Mary-Ellen Kelm and Laura Townsend. Toronto: University of Toronto Press, 2006.

_____. *The Importance of Being Monogamous: Marriage and Nation Building in Western Canada to 1915.* Edmonton: University of Alberta Press, 2008.

Cole, Sally. "Dear Ruth: This is the Story of Maggie Wilson, Ojibwa Ethnologist." In *Great Dames*, edited by Elspeth Cameron and Janice Dickin. Toronto: University of Toronto Press, 1997.

Cornell, George L. "The Imposition of Western Definitions of Literature on Indian Oral Traditions." In *The Native in Literature: Canadian and Comparative Perspectives*, edited by Thomas King, Cheryl Calver, and Helen Hoy. Toronto: ECW Press, 1987.

Cruikshank, Julie. *Life Lived Like a Story: Life Stories of Three Yukon Native Elders.* Lincoln: University of Nebraska Press, 1990.

_____. "The Social Life of Texts: Editing on the Page and in Performance." In *Talking on the Page: Editing Aboriginal Oral Texts*, edited by Laura J. Murray and Keren Rice. Toronto: University of Toronto Press, 1999.

Deloria, Philip. "Historiography." In *A Companion to American Indian History*, edited by Philip J. Deloria and Neal Salisbury. Malden, MA: Blackwell Publishers, 2002.

_____. "'These Have No Ears': Narrative and the Ethnohistorical Method." *Ethnohistory* 40, 4 (1993): 515–538.

DeMallie, Raymond J. "Male and Female in Traditional Lakota Culture." In *The Hidden Half: Studies of Plains Indian Women*, edited by Patricia Albers and Beatrice Medicine. Washington, DC: University Press of America, 1983.

Densmore, Frances. *Study of Some Michigan Indians.* Ann Arbor: University of Michigan Press, 1949.

_____. *Chippewa Customs.* Minneapolis: Ross and Haines, 1970.

Dickason, Olive Patricia. *Canada's First Nations: A History of the Founding Peoples from Earliest Times.* New York: Oxford University Press, 2002.

Dion, Joseph F., and Hugh A. Dempsey. *My Tribe, the Crees.* Calgary: Glenbow Museum, 1979.

Dorion, Leah Marie. "Opikinawasowin: The Life Long Process of Growing Cree and Metis Children." M.A. thesis, Athabasca University, 2010.

Dorion, Leah, and Darren R. Préfontaine. "Deconstructing Métis Historiography: Giving Voice to the Métis People." In *Resources for Métis Researchers*, edited by Lawrence J. Barkwell, Leah Dorion, and Darren R. Préfontaine. Saskatoon: Gabriel Dumont Institute, 1999.

Duran, Bonnie, Eduardo Duran, and Maria Yellow Horse Braveheart. "Native Americans and the Trauma of History." In *Studying Native America: Problems and Prospects*, edited by R. Thornton. Madison: University of Wisconsin Press, 1998.

Ermine, William J. "A Critical Examination of the Ethics of Research Involving Indigenous Peoples." M.A. thesis, University of Saskatchewan, 2000.

Fixico, Donald. "Ethics and Responsibilities in Writing American Indian History." In *Natives and Academics: Researching and Writing about American Indians*, edited by Devon Mihesuah. Lincoln: University of Nebraska Press, 1998.

Farrell Racette, Sherry. "Looking for Stories and Unbroken Threads: Museum Artifacts as Women's History and Cultural Legacy." In *Restoring the Balance: First Nations Women, Community, and Culture*, edited by Gail Valaskakis, Madeleine Dion Stout, and Eric Guimond. Winnipeg: University of Manitoba Press, 2009.

Fine Day. *My Cree People: A Tribal Handbook.* Invermere, BC: Good Medicine Books, 1973.

Flannery, Regina. "The Position of Women among the Eastern Cree." *Primitive Man* 8 (1935): 81–86.

_____. "Infancy and Childhood among the Indians of the East Coast of James Bay." *Anthropos* 57 (1962): 475–482.

Flannery, Regina, John S. Long, and Laura L. Peers. *Ellen Smallboy: Glimpses of a Cree Woman's Life.* Montreal: McGill-Queen's University Press, 1995.

Fogelson, Raymond D. "The Ethnohistory of Events and Nonevents." *Ethnohistory* 36, 2 (1989): 133–147.

Friedan, Betty. *The Feminine Mystique.* New York: Norton, 1963.

Green, Rayna. "Review Essay: Native American Women." *Signs* 6 (1980): 248–267.

Hallowell, A. Irving. "The Incidence, Character, and Decline of Polygyny among the Lake Winnipeg Cree and Saulteaux." *American Anthropologist* 40, 2 (April–June 1938): 235–256.

_____. *Ojibwa of Berens River, Manitoba: Ethnography into History.* Edited and with a preface by Jennifer S.H. Brown. Toronto: Harcourt Brace Jovanovich, 1992.

Hart, Michael. *Seeking Mino-Pimatisiwin: An Aboriginal Approach to Helping.* Halifax: Fernwood Publishing, 2002.

Hilger, M. Inez. *Chippewa Child Life and Its Cultural Background.* 1951. Reprint, St. Paul: Minnesota Historical Society Press, 1992.

Hill, Barbara Helen. *Shaking the Rattle: Healing the Trauma of Colonization.* Penticton, BC: Theytus Books, 1995.

Howe, Craig. "Keep Your Thoughts Above the Trees: Ideas on Developing and Presenting Tribal Histories." In *Clearing a Path: Theorizing the Past in Native American Studies,* edited by Nancy Shoemaker. New York: Routledge, 2002.

Hulan, Renée, and Renate Eigenbrod, eds. *Aboriginal Oral Traditions: Theory, Practice, Ethics.* Halifax: Fernwood Publishing, 2008.

Indian and Northern Affairs Canada. *National Assessment of Water and Wastewater Systems in First Nations Communities: Summary Report.* Ottawa: Indian and Northern Affairs Canada, 2003.

Jenness, Diamond. *Ojibwa Indians of Parry Island, their Social and Religious Life.* Ottawa: National Musuem of Canada, 1935.

Johnston, Basil. *Ojibway Heritage.* Toronto: McClelland and Stewart, 1976.

Kegg, Maude, and John D. Nichols. *Portage Lake: Memories of an Ojibwe Childhood.* Edmonton: University of Alberta Press, 1991.

Kermoal, Nathalie J. *Un passé Métis au féminin.* Quebec: Les Éditions GID, 2006.

Knight, Diane, ed. *The Seven Fires: Teachings of the Bear Clan as Told by Dr. Danny Musqua.* Muskoday First Nation, SK: Many Worlds Publishing, 2001.

Kovach, Margaret. *Indigenous Methodologies: Characteristics, Conversations, and Context.* Toronto: University of Toronto Press, 2009.

Kugel, Rebecca. "Leadership within the Women's Community: Susie Bonga Wright of the Leech Lake Ojibwe." In *Native Women's History in Eastern North America before 1900: A Guide to Research and Writing,* edited by Rebecca Kugel and Lucy Eldersveld Murphy. Lincoln: University of Nebraska Press, 2007.

Kugel, Rebecca, and Lucy Eldersveld Murphy, eds. *Native Women's History in Eastern North America before 1900: A Guide to Research and Writing.* Lincoln: University of Nebraska Press, 2007.

Kulchyski, Peter, Don McCaskill, and David Newhouse, eds. *In the Words of Elders: Aboriginal Cultures in Transition.* Toronto: University of Toronto Press, 1999.

Ladner, Kiera. "Nit-acimonawin oma acimonak ohci: This is My Story About Stories." *Native Studies Review* 11, 2 (1996): 103–115.

Landes, Ruth. *The Ojibwa Woman.* 1938. Reprint; Lincoln: University of Nebraska Press, 1997.

Leacock, Eleanor. "Women's Status in Egalitarian Society: Some Implications for Social Evolution." *Current Anthropology* 19, 2 (1978): 247–276.

Lee, Mary. "Cree (Nehiyawak) Teaching." *Four Directions Teachings.com*. http://www.four-directionsteachings.com.

Lightening, Walter C. "Compassionate Mind: Implications of a Text Written by Elder Louis Sunchild." *Canadian Journal of Native Education* 19, 2 (1992): 215–253.

Livingstone, D.W. "Adults Informal Learning: Definitions, Findings, Gaps and Future Research." SSHRC Research Network, New Approaches to Lifelong Learning Papers. Toronto: Centre for the Study of Education and Work, OISE/University of Toronto, 2001.

Loppie, Charlotte. "Grandmothers' Voices: Mik'maq Women and Menopause." Ph.D. diss., Dalhousie University, 2004.

Mandelbaum, David Goodman. *Plains Cree: An Ethnographic, Historical, and Comparative Study*. Regina: Canadian Plains Research Center, 1979.

Markstrom, Carol A. *Empowerment of North American Indian Girls: Ritual Expressions at Puberty*. Lincoln: University of Nebraska Press, 2008.

McLeod, Neal. *Cree Narrative Memory: From Treaties to Modern Times*. Saskatoon: Purich Publishing, 2007.

McNally, Michael D. *Honouring Elders: Aging, Authority, and Ojibwe Religion*. New York: Columbia University Press, 2009.

Mihesuah, Devon. *Natives and Academics: Researching and Writing about American Indians*. Lincoln: University of Nebraska Press, 1998.

Middelton-Moz, Jane. *Children of Trauma: Rediscovering your Discarded Self*. Deerfield Beach, FL: Health Communications, 1989.

_____. *Shame and Guilt: Masters of Disguise*. Deerfield Beach, FL: Health Communications, 1990.

_____. *Boiling Point: The High Cost of Unhealthy Anger*. Deerfield Beach, FL: Health Communications, 1999.

_____. *Values from the Front Porch: Remembering the Wisdom of our Grandmothers*. Deerfield Beach, FL: Health Communications, 2005.

Miller, Christine, and Patricia Chuchryk, eds. *Women of the First Nations: Power, Wisdom and Strength*. Winnipeg: University of Manitoba Press, 1996.

Miller, J.R. *Shingwauk's Vision: A History of Native Residential Schools*. Toronto: University of Toronto Press, 1996.

Minde, Emma, Freda Ahenakew, and H. Christoph Wolfart. *Kwayask ê-kî-pê-Kiskinowâpahtihicik. Their Example Showed Me the Way: A Cree Woman's Life Shaped by Two Cultures*. Edmonton: University of Alberta Press, 1997.

Mintz, Steven. "Teaching Family History: An Annotated Bibliography." *OAH Magazine of History* 15, 4 (2001): 11–18.

Mosher, Liza. "We Have Gone Back to the Original Teachings." In *In the Words of Elders: Aboriginal Cultures in Transition*, edited by Peter Kulchyski, Don McCaskill, and David Newhouse. Toronto: University of Toronto Press, 1999.

Murray, Laura J., and Keren Rice, eds. *Talking on the Page: Editing Aboriginal Oral Texts.* Toronto: University of Toronto Press, 1999.

Nathoo, Tasnim, and Aleck Ostry. *The One Best Way? Breastfeeding History, Politics and Policy in Canada.* Waterloo: Wilfrid Laurier University Press, 2009.

Ontario Federation of Indian Friendship Centres. *For Generations to Come, the Time Is Now: A Strategy for Aboriginal Family Healing.* Toronto: Ontario Federation of Indian Friendship Centres, 1993.

Paget, Amelia M. *People of the Plains.* Regina: Canadian Plains Research Center, 2004.

Payment, Diane. "'La Vie En Rose?' Métis Women at Batoche, 1870 to 1920." In *Women of the First Nations: Power, Wisdom, and Strength,* edited by Christine Miller and Patricia Chuchryk. Winnipeg: University of Manitoba Press, 1996.

Peacock, Thomas, and Marlene Wisuri. *The Four Hills of Life: Ojibwe Wisdom.* Afton, MN: Minnesota Historical Society Press, 2006.

Peers, Laura. *Ojibwa of Western Canada, 1780 to 1870.* Winnipeg: University of Manitoba Press, 1994.

————. "Subsistence, Secondary Literature, and Gender Bias: The Saulteaux." In *Women of the First Nations: Power, Wisdom, and Strength,* edited by Christine Miller and Patricia Chuchryk. Winnipeg: University of Manitoba Press, 1996.

Peers, Laura, and Jennifer S.H. Brown. "'There is no End to Relationship among the Indians': Ojibway Families and Kinship in Historical Perspective." *The History of the Family* 4, 4 (1999): 529–555.

Poelzer, Dolores T., and Irene A. Poelzer, eds. *In Our Own Words: Northern Saskatchewan Métis Women Speak Out.* Saskatoon: Lindenblatt and Hamonic, 1986.

Portelli, Alessandro. "What Makes Oral History Different?" In *The Oral History Reader,* edited by Robert Perks and Alistair Thomson. London: Routledge, 1998.

Preston, Richard J. *Cree Narrative: Expressing the Personal Meaning of Events.* 2nd ed. Montreal: McGill-Queen's University Press, 2002.

Preston, Sarah, and Alice Jacob. *Let the Past Go: A Life History.* Ottawa: National Museums of Canada, 1986.

Sayers, Judith F., et al. *First Nations Women, Governance and the Indian Act: A Collection of Policy Research Reports.* Ottawa: Status of Women Canada, 2001.

Shoemaker, Nancy, ed. *Clearing a Path: Theorizing the Past in Native American Studies.* New York: Routledge, 2002.

Skinner, Alanson. *Notes on the Eastern Cree and Northern Saulteaux.* New York: The Trustees, 1911.

Sleeper-Smith, Susan. *Indian Women and French Men: Rethinking Cultural Encounter in the Western Great Lakes.* Amherst: University of Massachusetts Press, 2001.

Smith, Andrea. *Conquest: Sexual Violence and American Indian Genocide.* Cambridge, MA: South End Press, 2005.

Smith, Linda Tuhiwai. *Decolonizing Methodologies: Research and Indigenous Peoples.* London: Zed Books, 1999.

Stremlau, Rose. "To Domesticate and Civilize Wild Indians: Allotment and the Campaign to Reform Indian Families, 1875–1887." *Journal of Family History* 30, 3 (2005): 265–286.

Tabobondung, Rebeka. "Women Sharing Strength for All Generations: Aboriginal Birth Knowledge and New Media Creation." M.A. thesis, Ontario Institute for Studies in Education/ University of Toronto, 2008.

Trimble, Charles E., Barbara W. Sommer, and Mary Kay Quinlan. *The American Indian Oral History Manual: Making Many Voices Heard.* Walnut Creek, CA: Left Coast Press, 2008.

Vanderburgh, R.M. *I am Nokomis Too: The Biography of Verna Patronella Johnston.* Toronto: General Publishing, 1977.

Van Kirk, Sylvia. *"Many Tender Ties": Women in Fur-Trade Society in Western Canada, 1670–1870.* Winnipeg: Watson and Dwyer, 1980.

Vecsey, Christopher T. *Traditional Ojibwa Religion and Its Historical Changes.* Evanston: Northwestern University Press, 1983.

Vogel, Virgil J. *American Indian Medicine.* Norman: University of Oklahoma Press, 1970.

Wahrus, Mark. *Another America: Native American Maps and the History of Our Lands.* New York: St. Martin's Griffin, 1997.

Weiner, Michael A. *Earth Medicine—Earth Foods: Plant Remedies, Drugs, and Natural Foods of the North American Indians.* New York: Macmillan, 1972.

Weist, Katherine M. "Beasts of Burden and Menial Slaves: Nineteenth-Century Observations of Northern Plains Indian Women." In *The Hidden Half: Studies of Plains Indian Women,* edited by Patricia Albers and Beatrice Medicine. Washington, DC: University Press of America, 1983.

Wheeler, Winona. "Decolonizing Tribal Histories." Ph.D. diss., University of California, Berkeley, 2000.

_____. "Indigenous Voices, Indigenous Histories, Part 3: The Social Relations of Oral History." *Saskatchewan History* 51, 1 (1999): 29–35.

White, Richard. "Using the Past: History and Native American Studies." In *Studying Native America: Problems and Prospects,* edited by Russell Thornton. Madison: University of Wisconsin Press, 1998.

Willis, Jane. *Geniesh: An Indian Girlhood.* Toronto: New Press, 1973.

Wilson, Shawn. *Research Is Ceremony: Indigenous Research Methods.* Halifax: Fernwood Publishing, 2008.

Wilson, Waziyatawin Angela. "Power of the Spoken Word: Native Oral Traditions in American Indian History." In *Rethinking American Indian History,* edited by Donald Fixico. Albuquerque: University of New Mexico Press, 1997.

_____. "American Indian History or Non-Indian Perceptions of American Indian History?" In *Natives and Academics: Researching and Writing about American Indians,* edited by Devon Mihesuah. Lincoln: University of Nebraska Press, 1998.

_____. *Remember This! Dakota Decolonization and the Eli Taylor Narratives.* Lincoln: University of Nebraska Press, 2005.

Wolfe, Alexander. *Earth Elder Stories: The Pinayzitt Path.* Saskatoon: Fifth House, 1988.

Index